Raising a Large Family

RAISING A LARGE FAMILY

Katherine Schlaerth, M.D.

COLLIER BOOKS
Macmillan Publishing Company   New York

Collier Macmillan Canada   Toronto

Maxwell Macmillan International
New York   Oxford   Singapore   Sydney

Collier Books
Macmillan Publishing Company
866 Third Avenue
New York, NY 10022

Collier Macmillan Canada, Inc.
1200 Eglinton Avenue East, Suite 200
Don Mills, Ontario M3C 3N1

Library of Congress Cataloging-in-Publication Data
Schlaerth, Katherine.
    Raising a large family / by Katherine Schlaerth.
        p. cm.
    Includes index.
    ISBN 0-02-081911-0
    1. Child rearing—United States. 2. Family size—United States.
    3. Parent and child—United States. I. Title.
    HQ769.S289 1991
    649'.1—dc20   90-20392

Macmillan books are available at special discounts for bulk purchases for sales promotions, premiums, fund-raising, or educational use. For details, contact:

    Special Sales Director
    Macmillan Publishing Company
    866 Third Avenue
    New York, NY 10022

10 9 8 7 6 5 4 3 2 1

Design by Glen M. Edelstein

Printed in the United States of America

To my husband and children,
whose patience, humor, and inspiration allowed me
to complete this projecct.

To my mother, Mary I. Dowling,
who unfailingly encouraged my interests
in childhood and beyond.

To the wonderful families
who participated in this work.

And to my (deceased) little brother Johnnie,
whose brief and painful life would seem meaningless to many
people, but whose existence has had such a profound impact
in so many ways.

CONTENTS

vii

CONTENTS

$\mathscr{P}$REFACE

LONG ago, as a medical student, I decided that I would never marry. Physicians needed to be devoted to their profession.

Then I met John.

Our courtship took place on the hospital wards, where I learned more about him than many women learn in years of being wined and dined by future spouses. I learned how deeply he cared about children the night he stayed up till dawn to reassure a scared eight-year-old boy with hemophilia. I knew he would become a superb surgeon when he was the only medical student on our ward able to do a successful cutdown (a surgical procedure to get into a blood vessel to deliver fluid and medicines) on a very sick elderly gentleman. The day he lost his first patient, I saw how very hard he tried to do all he could for each and every person he cared for.

We were married while in medical school and graduated together one year later. John didn't expect me to give up my career to become a mother, but he really did want at least one child. I didn't give up my work, but we now have five sons and two daughters. They keep one another company when John and I have to be at work at the same time. Having a large family was the best decision we never made. I say "never made" because that's exactly what happened. After each child, having another one seemed like a good idea, but we never actually set out to have seven. And John is just as wonderful a father as I knew he would be the night I saw him comforting that little boy on the pediatric ward.

Since I'm a pediatrician/family physician and we have a relatively large family by today's standards, I often give talks to medical and lay personnel about child development. About three years ago it struck me that all the articles I had seen on raising children talked about families of one or two. I knew from personal experience that raising seven was *nothing like* raising one or two. To my surprise, practically nothing had been written about how to manage a large family, yet 10 percent of young families have more than two children. So I set to work to learn something about large families other than my own.

First I designed a research project, had it accepted by our research committee, and then recruited the parents of nearly sixty families with four or more young children to describe their thoughts and experiences in raising them. These parents come from different socioeconomic, ethnic, and religious backgrounds, but all are doing their best to raise confident, happy children in healthy, intact families. These families were amazingly generous in sharing their time and thoughts, even though they were as busy as they could be. They mentioned how isolated parents of big families feel in our society, and they wanted to reassure other parents that a large family can be worth the effort if you really want it.

That's why I promised these families that the things I learned from them would be passed on to other parents and to medical personnel. All of the information that follows comes directly from these parents and their children, and from my own background as a pediatrician.

If you have already raised a large brood, it should be interesting to see how young mothers are struggling with the same problems you must have confronted when your children were little. If you are currently raising several children, the experiences of your contemporaries may be helpful and even reassuring. If you are trying to decide whether to have a third child, perhaps you will be able to see more clearly whether a third is right for you. And if you yourself are one of a large number of siblings, I suspect you'll chuckle as you recall how it was when you were a child.

By the way, if you want to know how I've found the time to write a book, I'll tell you: I have a standing date with my computer at four-thirty each morning.

ACKNOWLEDGMENTS

I'D like to acknowledge all the parents who participated in my study and gave unselfishly of their time, ideas, and talent to help and encourage other large families.

My thanks, too, to my co-workers and colleagues in the Department of Family Medicine at the University of Southern California School of Medicine, at the Family Medicine residency program at California Hospital, and at El Monte Comprehensive Health Center, who supported my work and suggested potential families to be included in the study.

And, of course, I'm grateful to my husband and older children, who kept the little ones busy as I clicked away at my computer.

Lastly, I'd like to thank major league baseball, pro football, and pro basketball for providing diversion for my family so that I could work in peace (some of the time).

Raising
a Large
Family

CHAPTER
1

One, Two, Four, or More?

PERHAPS you are asking yourself the *big question* right now. Maybe other people are asking you. It's one of the most important decisions of your lifetime. In the last analysis the answer will depend more on intangibles than on any listing of pros and cons.

The question, of course, is: "Shall we have another child?"

At the end of the eighteenth century this wasn't a decision people had to make. Nature made it for them. The average woman in those days had seven children. As the twentieth century dawned, people were a little more sophisticated and the average dropped to four or five. The midcentury

1

mother had three or four. Now women are giving birth to less than two children each, and half of all adults think two is the ideal number of children to have.

We all know people who turn out to be wonderful only-child parents. One couple I know is doing a beautiful job of raising their eight-year-old girl; she isn't spoiled because she does plenty of sharing in her after-school play group while Mom is at work. Another family of three—Mama, Papa, and little sport—focus all their attention on their nine-year-old. He is a promising athlete, and his parents' spare time is devoted to encouraging him. Both of these families are thriving because they like having an only child. They admit they would become unglued with a large number of children.

Lots of other parents, the majority, like having two children. But what about you? Is two children, or perhaps one child, ideal? Or do you feel that you would miss something important by having such a small family? Have you wanted a family of three or four children but felt awed by the responsibility? Or have you worried that having a bigger family won't allow you enough time to spend quality time with each child? If you are thinking of having more or already do have more, you might like to know what the future will be like for your growing family.

Why People Decide to Have the Number of Children They Have

Some mothers of only children have had a difficult time with pregnancies either because they can't get pregnant easily or because medical problems make it risky for them to have a second child.

Other parents like having just one child and find that being the parents of an "only" is suited to their temperament as a couple. With just one child they are free to do many of the things that childless couples do, yet still enjoy being a complete family. Sometimes parental careers are so time-consuming that parents don't think it would be fair to have a second child. There are couples who feel that a large family would distract from the attention they are able to give one another. And some parents find their first child so talented that they want to spend all their time helping him. A second child, they feel, might interfere with their first child's development.

My friends with two children are generally very pleased with their families. Two is a manageable number, they say, even if you have a career. Two won't send you to the poorhouse. Two means there is always a lap for each one. Two means each child will have company on rainy days. Two means variety without confusion. And people don't give you dirty looks when you bring two children into the store with you.

So why even consider having three or six or twenty? (Yes, I *do* know a few families with twenty children.)

Let me say, first off, that it is the rare family today that has many children because their religion prohibits birth control. Most religious couples know about acceptable methods of birth control that are more sophisticated than "rhythm," such as the so-called Billings method. Contraceptive failures may explain an extra pregnancy or two, but seldom ten or twelve. Almost all major religions take the number of children and the mother's physical and emotional health into account.

Deciding to Have a Third Child

Let's say you are trying to make a decision about whether to have a third child. Your second child may already be out of diapers or may even be in school when you feel a deep pang to hold another infant. Somehow your children are growing too quickly, and you want to relive those peaceful yet exciting baby days (but probably not those fatiguing baby nights!). You're a little worried, though. Would it be fair to the other children? Are you too old to stand the physical side of having a third baby? Can you afford it? And what on earth will your in-laws (friends, boss) say if you get pregnant again?

You talk it over with your husband, who is enthusiastic or perhaps just resigned. Maybe he brings up the subject himself. At any rate, he has no serious objections.

Or let's say you are the father of two. You've always wanted to have enough children for a basketball team but will settle for three. Your wife is willing, but still you have vague worries. Will your salary cover a third child, especially if they all want to go to college? Will your wife have to quit her job? Will you end up moonlighting? Will this be the end of luxuries such as tickets to an occasional pro-football game or a new car every so often? Will you be an adequate father to so many? And if the baby is born with a medical problem, do you have the wherewithal to handle it financially and emotionally?

Jumping from two to three is far more difficult than going from three to four or more. You really do change the structure of your family in an irretrievable way. Here are some questions to ask yourself as you ponder your decision.

Do we have the physical stamina to deal with three or more children? A large family takes plain old stamina. The workload is heavy, and it is constant. If you forget the wash for a day, you'll be up to your ears in dirty clothes the next. Babies and children have to be lifted, hoisted, carted all over. Sleep is a real luxury until they are all well past puberty. Even hauling in the groceries is an exercise in weight lifting. Several mothers I know are actually in training; they walk or run daily to keep up their strength.

If you are an active, healthy individual, a third child will be a stress but not an impossibility.

Age doesn't seem to be a big factor physically but may be psychologically. Men in their forties and above worry about such things as being able to play basketball with their youngest when he is a teen and they are in late middle age. Be assured this isn't a problem; your son or daughter will most certainly have his or her own friends and would probably be mortified if you expressed an interest in joining their game. Remember, too, that having a third child when you are mature will certainly keep you younger than your contemporaries!

Are we financially able to have another? Every responsible family must answer this difficult question. How much money do you need to feel comfortable? Are you willing to give up some components of your life-style to have another child? Are both parents working, or might this be an option as the children get older? And what about future prospects such as job changes or promotions to a higher salary? Some parents don't feel safe unless they have a large financial cushion, and others feel that somehow things will all work out financially.

Are we emotionally ready for this commitment? Sally, who knows she can handle a large family, says, "Well, I have four brothers and four sisters. I was brought up in chaos, and it doesn't bother me too much. I am flexible and like to organize (everyone else but me). So far I have insecurities as a wife and woman but very few as a parent. I feel sure of myself as a parent."

Nan feels the same way: "I love children, can handle confusion, and have a good sense of humor (very important). I'm not afraid to discipline constantly."

And Abigail, who describes "the desire to do so" as the main thing that makes her a good parent, adds, "All of us, children included, have a sense of humor. We have the ability to take the long view and realize that children go through stages: "This too shall pass." We're not compulsive about cleanliness—things need to be neat, not perfect."

All of these parents are ready to accept the ups and downs that come with a large family and don't look on life as having to be perfect all the time. Knowing whether you are emotionally capable of giving to a third child is an important part of your decision and demands a lot of personal honesty.

Can we handle serious setbacks? Some children (maybe most) are born less than perfect. If your third has a handicap, are you going to be able to deal with it? I can talk about this personally because our third was born with a cleft lip and has gone through several surgeries. (He's a strong, handsome teenager now.) Somehow you don't expect these things to happen to your child, but they do, and they are a risk you must accept with every pregnancy.

How will a new child affect the other children? Your other children are your main concern here; but children usually adjust to a new sibling in time. If either of your older children is a "high needs" child, you might be more worried about sharing your time with a new baby.

What Really Counts

You've gone through your checklist. You've reached the conclusion that it would be absurd to have another child. Too risky. But in the face of all that's practical, you still want another child. That's your best reason to have another because ultimately the decision about your family's size is not one of the pocketbook but one of the heart. It's a decision you have to intuit, not calculate.

And guess what! I can almost promise you that if you

want another one this strongly, you will never be sorry that you had a third baby.

Once you've had your third, decisions about having more come fairly easily. Once you have three, *they* outnumber you. Adding more will not proportionally increase your workload or your anxiety about how to divide your time. It will increase your financial responsibilities. This may become your major concern, especially as your children get older and need pricier things such as orthodontia and education.

When Parents Disagree About Family Size

I don't want to leave the impression that all couples, when they become engaged, talk about how many children they will have, arrive at a mutual decision, and stick with that decision through the years. That may be the way it should happen—and in fact does in some cases—but it doesn't all the time.

You and your spouse may both have thought two children would be ideal for you when you married. Now you are a decade older and want a third, but your spouse is happy the way things are. This represents a real dilemma for both of you.

One way of resolving the conflict is to choose a quiet time when there will be no interruptions. (You may need an impartial third party, preferably a professional, to guide the discussion. Remember, we're talking about another life, which is hardly a trivial concern.)

Each of you needs to have uninterrupted time to discuss your feelings. The other should try to restate those feelings to be sure he/she understands correctly. For example, a husband may say, "I am worried about whether I can support another child on my income." The wife would respond: "You are worried about the financial responsibilities of having another baby." Then the wife may express the feeling, "I just really want another baby. I don't think I feel as though I'm through having babies yet." This is a tough one for a man because his wife is really expressing a biologic drive that perhaps he cannot quite understand. So he may say something like, "You feel the need to be pregnant and have a baby again. I don't pretend to know what that craving feels like, but I know that it's important to you."

At this point luckier couples will arrive at a compromise. It may be that the wife will agree to get a job when the youngest is in first grade or leave work until the youngest is in first grade so she will be home to raise him. If the husband wants the baby, the wife may want household help for the first several years; to secure this help the husband may agree to work overtime to pay for it or he may agree to provide it himself.

Sometimes compromise doesn't come easily. Some women have gotten pregnant anyway and forced their husbands to deal with that reality. It's a bit harder for a husband if he's the one who wants the baby and his wife does not.

Sometimes a pregnancy that is "unexpected" by one partner works out just fine. Sometimes it doesn't. There are ethical and practical questions here. The partner who "brings on" the pregnancy has to be ready for the worst, which may be the breakup of the entire family or, at the least, the loss of marital trust. He/she also has to consider whether he/she has behaved in an honorable way toward the spouse.

Ideally, then, the decision to have a third or a tenth is a mutual one based on a couple's philosophy of life and personalities, and their pleasure in the little ones they already have.

(True accidents do happen. Not a few couples have

found themselves expecting a third they did not anticipate. Talk to these parents a few years later, and they're frequently glad that the event happened! Sometimes a surprise pregnancy can be quite hard on the mother at first. Biologic acceptance can take a little while. A few mothers reported being very depressed during the first trimester, but they felt much more positive as the pregnancy progressed—when they were less nauseous and sleepy, and the baby started to move.)

Most couples who have big families have taken life day by day. They found two children enjoyable, so they had a third. Things were still going well, so they added a fourth. They found they were really getting good at this "parenting" thing, so why not try for a fifth, and so on. Deep down, their children have given them a sense of fulfillment, and the work really isn't so difficult when you're "in training" and everyone pitches in. These parents usually say they have been "open to the possibility of whatever children are sent to us" and often are a little surprised at how large their families have become, but they can't imagine life without each one of their children.

The Benefits of a Large Family

You've always wanted a large family, and so does your spouse. Yet everything you hear at work or from your friends and relatives serves to discourage you. Everybody talks about how hard it is to work and at the same time take care of one or two children. They mention expenses such as designer-label clothes that their preteens must have to keep in sync with their peers. They hint that, were you to have three children, you would be committing a crime against that most important person in your life: yourself. They drag out research which implies that an only child already has a two-lap head start at the beginning of the "status race" each child in our society is forced to run. (The child is forced to run this race to demonstrate that his parents turned out a good "product." It's considered far less likely for each child in a large family to turn out "perfect" because parental egos are not totally tied up in one child.)

By this time you feel guilty for even having considered a third child. You begin to dissuade yourself of your desire for another by silently repeating what others have said to you whenever you mentioned that an urge for another had begun to surface.

Here is a heretical idea: We live in an age of "things" and of "personal bests." Keep in mind, however, that a family fortune rarely lasts more than a couple of generations, and you may hold on to your "top salesman" award for a year, and designer jeans self-destruct in about two months—but *a child lasts forever.*

The Large Family and Society

You have three, maybe four, children. They were all planned, more or less. You're very happy to have them. You wouldn't trade any of them for the world. Then why do you feel so out of place when people ask you how many children you have?

You have two children, two years apart. They're seven and nine years old, both in school full-time. Out of the blue comes an urge for another baby. You tell your friends, and they look at you with pity. They've never heard of such a (foolish) thing as to want another baby when you've finally put the years of diapers, night awakenings, and nursery school behind you.

You have three children. You call the obstetrician's office for an appointment when you suspect a fourth is on the way. When you arrive, the first question the nurse asks is, "Do you want to keep this one or have an abortion?"

If something similar to one of the above situations has ever happened to you, you are aware that society is often less friendly now toward large families than in previous generations. This really hit home for me recently when I was asked to be on a panel of medical school faculty women to discuss combining career and family before a group of female medical students. The minute I mentioned that I had a large family, no household help, and actually scrubbed my own floors, there was instant tune-out. I left the meeting crestfallen, mildly embarrassed, angry, and determined never to be on such a panel again.

It's only fair to mention that in some quarters the large family is a respected institution. A friend of mine tells the story of the time she and her husband were traveling through Utah and stopped at a gas station. The attendant saw four small heads bobbing up and down in the back of the car. He inquired if she and her husband were Catholics. My friend said no. "Well, then," said the attendant, assuming they were Latter-Day Saints (which they were not), "Welcome home, strangers!"

Susan, a rabbi's wife, also finds her community supportive, commenting, "In general we have very positive feedback from most areas (we do stick out in a crowd), with a few sourpusses who make comments such as, 'But now you've had enough, right?' For the most part, though, we get lots of positive treatment and comments from everyone."

With six children, Kit said, "People in general look at me in one of two ways: either with respect and the attitude that I know what I'm doing, or that I didn't realize how babies were made so it just happened because no one ever had six children by choice."

And Linette said, "I have encountered a few individuals

and groups which have commented that people with big families are 'crazy.' For example, when I tell people that I have five children, they say, 'Are you crazy?' or 'You must be crazy.' But I have found that generally people respect and admire parents of large families. I get as many comments (or more) on the positive side, such as, 'It's great that you have so many kids' or 'It's nice to see people having large families these days.' Those comments are nice to hear."

Linda is more cynical: "People in general try to figure out what is causing this bizarre manifestation of lower-class behavior from a couple that should really know about birth control, the economics of children, and that we are supposed to have only two."

It's one thing to field negative comments from strangers. You can either ignore them or say something like "Don't complain. My children will probably be paying for your Social Security." But when friends and family members disapprove of your family size, it hits closer to home. How do you handle these situations?

First, you must look at the reasons for your family's disapproval. Maybe they themselves could never handle a large family, so they assume you won't be able to either. Perhaps they feel they may be called upon to assume some degree of responsibility for your children if something should happen to you. Sometimes they even feel a bit jealous of all the time and attention your children take. There's not much left over for them.

Some grandparents can't deal with the noise and confusion of several children. Others fear that their own children's health and happiness may be impaired by the stress of a large family. A few equate large families with lower socioeconomic status so they comment negatively on each pregnancy and say "I told you so" when things get tough, instead of listening and sympathizing when you talk about the inevitable problems that come up when you have several children. They may even make subtle remarks about birth control.

Here is what you can do when those close to you disapprove of your large family or have trouble understanding why you want a large family:

Realize that their disapproval most likely has nothing to do with how good a job you are doing as a parent.

Allow them to accept you and your family as you are or not at all. Their approval and support are nice to have but are by no means necessary. You're all grown up now.

Reassure your children, when possible, that Grandma loves each of them individually. She just has trouble dealing with a lot of little ones at the same time.

Don't permit yourself the luxury of taking things personally. Chances are that your parents, in-laws, or friends object to your family's size for reasons that date back to their own childhoods and really don't have anything to do with you personally. An only-child grandparent, for example, may have grown up in a very quiet, neat home and feels vaguely disoriented when visiting a household with several active children.

Dealing with Professionals

The nice thing about being a many-time parent is that you learn to trust your own judgment and you learn what's really important. Believe it or not, many "authority figures" like working with large families. Parents and physicians, for example, can grow to know and trust each other over the years. When this type of relationship exists, everybody benefits. Kit, a mother of six, says, "The family doctor has learned to trust my feelings and abilities, so if I call and say that someone is ill, things are often done by phone rather than going in. Schoolteachers and administrators are helpful [about trying to make things a little easier], but I've always tried to do what I could each year and at each school."

Susan has a good relationship with her physicians: "Our gynecologist and pediatrician both know us very well—no worry about just being a number. Because I see them so often, I feel I get special treatment: immediate calls back, home phone numbers, and so forth. They also know I don't panic or call unnecessarily, so when I do call, I get taken very seriously."

Two of Kathy's four children were born with cleft lips. She has some complaints about physicians who expect her to know everything and who tend to rush her. She admits she's "aggressive with physicians. . . . I know the questions to ask and have expectations to be fulfilled." She had one pediatrician who understood the needs of a large family, but she felt that others did not. Many physicians have said they received little information during their training about how large families function. Not a few felt they learned about large families by having one of their own, or sometimes through their patients.

Teachers are in the same boat. Their expectations about parental involvement may have to do with their experience with the far more prevalent two-child family, and this is similar for coaches, team mothers, and scout leaders.

This means that you will often have to educate authority figures about large families. Here are ways to do that:

> When two physicians are equally competent, consider choosing the one on the same wavelength as you about large families. We did this when choosing our pediatrician. He was blessed with eight children at the time he became our doctor. He now has thirteen! (Yes,

doctors have other doctors to look after their families. As the old saying goes, "The man who is his own physician has a fool for a patient.")

If a professional asks you to do something that is too difficult, tell him or her. A teacher may want you to work an hour a night with one child. When you have six, it just can't be done! Tell the teacher this and suggest an alternative, such as having an older child help or spending a more manageable fifteen minutes with your child.

Don't be afraid to speak up if you don't know how to do something. A doctor or nurse may assume that because you have a large family you know everything about child care. He or she may not wish to insult you by offering too much advice. Never be afraid to speak up; honest communication is the most important factor in good health care, good learning, and just plain good relations with others.

Sometimes you may actually have more insight into a situation than a professional. Again, don't be afraid to voice your opinion. Cecelia had this experience. Her child was doing poorly in seventh grade, and she just knew that repeating the year would be best for her. The teacher felt differently. The principal decided to let Cecelia have her way, and her child improved dramatically during a second year in seventh grade. Chris had an opposite experience. Her second grader was labeled immature, and she was told he should repeat the year. Chris knew he was like his older brother and would catch up. Instead of having him retained, she switched schools. Her son did very well in third grade the next year. Both women were able to predict their children's academic needs better than school professionals because they knew their children best.

Say no when you are overburdened. The team mother may not understand why you can't man the snack booth at the soccerama for three hours when you're breast-feeding a newborn. Too bad. She may not remember how demanding a newborn can be. You have to take care of yourself and your family first, regardless of social pressure.

The Etiquette of the Large Family

When the Davises go out to eat with their seven children, they try to dine before six o'clock. The children can be noisy, and their family requires a lot of "waitressing." By going early they avoid the crowds and don't overstress the waitress or waiter. (See Chapter 8 for other helpful hints on dining out.)

The Browns try to stagger their dentist and doctor visits. They know these professionals would be overwhelmed if all twelve children were in the waiting room at once, and they want each child to be treated as an individual, not part of an assembly line.

The O'Haras always go to the children's church service, when child care is offered for children under six. They don't want their younger children to interfere with the worship of other parishioners.

When you have a large family, you need to be aware of the needs of others and pay attention to how your family can respect those needs. This awareness is good basic training for your children, and common courtesy to others in your community. Some points to remember:

1. The frail elderly person may be disturbed and even frightened by a rowdy group of youngsters. Let your children know this so they don't run wild when older citizens are around.

2. Teach your children good public manners—no fighting, pushing, yelling, or crowding others.
3. Encourage your children to remember the family's reputation when they appear in public. They should act in a way that does credit to the family.
4. When others are participating in an activity such as listening to a concert or worshiping, don't permit your children to disturb them. Remove your children from the event if they cannot respect the legitimate needs of others.
5. Make sure your children respect your neighbors' property and privacy.

Profile

Christie, mother of seven, has some very interesting things to say about people in authority.

Most health-care personnel assume I already know everything (which I certainly don't). I don't mind this, however, because I don't always take my kids in for routine checkups, and at least they don't give me a hard time about it. As for teachers, I sometimes sense a suspicion that I couldn't possibly give all those children all the time and attention they need. I feel extremely guilty when any of my children are not in the top reading and math groups, and so forth, because I can't spend enough time coaching and practicing with them. I am now realistic enough to accept that not every one of my children will be academically gifted, and I have self-confidence enough to feel sure that every one of them will do well, be successful, and reach his/her potential. But I feel that teachers still automatically suspect that there may be some neglect in big families. Teachers seem all too quick to blame every problem in a child from a big family on the fact that he/she comes from a big family. Who knows but that the problems might be even worse if he/she were in a small family? They seem prone to jump on the large size of the family as the cause for anything (stuttering, reading difficulties, whatever).

People in general are almost always amazed at our "brood," awed that we would choose to have so many, glad that it's us and not them. I haven't gotten much negative "zero population" criticism. Occasionally a little grandmotherly type (always a total stranger) will approach me with a lecture on family planning, but usually people are amused, overwhelmed, and relieved someone else is supplying children for our waning school system and Social Security contributors.

Sometimes I feel as though we are a bit of a spectacle. I hesitate bringing them all to the grocery store, for example, especially if they are not dressed up. I feel more pressure to keep my kids looking neat and tidy just so others won't accuse me of having more than I can care for. And I always give them a lecture about being quiet and orderly so we can avoid stares and help restore the image of big families. Restaurant personnel always compliment us on how surprisingly well behaved our kids are (they always prepare for the worst when they see us coming), which makes me exceedingly proud of them. I always feel bad when I don't have them all with me, and I usually find some way to tell the world I have seven children, not just these two or three. I really do love having our little army around—seven doesn't seem like quite enough. Maybe we'll go for a dozen.

The mothers of the preceding generation—the mothers whose children are now grown—raised their children in a different, and perhaps easier, time. It may be that the world current young mothers will face after all their children have grown will be quite different from the world of today. But though the world may change, raising many children will

always demand a lot of commitment, love, and the ability
to go without much sleep.

The winter/spring 1989 special issue of *Newsweek* was
devoted entirely to the family. Writer Jerrold K. Footlick
commented, "We have just begun to admit that exchanging
old-fashioned family values for independence and self-
expression may exert a price." And Melinda Beck, in her
article on the graying of America, predicted that "at least
some grizzled baby-boomers may look back on their busy,
self-centered lives and decide that what meant most to them
was their legacy: the families they will leave behind."

The large family has to instill certain values such as trust,
respect, and concern for others. It would not even be able
to function if children didn't cooperate a little bit. Working
together and getting along, learning to share and support
one another are skills and qualities that our society needs
desperately. Strong large families are good for our society,
and good for family members, too.

So don't feel antisocial or even self-destructive if you
choose to have a large family. Someday you may even find
yourself in a situation similar to eighty-year-old Magdalena
who tearfully told me about her daughter, her first baby
girl, who had died at the age of sixty-one. It was a great
sorrow to her, she said, but then a peaceful smile crossed
her face. "I still have many more. And so many grandchildren. And great-grandchildren. Did you know I am a
great-great grandmother? And all so wonderful. I am
lucky."

A lady named Pat Burke wrote a letter to *Parents* magazine several years ago, explaining why she and her husband had a large family:

> Our five children range in age from four months to twelve
> years, and we have three sons and two daughters. If there
> is one thing that can be said about a large family, it is that

there is never a dull moment. Although this life-style is not for everyone, let me share some of my feelings about my own family.

There is seldom a time when someone needs a sounding board and finds no one will listen. On weekends and afternoons my children enjoy being with one another, and often they will turn down their friends' invitations to spend time with their family (which certainly warms the heart of this parent). . . .

In an era when people are labeled self-centered, our children have learned to share at an early age and to see the happiness that sharing can bring both to the receiver and to the giver. It is wonderful to see the planning that goes into birthdays. The looks of affection that can pass at these moments make all the laundry worth it.

Those of us with large families can tell you there is nothing better than watching your children grow except maybe watching them watch each other grow.

Every time I see my older boys helping a little one hold a bat or lifting the youngest up so he can dunk a basketball; every time my daughters' friends tell them how much they like to stay at our house ("There's always something going on at your house, Liz!"), I get the feeling it's all worthwhile.

Rumor has it that Saint Francis could speak with the birds and beasts, but he must have had large families in mind when he composed his famous prayer. One line of it says, "For it is in giving that we receive." That about sums it up.

CHAPTER
2

When Baby Makes Five

MANY parents feel overwhelmed with two babies close in age. When they find that a third is on the way, they sometimes become depressed and worried. Where will they find the strength to be good parents to three babies at once? Where will they find the money to raise three who are so close together? Down the line, how will they manage with three in college?

Let's assume you've decided to have your first two babies close together, and then a third one comes along soon after. Possibly you've planned it this way, but possibly it is a surprise. (Pleasure when the pregnancy is confirmed is far likelier if the third is planned.) Either way, you have a big challenge ahead of you.

Pregnancies Differ

Lenore couldn't believe how different her third pregnancy was from her first two. This baby was so much more active, kicking at her ribs and never settling down. Her back hurt all the time. She was tired from morning to night, yet couldn't sleep because of heartburn. She wondered why things were so hard this time.

No two pregnancies are the same because no two babies are the same. Each pregnancy causes a little more wear and tear on your body, and with each successive pregnancy you are a little older. You are also more tired now that you have to care for your other children while you are expecting. Another important issue in closely spaced pregnancies is nutrition. If you have several babies in close succession, you may have depleted body stores of some elements and minerals such as iron. Be sure to follow your physician's recommendations about diet and supplementary vitamins and minerals.

Mothers who have been pregnant several times can tell you how their babies differed when they were still *in utero*. Some babies were quiet, some very active. The places where they kicked differed, and their movement or positioning could even be painful. Their sleep-wake cycles varied, as did their responses to stimulation and to what soothed them.

It's important to realize that all your pregnancies will not be the same. You will worry less about minor differences, but you will be able to identify real problems earlier if you learn to recognize each baby's individual patterns of activity *in utero*. For example: a baby whose activity is great at night may not concern you if he is relatively quiet all day, with only an occasional flutter of movement. You know this *in utero* behavior is normal for him. But your next baby may be very active during the day. If you notice a prolonged, unusual period of daytime inactivity in this fetus, it could be cause for alarm and you would want to let your doctor know about it right away.

Nursing a Baby and Taking Care of Toddlers

Many mothers become pregnant while still nursing an infant or toddler. In this event you can continue to nurse if you pay close attention to diet because being pregnant and nursing at the same time will place enormous nutritional demands on you. You are, after all, feeding three people! To ensure adequate growth of both your fetus and your nursing child, you must have a very good diet, and the best way is to go to your obstetrician or family physician and let him/her know you are nursing. Your nursing baby should also have ongoing medical attention to be sure his/ her nutritional intake is adequate for growth. Supplemental vitamins may be prescribed for both of you, but always use them under your physician's guidance. Taking too many vitamins can also cause trouble.

(Some mothers prefer to wean when they become pregnant. That's fine too.)

Most pregnant mothers who are breast-feeding will already have their infants or toddlers on supplementary foods. If so, they can breast-feed on demand, knowing that their baby has other sources of nutrition besides their own milk. In the rare case where a woman becomes pregnant while breast-feeding exclusively, she may wish to check with her doctor about starting her nursling on other foods too. According to Karen Pryor, author of *Nursing Your Baby* (revised edition; Pocket Books, 1984) a mother who is nursing and pregnant is in a risky position nutritionally.

Both the fetus and the nursling will receive nourishment, but this may occur at the mother's expense. She needs extra dietary guidance and, most especially, extra calcium.

Some children will gradually self-wean as the pregnancy advances. This is usually done by dropping one feeding every few days. You can initiate this process yourself if nursing is becoming too difficult for you.

Some babies will continue to nurse right up until their sibling is born. The newborn should get the colostrum, or extra-nutritious milk produced right after birth. After a few days, both babies can tandem-nurse, again with special attention paid to everyone's nutritional needs. Many mothers find that the toddler needs just occasional access to the breast to know that he/she is not being displaced. Think of your own needs as well, and wean the older child when necessary, while giving him/her plenty of rocking and hugs in the process.

When you were pregnant for the first time, you probably had the luxury of taking occasional naps or putting your feet up once in a while, even if you were working or studying full-time. Now you have a couple of children, maybe an outside job too, so you need "down" time much more than you ever did with your first pregnancy. Yet it's harder than ever to get.

Don't consider yourself selfish if you feel you need more sleep during this pregnancy. Nature has programmed women to crave this rest, especially during the first trimester. Though there are not much scientific data in this area, the increased fatigue during this part of a pregnancy probably serves an important physiological need.

So how do you get the sleep you need with toddlers around? Toddlers are physically demanding, and their needs seem endless. Fortunately, most do nap. Those who don't must be retaught to do so, as you must reteach yourself. You may have been in the habit of doing chores or socializing while your little one(s) slept, but when you are pregnant and have toddlers, you must use this time for yourself. Quiet time and even mealtime can give you an opportunity to put your feet up and take some deep breaths. You can play games with your children on the floor, and as they become involved with their toys, take a few seconds to close your eyes or stretch. Or you may do what Katy did while pregnant: She put her one-year-old and her three-year-old in the middle of her king-size bed each afternoon, got out some books, and everybody read until they got drowsy and fell asleep. This little arrangement turned out to be something the children really looked forward to, and so did Katy.

Telling Children About a Pregnancy

Children's concept of time is different from adults. It's hard for them to think in terms of hours, let alone months. Because of this, and also because there is a chance of a miscarriage in early pregnancy, most parents wait until the baby "shows." Toddlers seem to understand the concept of "a baby growing inside Mommy" if they see tangible evidence.

Amber was seven when her mother became pregnant for the third time. She had been a keen observer of her mother's second pregnancy, which had occurred when she was four. One day when Mom was about seven months along, she decided to tell Amber that she was soon to become a sister for the second time. "Guess what, Amber," Mom said. "The doctor said we are going to have another baby!" "Gee, Mommy," Amber said with a look of mild disgust at her mother's stupidity in not recognizing the obvious for so long, "you should have asked me. I knew you were going to have another baby for about a year!"

On the other hand, parents who have been trying to

have a baby for a long time sometimes want to share their news sooner. Eight-year-old Grace had been asking her mother to have another baby for years, as one after another of her friends acquired a second or third sibling. Grace's mother and father desperately wanted another baby too, but pregnancy eluded them. Finally, one glorious early spring day, Grace's mom's home pregnancy kit indicated "positive." Mom didn't even wait for her doctor's confirmation. By the next day all of Grace's second-grade friends had heard the news. Grace now had to wait a long eight months for her little sister. If you've ever taken a car trip with your children and answered the question "are we almost there yet?" a million times, you'll know how Grace's mom felt throughout those eight months. When her third daughter was on the way, Grace's mom kept the news to herself a good deal longer.

When you are well along in your pregnancy, and if you feel comfortable doing so, you might want to have the little ones see or feel the baby kicking. Fetal movements are so pronounced in some women that they are visible through clothing. Also helpful and available in all libraries are simple books with drawings that can give children an idea of their new brother's or sister's activities "inside." By doing these and other things, such as involving the children in name selection, you are helping to establish bonding even before birth.

Today, many parents are aware of the sex of their baby before it is born. The vast majority share this information with their children when it becomes available.

Luckily, kids in large families are less at risk for pregnancy-induced jealousy. They get used to the idea of a new baby every so often. In general they have never had their parents' complete attention; sharing their parents with their brothers and sisters is something they have always done. And they have their own support system, because an older sibling will often pay closer attention to a younger one when Mother is busy with the new baby. Kids are great at instinctively recognizing and helping the displaced ex-baby.

The emotions children feel around a new baby also depend on their own personalities. Mothers and fathers may recognize that one of their children is particularly vulnerable to feeling left out and so spend a little extra time during pregnancy reassuring and preparing that particular child. Sometimes a grandparent can make a child his or her "project" for reassurance.

And remember: The vocal child who expresses his or her fears and anger and allows you to reassure and comfort is usually not the one you need to worry about. The silent child, the one who is "too good," may be the one who needs help in letting out his/her feelings. The child who seems to be coping the best by not voicing opposition may need the most attention and reassurance.

Teens are often surprised by a parent's pregnancy unless there has been a new baby in the family every year or two. They may be thrilled about the new sibling, or they may feel a bit uneasy or embarrassed about the new arrival. On the whole, teens tend to have mixed feelings about Mom's pregnancy and how it will change family dynamics.

One little six-year-old, who had four brothers, was told that the new baby would be special for her. She took this to mean that she would be responsible for it. When the baby turned out to be a girl, she became convinced that her parents had the baby just for her. She worried about doing a good job of bringing it up and protecting it from all its brothers. This illustrates that children can have anxieties about a sibling-to-be that you may never have guessed. However, the most common anxiety is that the baby will forever supplant them in their parents' affection. Or as one ten-year-old with two younger siblings put it, "I was afraid that the baby would get as much attention for the rest of his life as he got in the beginning."

Pacing Yourself at Work and When to Stop

When Chris was first pregnant with her third baby, it was hard to keep up the pace she was used to at work. Sometimes she'd even have to put her head on her desk and close her eyes for a little while. This general slowdown didn't go over too well with her colleagues. Her tiredness did begin to improve as her pregnancy progressed, and Chris persisted at her job until delivery. Luckily, Chris had a sympathetic boss who set an accepting tone in the office because she didn't have the luxury of being able to quit.

Working while pregnant with your first one or two is difficult enough, but by the third or fourth you may no longer feel that you are as efficient at your job. Your fatigue, bulkiness, and preoccupation with the baby may blunt your work skills, especially if your job calls for physical or mental agility.

Pregnancy may be the time to focus on performing adequately at work, but put your professional ambitions on the back burner for a while. Realize that you are under increased physical stress, and don't be angry at yourself if you can't put in the twelve-hour day required for promotion to vice president. Your priorities are your baby, your family, and yourself for these nine months. Unfortunately, the workplace wasn't created with the pregnant woman in mind, but attitudes and occupational laws are softening toward the pregnant woman as women have babies and continue to work.

Some criteria for knowing how and when to cut back are as follows:

1. Recognize that the first three months are the most difficult for many mothers, and minimize housework and extra office work during that time.
2. Though you may not require it when not pregnant,

consider extra household or babysitting help now
if you can possibly afford it.

3. Let your husband know what your needs are. He
   has never been pregnant and won't know what
   you're contending with if you don't tell him. This
   could be a time for him to build strong ties with
   the older children as he helps you out.

4. Let your doctor know about the special stresses in
   your life so he/she can be more realistic about medical advice and more alert to possible problems.

5. Accept the fact that your energy for cleaning and
   other activities will be diminished. You won't be
   able to take the kids to the park every day as you
   used to.

6. If you work with substances or under conditions
   that could possibly harm your unborn child, request a transfer when you first suspect that you
   are pregnant.

If you are employed outside the home, at what point in
your pregnancy should you stop working? Again, your
physician is the best one to advise you, but he/she must be
told exactly how strenuous your job is and how far you
must commute each day. For example, a secretary who
works close to home and doesn't have to drive several
children to the babysitter may work until a few weeks
before delivery, provided all is well with her pregnancy and
she isn't on her feet a lot. On the other hand, a lineman
(linewoman) for the phone company would either have to
take a temporary transfer or stop work relatively early in
her pregnancy.

Some people (especially physicians) work right through
early labor. This is not too advisable. One of my friends
went into labor in the clinic, kept on working, and almost
had the baby in her office. This little episode shook up the

clinic director so much that she ordered all pregnant physicians to stop working at least two weeks before their due
date.

Many companies have policies about work and pregnancy. If they do not, eligibility for state disability occurs
at thirty-seven weeks (eight months) in some states (check
local regulations). Company policies have three main goals:
to protect the company's interest, to protect your interests,
and to prevent litigation against the company. With this
in mind, be prepared when you become pregnant to be
given a lighter work load, a different position, or less work
that leads to career advancement.

Some people may have to take a medical leave of absence
during pregnancy for a specific problem, such as a threatened miscarriage, and can sometimes return to work after
the problem is over. Here again, your physician, with your
input, can assist you in making the decision that is best for
you and your baby.

You may find yourself dealing with a lot of mental stress
during your pregnancy too. It could be anything from tremendous mood swings (a heightened tendency to shed tears
at work) to feeling a constant fear for your baby's future
health. Most of us are a bit more emotional during pregnancy, and things bother us that ordinarily wouldn't. (Even
old wives' tales warn about the effect of mental stress on
the baby. In some cultures a birthmark may mean that a
mother was frightened by something and a birth defect
that she was angry.) If the going gets too tough, be easy
on yourself. Confide in a friend and take a few days off.
Stress on you means stress on the baby too.

Remember that the things that happen during your pregnancy can affect you and your baby for a lifetime. Don't
let your compulsion about work or pressure from your co-
workers get in the way of making prudent decisions about
when to stop work. But do realize that most women can
have normal pregnancies and still work if they need to,

provided they cut back on physical and mental stress, and work hand in hand with their physicians (See also Chapter 11 for more helpful thoughts on the working mother.)

Preparing the House

With the baby on the way, you must rearrange your house to make room for another person. This frequently means changing sleeping arrangements for your other children. It's wise to do this a month or two before your baby comes so that your other children don't feel they're being displaced at the last minute. In this way the bed or room change won't be associated so much with the baby as with their perception that they are "growing bigger" and need a new bed or a new roommate. If they can be involved in choosing furniture or in decorating their new room, so much the better. Involve the children as much as possible so they feel more a part of the situation and less as if it is something forced upon them that they must endure.

If your other children are older, you may already have safety-proofed your home, but it's a good time to rethink this for the baby: Get out the electric outlet guards and the cabinet locks, and crawl around on your hands and knees to look for menaces that lie below adult eye level.

When the Baby Is Born

Toddlers and even older children can be frightened by labor unless they understand ahead of time what will happen. Some hospitals offer programs for siblings that prepare them for their mother's stay in the hospital and teach them "sibling skills." If you plan to deliver at such a hospital, you would do well to take advantage of this service.

Children need to know something about labor and delivery, at their level of understanding. (There's no need to emphasize the discomfort of labor, however.) If you intend to deliver at a hospital, you may want to show your children where the hospital is; perhaps go into the lobby or even up to the maternity ward if that's permitted. You'll want to reassure the children that you'll call them daily while you're in the hospital. You may not want to make any firm promises about how long you'll be there, however. Many mothers and babies go home after a twelve-hour stay, but there's always the possibility of a complicated labor or a cesarean delivery. Sometimes babies need to stay at the hospital after Mom is discharged—for example, if the baby is a bit too jaundiced and must be kept under bililights for a short while. This should be carefully explained to the older children.

At this time, too, you may want to tell your children a little about nursing a baby, especially if they haven't seen you nurse another sibling. Pictures may help here, and be prepared for a few giggles.

Be sure the children know who will be staying with them while you are having the baby. If they don't know the person, arrange for them to spend a little time with her/him beforehand. An unknown caretaker can be the scariest part of a delivery for little children, and Dad may want to be home as much as possible while Mother and baby are in the hospital.

Consider saying something like this to your children beforehand: "You know that very soon the baby will be coming. I will know when it is time to go to the hospital, although we can't know exactly when that will be. When I know, Daddy will call the doctor who will help the baby be born. Then he will call Aunt Suzy to come over here to be with you. My bags will be packed for the hospital. You can help me pack them ahead of time and pick out the outfit the new baby will wear home. Remember that the baby might decide to come in the night. I will say good-bye if you are awake, and Daddy will call you as soon as the baby is born."

Some parents want a family delivery. I generally believe (and studies have shown) that this is a bad idea, especially if you have young children. The activity, the blood, and the whole "ambiance" can be very traumatic for small children, who may even think you are dying. If any problems do arise, there will be no time to reassure them. They may even get in the way. Having children see their new sibling after birth is a much better way to go.

While it is true that most home deliveries go well, it's the few that suddenly turn sour that worry me as a physician. You just cannot predict when things will go wrong. And if they do, there often isn't time to get to a hospital, even if it's only across the street.

My second delivery as a medical student is a good example of an "easy" birth that went sour for the mother. I was assisting a seasoned obstetrician in delivering the baby of a healthy nineteen-year-old mother who had a toddler already. The baby was delivered uneventfully and handed to a nurse. Suddenly, as I was chatting with the new mother, she started to hemorrhage. Luckily, because she was in the hospital, we were able to act quickly. Had her child been delivered at home—a good possibility, since there was no reason to anticipate any problems—this new mother of two might have died.

Many hospitals offer homelike deliveries in special suites that resemble your bedroom. Husbands or select others who have taken prenatal classes are encouraged to stay with the mother. Research has shown that labor and delivery are much better (and even faster) when Mom has her own personal coach. Rooming in with the baby is also a highly desirable option, especially if you are nursing. Being right there to offer the breast to the baby when he/she wants it helps prevent excessive engorgement of the breasts and gets the feeding process off to a much better start.

Whether or not your hospital offers homelike deliveries or rooming in, you still have the challenge of maintaining contact with the other children. Fathers are a tremendous help here. (Perhaps you can even remember your own father being with you after a brother or sister was born.) Dads can take the children to see you and the baby as soon as this is reasonable. They may take the children shopping for a gift for the new baby, then out to a restaurant for lunch. They can offer reassurance that Mom is fine and will be home soon. And you can call several times a day, letting the children know each time when the next call will be.

Dealing with Complications

Unfortunately, things do not always go well. Your chances of having a cesarean delivery vary but may be as high as one in four or five. Premature delivery is also a common problem, and about 4 or 5 percent of babies are born with a minor or major congenital malformation. As a nation we also have a significant perinatal death rate. How do you help your other children cope when things go wrong?

If the problem is a cesarean delivery, you will need to explain that "Mom had to have an operation to keep the baby healthy, so she will be in the hospital a little longer than we expected. But Mom and your new sister (brother) are doing fine." Since a few days seem like a year to young children, Mom will need to be especially faithful about calling them and having them visit daily if possible.

When a new baby is born ill, the problem becomes much more difficult. Mother and father are usually so preoccupied with the new baby that they don't have much emotional reserve for the other children at that critical time.

Relatives, clergy, and friends can be very important to the other children. Parents need only make the phone call that will mobilize others to help. Also, ask your doctor what to tell the other children. He or she can be a tremendous help if you take the initiative and make your family's emotional needs known.

If the baby is born with a significant birth defect, you will need your physician's help to know the prognosis and the special needs of your new child. Perhaps your physician can hold a small "family conference" to let the other children know what is going on and to give you the words to explain to others.

Sometimes children feel guilty about "what happened to the baby," and parents don't even realize it. One child, for example, felt that she had caused her brother's cerebral palsy because her mother had tripped over something she had left on the floor when the mother was pregnant. When explaining why the baby was born ill, her mother had said that "anything could have caused this—a virus, a mother getting hurt, anything." The little girl immediately remembered the time her mother had tripped, although the mother had long since forgotten this trivial accident.

An ill child or one with a birth defect can cause worry and upset for your other children, but a tragedy can also be a time of growth for them. They can learn the world is not perfect, and they can learn to love and help a handicapped child. These lessons can make them better adults, stronger and wiser. If you have religious beliefs, these can also reassure children.

Let them see you mourn; don't hide your sadness, because children can see through the barriers you put up. They need to know that you love the baby, no matter what his/her problems. As you grieve for the baby's illness, you show them that you do all you can to help and love the baby. At this time you are also thankful for your other children and show that you are always there for them too.

Be especially careful not to burden your other children beyond their years by giving them excessive responsibility for the care of the new baby. (See also Chapter 10, which discusses special children.)

At Home with the Newcomer

"When we brought each baby home," said Margaret, the mother of fifteen, "that baby would give a present to each one of the older children."

Another mother of four gave a baby doll to each youngster when the new baby came home from the hospital so that each one would have his/her own baby.

In a third family, each child ceremoniously presented the new baby with a gift that had been chosen as a welcome into the family.

A fourth family with seven children had the next youngest sit on the sofa for the first official "holding" of the new baby. Then the other children, in reverse age order, held their new brother or sister (with close parental monitoring, of course), and photos were taken of each one.

A "welcome into the family" ritual does two things: It formally introduces the new baby into the family, and it serves to assuage some of the normal jealousy the other children might be feeling. When you are devising this kind of ritual for your family, you need to make it something in which all the children can get involved. It should also be a ceremony that highlights the other children in some way.

What follows after the baby gets home might well be the toughest two or three months in a parent's career. Almost all new babies get up to feed several times a night. In the morning parents must be fresh for the other children, who may need extra attention because they see themselves being displaced by the new sibling. If the mother is nursing, she can count on about ten feedings a day as her milk supply builds up over the first several weeks.

There is no good way to handle the fatigue of the first several months except to put everything but essentials aside. Jenny wants to play T-ball? Next season. Patrick is clamoring for a big birthday party? Sure, but it will have to be this summer when he's seven and a half, not when he actually turns seven, because the baby will be only two weeks old on his seventh birthday.

Get everyone you can to help out, to go shopping for you or to take the older children for an afternoon. And rest whenever you get the chance, just as you did in early pregnancy. Should you find yourself getting depressed, easily upset, or angry with the baby or others, be sure to bring these feelings to the attention of your physician.

Relatives and visitors are of two types. Grandma may come over and scrub all the floors each week, then take the older children to the park for several hours. She's a good visitor. Aunt Bernice might come over and expect to be fed dinner. She may be aghast at how untidy your house is but in spite of this will choose to stay until late at night. She's a bad visitor.

A bad visitor is one who wants to hold the baby even though he has a hacking cough or one who expects to be entertained. Bad visitors are more than just an inconvenience when you have just had a baby. They may upset you because of who they are—a demanding, critical mother-in-law, for example. You must protect yourself from too many of these intrusions. Probably the best way to do this without hurting anyone's feelings is to use your physician as an ally. You may request that your doctor disallow visitors for the first six weeks (except those who scrub floors, that is). Your physician or nurse can provide an almost airtight excuse, and no one will be offended.

Janice did this when her fifth child was born. She wanted to nurse her baby but had so many visitors that the stress was interfering with the establishment of a healthy milk supply. A physician suggested that no one be allowed to visit until Janice had nursed successfully for a month. Janice could now say, "My doctor won't permit me any visitors at all," and she was able to breast-feed in peace for several months.

Jealousy is a very normal response to being displaced by a new sibling, and new babies *do* displace the older ones, no matter how hard parents try to prevent it. The good news is that children in large families have already learned to share their time with a sibling, so a new baby isn't the threat it would be to an only child.

Certain situations can trigger more jealousy than others, however. When children have been born very close together, only a small portion of the oldest one's life has been spent without a sibling. But when two children are followed by a third after a number of years, there's likely to be a little more resentment, especially on the part of the now-middle child. Another situation where you must tread carefully is where there have been several children of the same sex, followed by a much-desired child of the opposite sex. And remember: Some children's personalities are such that they have more trouble with jealousy than others.

Here are a few ideas that may help you handle jealousy:

1. Accept that jealousy is a normal and, in some ways, a healthy emotion. You may want to say something like this to your children: "I know you're angry sometimes because of the time I have to spend with your new baby sister. I think that's why the two of you always get into fights when I'm feeding or diapering her. If I were you, I'd probably feel upset too. You know I can't let you fight, but I will try to put her down for a nap, and then we can go out in the yard and plant those flower seeds together."

2. Verbalize your appreciation of your older children. Tell them how lucky you feel to have big children who are able to talk with you, who are so strong that they can carry the baby's toys to her, who say smart and funny things. Baby can't do any of those things yet, but perhaps one day they will teach her.
3. Watch for the child who can't express his/her jealousy. I worry less about—but watch more carefully—the child who tries to hit the baby over the head with his beach shovel than the child who is afraid to even say anything negative about the baby. The little one who can't express his jealousy may be more insecure. In any event, he has to know it's safe to talk about his natural feelings.
4. Know that jealousy is expressed differently by different children. Your teenager might be glad you have a new baby to occupy your attention, and a ten-year-old girl with two younger brothers will probably be thrilled by a new sister to show off to her friends. But either one might have a flash of jealousy if you can't take her somewhere because of the baby.

Juggling Three Babies

When Martha goes to the supermarket, she puts one infant in an infant seat in the body of a shopping cart, the one-year-old in the baby seat of the cart, and the two-and-a-half-year-old holds on to the cart. She pulls a second cart into which she puts the groceries. It takes Martha a long time just to get around the aisles with this entourage, and she attracts quite a bit of the "are all these yours" type of attention while she shops.

Sissy decided she had put on too much weight during her last pregnancy, so she put her infant in his front pack and took her two- and four-year-olds down to the local high school track, where everyone did a slow-motion jog. She thinks she lost two pounds the first day from dragging everyone around with her.

Mike's cub scout pack had a three-mile hike up a local mountain one Saturday when Regina's husband was at work, so Regina carried the baby and literally pushed Mike and his little sister up the mountain. About two thirds of the way up, she says, she felt she had done enough penance for all the sins of her past life.

Juggling three babies demands creative thinking, determination, versatility, and brute strength. Mothers who have done it offer the following advice:

1. Get the essentials done first, while you have the energy.
2. Be kind to yourself if your tasks aren't as thoroughly done as usual.
3. Recognize signs of fatigue, hunger, and sleepiness in your children (and yourself) before they get out of hand.
4. Take domestic shortcuts.
5. Keep in contact with others in your situation.
6. Give yourself positive feedback: "Self, you did a great job of handling that fight between Jeremy and Jason" or "Self, I don't know how you got the living room so clean today, with all you had to do."

Returning to Work or Staying Home

Many women return to work after having their first or second child, but returning to the work force when you have three or more youngsters may present some special dilemmas. (Additional situations will be discussed in Chapter 11, which concerns the working mother.)

Lisa had to return to work after her third child was born. The family's finances were too precarious to allow her the luxury of staying home. Though she loved her position as receptionist/secretary in an exciting academic setting, no child-care facility was available there, and the commute was nearly three quarters of an hour. Lisa had no trouble making up her mind to take a less challenging position with comparable pay near home where there was an on-site day-care center.

Gail's third baby was the straw that broke the camel's back—in this case, the caretaking abilities of the sixty-six-year-old woman who had been with her other two toddlers since birth. Gail didn't want to lose Aunt Ruby, as the children called their babysitter. She was almost a part of the family. Gail's solution was to pay a friend down the street to watch her oldest child, who often played with her friend's children anyway.

A parent who must find care for three or more children when she returns to work faces a real challenge. Many mothers in this situation find in-home caretakers to be less expensive than day-care centers, but they may be less reliable too. Sometimes a day-care mother will take all the children in a family, but often parents find themselves placing each child at a different site: an after-school program for one, preschool or day care for another, and a day-care mother for the third. This makes the morning dropoffs and afternoon pickups difficult, prolonging the drive to and from work by up to an hour.

The following suggestions may help you to cope with the problems associated with child care:

1. Ask friends and relatives, place ads in neighborhood papers and church bulletins, and consult

your minister, priest, or rabbi well before you have to return to work. All of these sources may help you find a reliable person to care for your children.

2. Interview and check references on as many prospective babysitters as you can.

3. Look for intelligent, warm, responsible caretakers who are doing the work not just for the money but also because they genuinely enjoy children. Mothers whose own children are grown and doing well are frequently ideal candidates.

4. Don't overlook the possibility of placing your children at different sites if this type of arrangement best meets the needs of each child.

5. If your children are cared for at several different locations, equip your car with toys and snacks for the trips back and forth because the first pickups will get hungry and bored as you make your rounds.

6. Follow your gut feelings. If your intuition tells you that a prospective employee with sterling references is just not right, don't hire her.

7. Make sure your child-care site provides age-appropriate stimulation for each child.

8. Try out the arrangement before you actually go back to work.

9. Watch your children closely to be sure they're adjusting well. Persistent negative behavior is often a sign that something is amiss.

10. If you are in an occupation where some of your work can be done at home, ask your employer if you can do this, at least while the baby is very young.

11. Sometimes newborns can be taken to work and kept in a portable crib in the mother's office. This arrangement usually becomes impractical as the

baby becomes more aware of his surroundings and sleeps less, somewhere between two and four months of age.

12. If you have a choice between a caretaker who will clean your house and one who will read to and play with your children, choose the latter.

13. Stop in unannounced from time to time to spot-check your children in day-care or caretaker arrangements.

"In the 'old days' a girl grew up, got married, and had a family," said one employed mother of ten who is now a grandmother in her sixties. The role of mother was a respected one in the community, and there was a good deal of social support and positive feedback for competent mothers.

No more. At-home mothers feel increasingly isolated and discounted. Unless there is strong church support for their roles, they need to have internalized strong feelings about the importance of what they are doing. They must combat the media portrait of a successful woman as one with maybe two children and an office with her name on the door.

Yet were it not for the dedication of at-home mothers, the world would probably not have had the talents of either Albert Einstein or Thomas Edison. Both of these geniuses had gifted mothers who supported and taught them during some rather rough times as they grew up.

These are the chief complaints of at-home mothers of small children:

Being swamped by little people day after day: At-home mothers don't have the over-the-fence social system of years gone by. Their neighborhoods may be quite empty during the day because all the adults, mothers and fathers alike, are away at work, which leaves only little people, with unending needs, to relate to. Often at-home mothers' own toddlers can't find playmates because every other child, it seems, is in day care. Some at-home mothers worry that their brains will turn to baby food!

Enduring financial straits because they don't bring in an income: It's hard to watch your employed neighbor jet off to Hawaii for two weeks while you make ends meet by sewing your children's clothes and praying there will be enough money to pay the mortgage.

Realizing that society doesn't appreciate the importance of the at-home mother: When the at-home mother goes to a party, she may as well be a piece of furniture. As soon as people find out she is not a corporate vice president, they often tune out. When the at-home mother picks up something to read, she finds a plethora of stories about women with glamorous careers and competent nannies. No matter how important you consider the time you spend with your children, it's hard to maintain your self-esteem with all this negative propaganda around you.

Fearing their lack of acceptance into the work force when they are ready to reenter after their children are in school or grown: Will they be too old to be hired? Too rusty? Will they have lost their big chance to get to the top in their career field? And if they can't get a job, how will the family have money for college educations?

Even with all these concerns, many families are willing to make the sacrifice involved in having a parent home full time while the children are small. Mothers with three small children who are functioning successfully do have a few tricks up their sleeves, and they offer the following:

1. Arrange naps so you have free time to sleep yourself, to catch up on housework, or on a particularly bad day, to do something nice for yourself.
2. Don't make a big deal of daytime meals. Most toddlers eat off and on all day anyway, so be sure

to provide nourishing snacks from time to time
and limit junk food.

3. Work out daily routines in such a way that they
   become almost rituals and your toddlers know exactly what to do. Bathtime, for example, might be
   three in the tub, right after dinner. The children
   know to get their towels and head for the bathroom as soon as their plates are clean. Have shopping time right after you drop your four-year-old
   off at nursery school. Your two-year-old and the
   baby will come to expect this and, it is hoped, be
   ready to cooperate.

4. Join or start a play group or mothers' group. Depending on its structure, you can share ideas and
   problems with other mothers, reinforce one another's self-esteem, rotate babysitting chores, and
   provide friends for your toddlers.

5. Maintain discipline and control in your household.
   Nothing will make your job harder than poorly
   disciplined children. Note that discipline almost
   never needs to be physical. The only time physical
   discipline is called for—and limited to a wallop
   on the rear end—is when the child places himself
   in physical danger. As you have probably heard
   before, discipline means teaching, so it usually involves explanations, time-outs, or other methods
   geared to the particular child. (Also, see Chapter 6.)

6. Be aware of situations that can get out of hand.
   Tired and hungry children get into more trouble
   than rested and fed children. Sometimes a particular playmate can provoke your children into
   doing things they ordinarily wouldn't. Or trouble
   can occur when a particular friend of yours comes
   over because you become so involved in conver-

sation that you tend to forget the children. If you notice that a certain situation is likely to cause problems, either steer clear of it or take precautions.

7. When you notice that your patience is wearing thin, call a time-out for yourself. Don't allow yourself to get to the point where you take out your impatience on the children in a way you'll regret tomorrow.

8. Enlist Dad's help when things get overwhelming. There's a good reason for the saying, "Wait till your father gets home." Dads offer a different type of discipline, one that children are somehow more likely to respect. Again, we are not speaking of corporal punishment here. Father's function must not be solely that of disciplinarian, but sometimes his authority and intervention are lifesaving for harried moms. Or he might intervene by getting the kids out of your hair for a little while, allowing you to revitalize yourself.

9. Be sure to tell yourself *every day* that the job you are doing is the most important one in the universe, no matter what the *Wall Street Journal* says. Because it is.

CHAPTER
3

Helpful Economies
and Strategies

GONE are the days of "cheaper by the dozen."

Most parochial schools have abandoned the practice of reducing tuition for each successive child, there aren't too many families that are large enough for group rates at amusement parks, and who ever heard of spending only two thousand dollars on each child per year—the deduction allowed by the federal government on our income tax? (Well, maybe on a farm, where you raise your own food, have inherited a house, and the children are bused to public schools.)

The cost of raising a child from pregnancy through age

eighteen is estimated to be nearly two hundred thousand dollars. If you plan to send your four kids to Harvard, add another hundred thousand per child ... and that's without the Porsche! Remember, these are not tax-deductible dollars.

Parents have dealt with these financial realities in innovative ways when raising three, five, or fifteen children, but these financial realities are the reason few families are as large as they were twenty-five years ago.

Housing

If you are currently house-hunting, you are probably finding the search more difficult than you expected. Large homes are hard to find, often need extensive repairs, and in many places are quite expensive. Newer tract homes are usually designed for the two-child family and are woefully lacking not only in bathrooms and bedrooms but also in closet and storage space. The built-in appliances don't meet the needs of a large family and garage space is limited.

If you decide to design your own house, expect much higher costs. If you can afford to, however, it's a good investment, provided you plan to live in it for several decades.

Renting puts parents of large families at an enormous disadvantage in a tight market. Large families are considered undesirable by many landlords and may have to accept housing that would be passed over by a small family, which has other options.

Room-Sharing

Regardless of what type of housing they have, most families with three or more children are unable to provide separate bedrooms for each child. But children who share rooms are not necessarily worse off than those who do not. Rooming with a sibling teaches a child how to negotiate living space. The child who has shared a closet with a sister will be unlikely, later in life, to fight with her husband over who gets which dresser drawers. She will also remember the security of always having someone with her when she was little, even on the darkest, scariest night.

Although at least two and sometimes all of the children share bedrooms in most families, an effort is often made to permit teenagers to have a room of their own. Even this is impossible in very large families and for most families in urban areas where housing costs are especially high.

Positive and negative things happen when children share rooms. On the positive side, roommates often develop strong sibling friendships. As mentioned before, they are seldom lonely at night, and in fact if a little one awakens, his older brother will often comfort him. Knowing that a big brother or sister is close by helps a little one fall asleep. One mother relates that when one of her sons went off to college where he had his own room, he was so lonely that he took to coming home almost every weekend. The problem was solved when he got a roommate.

Children who share rooms learn to negotiate problems with each other. They must cooperate on some level if the room is to remain functional, that is, if there is to be some place for everyone's clothes and toys and still space to walk around.

Some families have dormitories, with girls in one large room and boys in another. Space can be a problem with this type of arrangement, since there is usually little room for storage. One mother reported that the only floor space available in the boys' room was taken up by a big G.I. Joe aircraft carrier, while the girls' room was made impassable by a Barbie Townhouse.

When assigning rooms, parents usually take into account their children's ages, sex, and compatibility. Many shared rooms have bunk beds, so at least one child must be old enough to sleep safely in the top bunk. This usually happens when a child is five or six, but some older children are deep or restless sleepers and not yet safe in a bunk, while other, younger children do just fine in the top bed. There are safety slats that can be put up on the sides of the top bunk for as long as needed. Even these may be dangerous for very young children, however. (You might want to inspect bunks from time to time. The slats under the mattress can wriggle free and fail to support the mattress of the upper bunk.)

Drawers in dressers should be assigned according to a child's height, so a small child can get his own clothes out. Many parents find large plastic storage tubs to be great for holding either clothes or small toys with lots of pieces. Some plastic bins are even large enough for large toys.

Some same-sexed children share beds. This can work if neither is a restless sleeper. As adolescence is approached, bed sharing should usually be abandoned.

Some parents decree that once children are assigned to a room, any differences between assignees be settled by binding arbitration. If you sense that a mismatch has occurred, however, and the roommates are really incompatible, it might be time for reassignment. Some children do fine sharing a room for a number of months or years, and then they get out of sync developmentally and would be better off with a different sibling. For example, the preadolescent sister of a teenager who has just started dating may need to be switched to a room with a younger sister —for everyone's sake. Another preadolescent might thrive on sharing a room with a teenager, even if it means less sleep on weekend nights!

The Bathroom

"Mom, Craig's been in the bathroom for an hour, and I want you to make him get out now! I don't know what he thinks he's shaving. He doesn't have any beard anyway!"

"Dad, would you tell Carol that she used all the hot water, and I have to take a shower right now!"

"Mommy, can you get my doll (sandwich, sweater, G.I. Joe) out of the potty bowl?"

Other than the TV, the bathroom is probably the biggest source of argument in the large family, especially when the family has teenagers. Insufficient bathroom space is a real problem; most new housing has no more than two bathrooms, and adding another, complete with plumbing, is quite costly.

You can see that you'll need some hard-and-fast rules for bathroom use if you don't want to spend half your life refereeing. If you have more than one bathroom, consider assigning usage except in an emergency. It also helps to set reasonable time limits for occupancy and to assign bathing hours to be sure there is enough hot water to go around. (You may even want to enforce the use of an egg timer to limit actual water usage.) Kids can trade shower times if mutually agreeable. For any big projects, such as giving a friend a home perm, advance permission of everybody assigned to that bathroom is mandatory.

If you have small children, you will want to be sure everyone puts the seat and top down after using the commode. Toddlers have drowned in toilet bowls! Certainly, courtesy would decree that males put down the seat after commode usage too. (That would prevent a *lot* of arguments.)

In some large families the bathroom is the only place one can go for privacy. So, while bathroom doors need locks, they should be high enough that a toddler doesn't lock himself in. Children should also be told not to use electrical equipment such as hair dryers in the tub or near water. Another useful idea is to color-code towels. And lastly, if you have a child who is a bathroom reader, you may have to warn him not to spend a lot of time in the bathroom reading when other people need to use it.

You may wish to post some pointers such as the following on the bathroom door:

1. No showers after 10:00 P.M.
2. Stay in the bathroom for as short a time as you can.
3. If you use the last of the toilet paper, soap, or Kleenex, please replace it for the next person.
4. Make way for a bathroom emergency if you can.
5. True emergencies take precedence. Please do not cry wolf.
6. Use your own towel, washcloth, and toothbrush.
7. Don't use all the hot water.
8. All personal items left in the bathroom by those over the age of reason (age seven, for those of you not acquainted with Thomistic philosophy) will be confiscated.
9. Don't leave a mess in the washbasin.
10. Try not to get water from the shower on the floor, and if you do, clean it up.

Group Bathing: When you have a lot of dirty little ones, it's so easy to put them all in the tub at once and hose them down! This usually works great up until about age eight. They become capable of bathing themselves fairly successfully around seven or eight, and their emerging modesty demands more privacy.

For younger ones, though, group bathing saves water and time, and makes baths more fun. Usually you can fit two or three into the tub, with their respective toys. They might fight for the spigot end, where it is warmer, and you will have to rotate this position.

Many families have coed bathing. Some have special towels for each child. Some do toothbrushing in the tub. However you do it, a prime issue with bathing is safety. (Those of us in the medical field have too many tragic tales of children left in the tub only a moment while a parent went to answer a phone or the doorbell. My first admission as an intern was a beautiful brain-dead toddler whose mother took a phone call while bathing him.) Mom, Dad, or a responsible teenager should always be around. Skids on the bottom of the tub (you can get them in interesting shapes, such as alphabet letters and fish) can prevent slips and slides. No-combat rules must be enforced. Babies younger than walking age are best bathed separately. The number of toys in the tub must be limited, and they should all be of soft rubber or foam without sharp angles. Grips around the tub should be sturdy. Time in the tub must be limited so the children don't wrinkle like prunes.

Storage Space

Storage space is another big problem: There's seldom enough space to store a decent supply of food. The pots and pans don't fit into the allotted cupboard space. The kids' toys can't be put away neatly. The attic has limited access and even less space, so there is no room for winter clothes in the summer, and vice versa. Families solve these problems by erecting storage sheds, using plastic stacking trays and containers for toys and clothes, installing efficiency shelving in every nook and cranny of their closets, and eliminating things that are no longer useful.

Garage and yard space may also be at a premium. A fenced-in yard is a big help for a family with several small children, but sometimes a nearby park must substitute.

The Norberts have four teenage boys. Their house has a two-car garage, which has become a bedroom and weight-lifting room. Mom and Dad both work, and all four boys have their own cars adequate for work and school. With all the cars parked around the Norberts' house and driveway, it looks as if a perpetual party is going on. Luckily, they have a big driveway. Still, parking would be a big problem if they had to move all their cars off the street each night.

Unless you are one of the lucky few well-housed large families, you should plan on dealing creatively with problems caused by too little space. You might even be surprised to find that your kids will thrive in this atmosphere of "togetherness."

Furniture and Appliances

Very few furniture stores purchase their inventories with the large family in mind. This means it is going to be fairly difficult for you to buy reasonably priced family furniture to meet your needs, such as tables and dinette sets. Some families have their furniture custom-made, but this is very expensive. Other families buy used furniture and refurbish it themselves. Still others do what the Smiths, a family of seventeen including Grandma, have done. They bought three collapsible, picnic-type tables and installed them side by side the length of the family room. A very long, very durable tablecloth always covers these tables, and this arrangement serves the whole family, plus an occasional guest or two. It can even be used for group homework.

Major appliances are another problem. Standard four-burner ranges work fine if you have three children. Once you get beyond four or five, these ranges are too small. When cooking for a family of seven or eight, you must use big pots and pans, and they just will not fit side by side on the standard-size range. If you have the option, consider buying a six-burner gourmet range.

Refrigerators come in large sizes; nevertheless, they seldom have enough space. The Biggs, when faced with this dilemma, obtained a used model for the garage and a portable minimodel for the master bedroom, and they replaced their dishwasher (which was hopelessly inadequate for a family of nine) with yet another small refrigerator. They still don't have enough refrigerator space.

The Dillons have a freezer in the garage, and this helps them take advantage of sales and greatly simplifies meal preparation. Some butcher shops will even sell the Dillons a side of beef, then dress and package it. And when a friend asked the Dillons if they could use some deer meat, they had plenty of room to store it.

The O'Malleys rent freezer space at a local meat company, the way you would rent a wine locker. Why do they do it? Because they can buy in bulk, cutting far down on shopping time and expense.

The vacuum has yet to be invented that will adequately service the large family. It should be a canister type, with attachments that permit you to reach the bugs and spider webs encroaching on the corners of your living room ceiling. It must also have a pliable enough hose to permit the passage of small toys and Legos, which can be retrieved later from the dust bag. The hose also has to be strong so that the objects passing through it don't rip it. The motor must be very powerful and sturdy enough to resist all the banging and dragging inflicted by child-users. Even commercial-grade vacuums seldom function this well, so buy the best quality and be prepared for servicing expenses.

There are some commercial-type washers and dryers that will meet the needs of the large family. Most families with three or more young children will do at least fifteen loads of wash a week, and some will do thirty or more. Many families have learned how to service their own washers when something simple occurs—such as a belt or a sock getting caught in the outflow hose.

If you don't have a dryer or must use a Laundromat, you are probably frugal about children changing clothes often. Some clothes can be laundered by hand between trips to the Laundromat.

Bulk Food Purchases

Food is the major expense for most families. Many large families have gardens, and not a few do their own canning and preserving. The mother is often the person in charge of these activities, which can turn into a great teaching experience for the kids. (It's hard to beat the expression of pleasure on the face of a five-year-old as he offers you the first home-grown tomato from his garden.)

If you don't have space or time for a garden, consider purchasing vegetables in bulk. Most cities now have membership warehouse-type grocery outlets where you can make commercial purchases. These establishments are ideal for large families who can go through a 106-ounce commercial can of tomato sauce or mixed fruit in two or three meals. The cost is one half to two thirds as much as purchasing the same items in smaller units.

If your community does not have such a warehouse, you may be able to order at a reduced rate through a local grocer if you agree to buy in bulk. This arrangement works to the benefit of both buyer and seller. Most chain stores will not do this, so you may prefer to buy from them only "lead" items, those reduced to cost or below as a sales promotion. When these lead items are cheap, buy large quantities for storage. For example, paper towels may be a lead item one week, at thirty cents off the usual price. You use lots of paper towels, so buy a couple of cases if you can afford it. At twenty-four to a case, you will save

$14.40 on two cases. Your local paper will give you information on lead items and perhaps some coupons also. Many homemakers have a real genius for using coupons. Be sure that you use the items you purchase, though.

Other food bill cutters are farmers' markets (when things might be reduced at the end of the day) and butcher shops that sell in bulk. You may also prefer to bake your own desserts. You can whip up thirty-six cupcakes in about fifteen minutes at a cost of about eight and a half cents each, icing and all. These same cupcakes sell upward of four times as much in bakeries or in snack packs.

You can also do what the five-member Molloy family did in their zoned residential area: They built a chicken coop and had their own daily source of fresh eggs.

Coordinate your shopping trips with other activities to save gas and time. Fresh items can often be picked up when you are out taking the kids to an activity or someone to the doctor. When you have a trustworthy butcher, meat shopping can be done ahead of time by phoning in an order. Bulk buying is time-consuming; schedule it to be done on your way home from work or from the dentist, and make it your last stop. Whenever you can, shop when the stores are most likely to be empty. I have found that 5:00 or 6:00 A.M. is a great time to shop if you don't mind dodging stockers resupplying the shelves. (Most large communities have all-night grocery chains.)

Clothing

Mrs. Dixon has nothing but praise for the unisex look, long may it endure! Her three eldest are teenage boys. When they are finished with their shirts and shorts, the items go to their mother and fourteen-year-old sister. Then the clothing is worn by the ten- and eight-year-olds for play. The baby of the family is still waiting to grow into them. Dad shares boots, shoes, sweaters, and shirts with whomever.

Mrs. Lee also passes down clothes, but it's done strictly on a gender basis. She is very happy with her four girls and four boys, and wants to keep the girls looking like girls and vice versa.

Hand-me-downs don't just come from within the family. Parents of one- or two-child families will often pass outgrown clothes on to larger families in the neighborhood or through school.

Hand-me-downs are a fact of life in most large families. They also create problems. Teenagers want their own clothes—new! While teens will lend clothes to a best friend at the drop of a hat, there's frequently a war when a sister wants to borrow something. It helps to lay down the ground rules early. Preteens need to be told that clothing will be bought for them when it is financially possible. Children also need to know that their parents do understand how much they enjoy having new clothes. Some large families are wealthy enough to get new clothes for each child, but most aren't.

When children understand the financial and practical reasons behind sharing clothes and realize their parents are trying to do what's best for everyone, they're much less likely to feel "cheated."

Most of us try to save as much on clothing as possible. Here are some suggestions:

1. Buy at outlet stores whenever possible, even if it means a long drive. Plan ahead to make several purchases at once.
2. Thrift shops, garage sales, and fund-raising swap meets such as those sponsored by churches and schools are excellent sources of inexpensive, practically new clothes for babies and small children.
3. Membership warehouses and co-op stores gen-

erally sell almost identical merchandise at prices that are lower than most department stores.

4. Consider catalog purchases, especially big-chain, post-season sales catalogs. If merchandise is faulty, it can usually be returned.

5. Purchase next year's summer or winter clothes at end-of-season sales. Get a size the children will grow into.

6. When you're having a birthday party for your child, suggest to parents who ask what to get your child that clothing would be a great birthday gift.

7. Wait until after a department store sale to look for sales items that have not sold and are slashed still further in price.

8. If you're a skilled seamstress or even if you're not, make your children's clothes. Material such as flannel for bedclothes or prints for T-shirts and shorts is quite inexpensive. You can even use remnants for children's clothing.

9. When buying clothes that will be used by several children, you may want to invest in sturdy, versatile ones that cost more but last longer.

10. Check each item you buy for manufacturing quality. Look at size, type of fabric and thread, washability, and whether the seams are double-stitched and the buttons and decorations are securely attached.

11. Make sure older children like the clothes you buy. Items that a child refuses to wear are no bargain, no matter the price.

Medical and Dental Care

It is important for young families with marginal financial reserves and no medical insurance to remember that not a few doctors will provide care and set up a payment plan the family can live with. (The American Academy of Pediatrics seems to be very much concerned with these "medically orphaned" families and encourages its members to work out solutions.)

In addition, free clinics, public health clinics, and hospitals run by fraternal and charitable organizations can all be used. In most states children with congenital disabilities are eligible for state or federal funding for their care.

Using Community Resources

Large families contribute to the community, and the community can provide valuable help to the large family. Become familiar with the services that your local community supplies. These can range from supplemental food for pregnant mothers (the W.I.C. program) to library storytime hours for your toddlers.

Here are some ideas as to where you can get information on public and private programs that may be of help to your family:

1. Talk to other parents. They are your best source of information on such diverse things as childcare programs and how and where to enroll your children in soccer.
2. Call your city or town government offices. They can inform you of public programs: recreational events, fire department inspections for home safety, and so forth.
3. Your local health department often provides many free or inexpensive health services such as immunizations and prenatal care.
4. Private institutions such as Boy's Clubs have everything from inexpensive music lessons (you

can often rent the instrument very cheaply too)
to family all-you-can-eat dinners.

5. Your local community college may have classes
   on parenting, special offerings for children, and
   a host of other goodies.
6. Churches often have special programs for children and teenagers.
7. The Girl Scouts and Boy Scouts, Bluebirds, Future
   Farmers of America, American Legion, Campfire
   Girls, Little League, Y.M.C.A., and other youth-
   oriented groups have wonderful programs for
   children of almost any age.
8. Sometimes department stores and malls offer special programs.
9. Some communities have special programs such
   as babysitting consortiums. These can often be
   found advertised in the local newspaper.
10. And don't forget your library. Your librarian can
    help you find almost any program to meet your
    family's needs.

While speaking of communities, don't forget your neighbors. They are especially valuable in rural areas. Good
relations with your neighbors makes life pleasanter and
could save your life in the event of an emergency.

CHAPTER
4

It's Just Another Day

MOTHERS of large families will tell you that if they want to get anything done, they do it while everyone else is asleep. This often means getting up very early in the morning. Mothers often have fragmented sleep during the night anyway because they are nursing or feeding a baby, or because little ones, for a variety of reasons, visit them during the night. (My favorite is, "Mommy, can I sleep in your bed tonight? I think we're going to have another earthquake.")

If you happen to be at peak efficiency during the morning hours, you can get a lot of work done or you can use this time for yourself, for exercise, for spiritual refreshment, for letter writing, for reading, or for whatever else you want to indulge in without interruption.

Other things that mothers do before the children wake up include these:

1. Walk a half hour with a friend while your husband is home "on duty" with the children.
2. Work for an hour on a pleasurable hobby or craft such as sewing or painting.
3. Devote time to spiritual meditation, reading, or doing work for the office.
4. Enjoy special time with your husband for talking, lovemaking, or whatever—but only if he is an early riser too!
5. Prepare a casserole dinner, do wash or mending, or clean an unoccupied part of the house. This works well if you have an especially busy day scheduled.
6. Have uninterrupted time with one child to go over homework, teach a craft, or just to talk or play.
7. Take a long, relaxing, uninterrupted bath.

Most mothers, especially those with school-age children, get up at six or six-thirty, if not earlier. One working mother with six young children including a nursing baby must get up at 4:00 A.M. to pull the house together before she is due at work. (Farm families have been doing this for centuries.)

The Morning Rush

A minority of large families rate the morning time as the most difficult time of the day for them. (Dinnertime is the most stressful for the majority of large families.) Once the family is awakened, there is a predictable series of tasks to be accomplished: Breakfast must be made, then dishes done; beds must be made; the younger children have to be helped to dress; and perhaps a load of wash is started. If children go to schools without a lunch program, somebody has to make lunches for them, and maybe for Dad (and Mom) too. A young baby will have to be fed amidst all this activity. The kids must get to school. This may involve nothing more complicated than a good-bye wave from the door, but for many families it may mean walking a young child or driving one or more car pools. Working families with preschool children have the daily ritual of dropping off one or more children at the babysitter or child-care facility, along with bottles, toys, notes, lunches, snacks, diapers, and changes of clothing. A babysitter who comes to the home may have to be picked up; at any rate, the babysitter will have to be briefed on the day's game plan. By the time Mom gets the last child out the door, she has probably put in between two and four hours of frantic activity, and is ready for a coffee break.

Breakfast and Lunch Preparation

Toddlers and infants demand top priority at breakfast time. If you have a breast-fed infant, schedule a nursing right before breakfast so he isn't hungry when you are needed to help the other children. Your baby does not have to be fully awake to nurse. He will suck if put to the breast, and the milk in his tummy should keep him sleepy enough to doze through breakfast time. Toddlers, if awake, may need to be given a snack before breakfast time. They can also forage while the older children eat.

Breakfast does not have to be the traditional eggs and bacon either. In fact, if your family has a cholesterol problem, it had better not be! Think about having soup or pasta for breakfast. (Not too many families have caught on to this yet.) Both are nourishing, cheap, and warming on cold mornings. Cheese and fruits, vegetable juice, sliced meats, or last night's leftovers are also easy to prepare and are nourishing. Use your culinary imagination. And save the weekends for really traditional meals that everyone can help cook.

Parents do not have to make breakfast. If the ingredients are at hand, even a six-year-old can prepare her own. Mom's role can be pared down to getting out the juice, cereal, milk, sugar, spoons, and bowls. Or maybe bowls can be put on a low shelf so everyone can reach them. Having kitchen implements that are accessible to kindergartners but out of reach of toddlers can demand creative kitchen reorganization, but it pays off in time saved. A sturdy footstool can assist little people to reach higher shelves too.

There are also many shortcuts when it comes to making lunches. Have the kids make their own (but do spot inspections for excess quantities of cookies or a dearth of fruit and sandwiches). Make a pile of sandwiches, assembly style, on Sunday, put them in the freezer, and take them out as they are needed during the week. If you have soup for breakfast, the extra soup can be put in thermoses for lunches.

Always be aware that no matter what you put in the children's lunches, they will probably trade with their friends anyway. (One mother suggests filling the kids' lunchboxes with sweets and insisting that they trade these with the other kids at school for sandwiches, fruit, and fresh vegetables.)

Additional Challenges

It is the rare large family that doesn't have at least one member who must be pulled out of bed by the toes. If you have a child who is difficult to get going in the morning, give him or her an alarm clock. If the child is old enough—perhaps nine or more—and fails to get up after repeated warnings or forgets his alarm, allow him to miss the school bus, then take him to school late. He will have to enter the classroom or go to the principal's office alone. Since this is very embarrassing for a youngster in fourth or fifth grade, you are allowing your child to see the consequences of his actions.

A note of caution here, however. There are some children who lack that innate sense of time that most of us are born with. If you have a child who has a blind spot for the passage of time, you will have to work time-clue-giving into your morning routine. You may have to wake him repeatedly or stand by his bed until he actually gets up. Then in a neutral tone of voice you can feed him a constant stream of time messages: "Johnnie, go to the bathroom now, then get dressed." "Johnnie, are you dressed and did you go to the bathroom? Now put on your shoes and socks, and make your bed. Put your pajamas under the pillow." "Johnnie, are you done with your bed now? Okay, come downstairs and get yourself a bowl and pour some cereal." "Johnnie, are you finished eating? Now brush your teeth, comb your hair, put your lunch in your bookbag, and get your jacket from the closet." This kind of child is probably not being deliberately uncooperative, he just has a lot of trouble getting his act together, especially when he has just gotten up.

How can you tell if your child really has a time recognition problem? Usually the child with poor time recognition skills will have trouble in other settings also. His teacher may comment on the trouble he has getting organized at school. He is not being uncooperative, he really cannot pace himself, and punishment rarely works.

Kids always wait until the last moment to give parents the permission slip for today's zoo trip; it must be signed *now*, and of course the school bus is just about to pull away from the curb. The parent has the choice of signing the permission slip and driving the child to school, or not signing and being called at nine-thirty to pick the child up at school because he can't go on the trip without written parental permission. And you as a parent can count on having to sign all tests with grades of C- or less in the morning when you cannot possibly give these tests (and the child who did them) their deserved attention.

And among all the other morning-rush delays, you're bound to experience another unexpected one. It is a well-known fact that accidents happen when you are under stress, so you may as well count on breaking a glass or burning the bacon at least once or twice a month. (Most large families have sturdy plastic or rubber dishes and glasses, but these too can fracture after sufficient use.)

Mornings are especially challenging for the woman who works outside the home. She must leave the house in good order so that she doesn't have to do both morning and evening chores when she gets home from work. Often she has to drive young children to the babysitter too. This can be made somewhat easier by getting the babies' equipment ready the night before. Parents can share the driving, depending on whose schedule allows the greatest flexibility on any given day. Morning chores are also sometimes shared by fathers.

A mother employed outside the home may find it helpful to put a roast in the oven (if there is an automatic timer) in the morning so that dinner will be cooked when she gets home. (A Crockpot can be similarly used.) Meat can be taken out of the freezer to be defrosted by dinner time, or prefrozen casseroles can be defrosted. Peeled vegetables can sit in a pan of water in the refrigerator until dinnertime; some mothers peel their vegetables while the family eats breakfast.

Employed mothers with nursing infants need to schedule a feeding for right before they leave for work.

Here are a few rules for making the morning rush a little easier:

1. Have the kids get their bookbags packed the night before, including having notes signed and school excuses written.
2. Make it a rule never to sign in the morning those critical items that need parental input such as test papers and report cards.
3. Lay out all clothes to be worn the next day, including shoes.
4. Make sure car keys, umbrellas, coats, boots, and any sporting gear needed in school have a regular place and are returned there after use. Then the next child who needs them will not be thrown into a tizzy just when the school bus is leaving because he can't find what he needs.
5. If you have teenagers and limited bathroom space, consider posting a morning schedule for bathroom use (with exceptions for emergencies).
6. If you will be gone the whole day, before you go put the dishes in soapy water or in the dishwasher, or wash them and let them drain.

Midday

The rush is over, and now the preparation for the day's activities begins. There is wash to be done, car pools to be organized, and chores to be accomplished.

The Daily Wash Load: Wash must often be done daily in the large family, especially when there are infants and toddlers. Although most families nowadays use paper diapers or have a diaper service, a significant number also use cloth. Some babies have skin that is too sensitive for paper diapers, and some parents cannot afford the cost or are concerned about the environment. But even when you use paper diapers, babies make plenty of other wash.

When all your children are out of diapers, you generally have to do at least one wash load a day. If you have to go to a Laundromat, you probably save things up for a few days, but the loads are big when you do them. A small fraction of families must wash manually and use clotheslines to dry.

There are ways to make this chore easier. One working mother puts a load in the washer before leaving for work, and folds and puts away a load from the previous night at the same time. When she returns from work, she puts the morning's load in the dryer, then folds it after her children's baths, at which point she has another load for the washer and dryer, which she again folds in the morning, starting the cycle over again.

Another parent lets her teenagers do their wash on a rotating basis. They have bedroom hampers, and the teen on wash duty collects dirty clothes from these and returns the clean wash to be folded.

Ironing can be another problem. Most families purchase only drip-dry unless they have a lot of household help. Ironing is generally limited to Dad's and Mom's work clothes, and perhaps "special occasion" clothes, unless children wish to iron their own clothes (with supervision, of course). Many mothers have discovered that ironing can be done while watching a favorite TV show or talking on the phone or helping with homework.

As a general rule, children age ten to thirteen can begin to assume responsibility for their wash. However, if everyone does his/her own wash, the family sacrifices cost-effectiveness. Some families accept that it will cost more to have each person do his own wash, but the cost will be offset by time saved by parents. Other families rotate washing chores for the whole family. In still other families, Mom or Dad does all the wash but does not gather or fold it. That is the children's responsibility. In most families, however, especially when children are young, Mom just naturally expects to do all the work, perhaps sharing this chore with Dad.

The Car Pool: When your children cannot walk or take the bus to school, maybe you've considered or are in a car pool. Car pools are not for everyone. If you or your husband can drop the children at school or at the babysitter's on your way to work and pick them up on the way home, you don't need one. In fact, the time spent in the car with your children is a wonderful time to talk, to do times tables, or even to finish eating breakfast.

But if you are unable to drop off or pick up daily, a car pool can be a godsend.

Car pools are best arranged before the start of the school year or soccer season, or whatever you need one for. You may need to make the first move toward starting a car pool, but then you will have control over how it functions.

First, get lists of the names and addresses of all the other children in the school or on the team. Find out where they live, either situated on a map, by zip code, or even by telephone number prefix. The latter two methods are helpful if you live in a fairly large community. Given a choice, you may prefer to have families with children the same age and sex as your own. Once you have narrowed down your selection geographically and by age, consider how many families you want in the car pool. You need seat belts for each child; assuming you have these, anywhere from two to four families works nicely. Then call the respective families. Explain who you are and how you got their phone number: "Your son and my boys will all be going to St. Stanislaus School this September, and Sister Mary Rose gave me your phone number. We live close by, and she thought you also might be interested in a car pool."

You can do a lot of winnowing out on the phone. Find out if Mom works and wants you to do nine out of ten pickups. (No!) If Percival is the only child and must have absolute quiet on his way to and from school, or if the other mother smokes in the car and your kids have asthma, it may not be a good match either. Sometimes you can tell over the phone that parents feel a car pool is a great imposition on their time and are not really committed to working through details. These parents will usually bail out quickly and are best not included. Don't be afraid to ask tough questions, such as past driving record and use of drugs, medications, alcohol, and cigarettes (which are associated with a slightly increased risk). Certainly you need to know about their insurance, the condition of their car, and the number of seat belts they have. The other parents are entitled to the same information about your family.

You may wish to break the ice: "Mrs. Smith, we have a two-year-old station wagon with eight seat belts. My driving record is excellent, and so is my husband's. We have auto insurance, neither of us smokes, and we're careful never to take cold remedies that cause drowsiness when we're going to drive. I'm telling you this so you'll know how seriously we take auto safety. How about you?"

If over the phone you feel that this might be a good match, then invite the families over to get to know one another (unless, of course, you're already acquainted). This gives the children a chance to become friends too.

Your first meeting can be used to set up the car pool schedule. Everyone should bring calendars. Figure out how everyone's needs are best accommodated: Does each parent want to take a week in succession? Does one parent prefer to drive in the morning and another in the afternoon? Is there a working mother who can drive some days and not others? What about vacations? Pregnancies? Emergencies? What if one child is on an after-school sports team? Does the afternoon mother have to make two runs or will the other children stay late? Or will the athlete's mother be responsible for picking up her own child, even if it isn't her afternoon to drive? What will happen if one mother's child is sick and it's her turn to drive?

All of these questions must be dealt with before they arise. Everyone must exchange home and work phone numbers, and spouses' work numbers, and stipulate an emergency driver in case the designated parent can't drive. (For example, a grandmother may be available to drive the month a car pool mother's baby is due.)

At your initial meeting, be cautious if you sense that a parent doesn't seem too committed to being in a car pool. That parent will probably drop out if things don't go exactly his/her way. A group of employed mothers, for example, spent hours hammering out a schedule that would meet everyone's work obligations. One mother, who made more than her share of demands at the time the car pool schedule was originally set up, soon found it too hard to get up a half hour earlier several mornings a week. She hired someone to drive her own children, leaving the other mothers' schedules in disarray.

Beware, too, of parents whose approach to child care is a good deal more casual than your own. One parent related how she and two other mothers had formed a soccer practice car pool. One of the mothers thought nothing of leaving all three of their nine-year-old girls at the soccer field in the dark for up to a half hour or more when pickup time was inconvenient for her that day. Of course, the coach didn't appreciate this casual approach either; he couldn't allow the girls to wait alone and so had to stay late with them. That car pool didn't make it past the opening game.

But if you do find a group of congenial, cooperative, trustworthy parents, you will be repaid many times over for the time you spend setting up the car pool, and you probably will make some friends in the process.

Doing Chores with Toddlers: Everyone knows how hard it is to complete a chore with little ones around. They have to help with bed-making, want a snack when you have just warmed up the iron, or desperately need a Band-Aid and hug when you are on the phone. Actually, the most important thing you do as a parent is be available to your children when they need you. (This is what is so hard for the employed mother; she cannot be there when her child needs her during the day. Her child must rely on someone else.)

The most important teaching that you do as a parent takes place very informally as you are going about your routine activities. The self-esteem that your child develops when you stop what you are doing to answer a question or demonstrate to her how to polish a coffee table (and then praise her for how energetically she works) will stay with your child for a lifetime. Mothers (and fathers) should instinctively recognize this and generally plan on a chore taking about twice as long as it ordinarily would when they have one or two toddlers following them around.

Remember that preschoolers can learn a great deal from even the most routine activities. You, the parent, must guide them and can do so by asking questions such as: "Why do you think that Mommy has to wash the dishes after we eat?" A three- or four-year-old will then think about the consequences of not washing the dishes—she would have to eat off a dirty, icky plate. It might even have ants on it. Then you can ask why she thinks ants like dirty, icky plates. This can lead to an interesting discussion about insects. You might even get out a book about insects and look up some facts about them. What a tremendous amount of teaching from a simple household chore!

Or you might have your four-year-old spray the windows as you clean them. The two-year-old can wipe. It goes without saying that they will each want to do the other's chore (and you will have to do the whole thing over, so give them a practice window while you work on the others). But cleaning windows under supervision does give them exercise and teaches them visual-motor coordination. They learn how good it can feel to do a job that makes something better. (It might not look clean to you when it's all done, but they will think it's spotless. Don't let them see you redo it.)

Of course, it's great to teach your children as you do your routine chores. Children can work side by side with you, and the baby can be propped in an infant seat strategically located so he can see you yet still be safe from an inadvertent shove by a two-year-old. But let's face it, you need to have some time when you can work fast and furiously, and really get things done. How can you arrange such a time? It's never easy, of course, but knowing your children's activity patterns throughout the morning should help.

Toddlers have relatively short attention spans and will move from one activity to another. The great majority of infants nap at some time during the morning. Thus, to have some uninterrupted time, you might consider these suggestions:

1. Capitalize on the baby's morning nap. You can do this by nursing or feeding him and putting him down when he is sleepy after his feed at the same time each morning.
2. Have your toddlers work with you a little, then give them busy time with toys, paper, and crayons or another activity—in a safe place preferably somewhat removed from where you are working.
3. Check on your children often, of course, and if

you have a four-year-old preschooler, have him or her assist in a "babysitting" role.

4. You may wish to consider a rotating play group for your toddler if you live in an area conducive to starting one because it might actually be more difficult to arrange free time to do your work if you have only one child at home during the morning. A toddler wants lots of attention from you because there are no siblings to distract him. (A baby at home is somewhat easier, provided he naps well.)

After School Lets Out: You have spent your day working outside the home or at home with toddlers or alone doing household chores or doing community work; then the children come home from school, and the pace of your day changes dramatically.

The first order of the day after they troop in the door must be to put away books, lunch boxes, sweaters, coats, athletic equipment, and whatever else they will need tomorrow—clean and in a place where it can be easily retrieved in a hurry.

Kids generally come home from school with a huge appetite, one that, if completely sated, will ruin dinner. Snacks need to be available that are relatively nutritious but low in fat content. Fruits and fresh vegetables, if you can get the children to eat them, are great. If not, think about pasta, crackers, soup, cold sliced meat, or last night's leftovers. If you plan to have an early dinner, you may wish to prohibit eating in the hour or two before dinner.

Whatever your rules about the television set, a very common rule is "No TV until you *all* get your homework done." This puts sibling peer pressure on everyone to get homework done quickly.

Some children need free time to unwind after they get

home from school. Only when they've gotten the excess energy out of their systems can they concentrate on homework. Assuming this is the case for some of your children, it is wise to allow them to run around a little while before settling down. Others will wish to read or rest or talk with you before hitting the books. You can be with them as you prepare dinner, and they can help you with the preparation before they start their homework or chores.

For many children, after-school activities take the form of organized sports, scouts, 4-H, or other structured programs.

If you live in a small community that has safe streets, your children can bike or walk to after-school programs. Otherwise, you must drive them. This is a real problem for many mothers because meetings or practices are often scheduled right before or even during the dinner hour. And in the large family, more than one child is often involved —each child on a different team with a different practice schedule.

Many organizations require active parental participation, so with four school-age children you could find yourself driving four kids to soccer practice (or Little League or "Y" basketball, depending on the season) for eight practice sessions a week, being Brownie cookie mom and assistant den mother two other afternoons a week, and maybe even helping coach a team plus driving for music lessons or choir practice. Sound impossible? There are parents who do this.

How can you avoid an afternoon rat race if your children wish to become involved in extracurricular activities, yet still give them a chance to participate when they really have an interest in something? Here again, knowing and acting on the strengths and limitations of your family are important. For instance, you may decide that you can drive just two days a week; you can get very involved (say as a coach or leader) in one activity a year; and Dad is available on Saturdays. With this as background, your family will have to decide who does what. Children might be responsible for arranging car pools on the days you cannot drive. Teenage siblings might help out the afternoons they don't have other things going on. You may decide that each child has the choice of a fall, winter, or spring sport but not all three. One child might elect a sport; another, Campfire Girls; a third, guitar lessons. The fourth might need extra time to work on homework, and when grades are better, he also can have a choice of activities.

For some families, especially those with new babies or where both parents are employed full time, afternoon activities are impossible and the children have to realize this. Sometimes these families are able to hire a trustworthy teenager to drive and help out, but even this solution is often beyond reach.

You might consider these rules for after-school activities:

1. Decide what you as parents can reasonably do, and don't overextend yourselves.
2. Have the children bike or walk when it is safe and practical.
3. If you have more children with more activities than you can drive to or help out with, divide things up reasonably fairly among the children.
4. Make use of after-school car pools with other parents whenever possible.
5. Your own teenagers might be able to help out, but don't overextend them either. Hire someone else's reliable teen if you can afford it.
6. It's okay to let coaches, scout leaders, and others know that your family size may limit your ability to help out. If they are used to dealing with small families, they may not understand this.

7. You're not a bad mother or father if you're not present at all the games. Don't feel guilty for what you can't do.

Dinnertime

Carol has a family of fifteen and a very busy pediatrician husband who often works evenings. For Carol and her family, dinner is almost a sacred time. Dad comes home, even if only for a few minutes between patients and hospital duties. All the children are expected to be there, and absence is rarely permitted. Dinner is a time for the family to discuss the day's happenings and touch base with one another.

At the other end of the spectrum is Rosa, whose seven children seldom eat with their surgeon father because he is rarely home before 8:00 P.M. Sometimes the little ones get fed before the teenagers who are at school activities or work until late.

Although there are many different ways of handling the dinner hour, mothers of large families almost uniformly agree that the evening meal is the worst time of the day for them. Linda, mother of five, speaks for many mothers when she says, "The worst time of day is from 5:00 to 6:00 P.M. when the children are tired and hungry, I'm making dinner, and the baby is cranky."

At dinnertime the mother of a large family is contending with a lot of different issues. First of all, she has to prepare the meal, and as every parent knows, no two children like the same food.

Second, she has to deal with a very primal need: hunger. Somehow she has to keep the kids from snacking on foods that are not good for them, will spoil their appetite, or will start a fight, as in: "But Bobby had a cracker. Why can't I?"

Third, kids frequently need to be picked up and school meetings start right around the dinner hour. Babies also need a lot of attention around this time, it seems. And often Mother has to make dinner while simultaneously helping three children do their homework.

But worst of all is the commotion. It's amazing how hunger can make even a placid child into a whirling dervish. That's one of the reasons fights generally occur around dinnertime.

If Dad is home at dinnertime, he can be a great help, if only to keep the kids in line. If he is not, Mom knows that there will have to be a second dinnertime for him. He should get accustomed to making his own dinner or heating up what has been prepared earlier.

Almost everyone would agree that, ideally, dinnertime is a time for the family to eat together, share the day's events, and enjoy each other's company. Some families actually approach this ideal by making it a top priority in their planning. Most families do not.

In the families that prioritize dinnertime, Dad's schedule is generally flexible enough to allow him to be home for dinner every day. (So is Mom's.) Mealtime is rather early because little ones cannot wait until 8:00 P.M. to eat. A ritual has been established that permits the serving of a meal in such a way that Mom does not have to spend the whole dinner jumping up and down to get a glass of milk for one, a replacement fork for another.

Rules are strict. There is no verbal or physical skirmishing at the table—ever! And the conversation generally is so structured by tradition (or strict enforcement) that no topics are brought up which could lead to sibling confrontations, such as, "Do you know what dummy got her report card today?" or "Danny borrowed three dollars from me last week, and he never paid it back. Did you, Danny?"

Some families, especially those in which the children are

younger and the parents have regular schedules, can and do have lovely dinner hours, but for many families the only time everybody can manage to be together in one place seems to be Thanksgiving or some other holiday. This is especially true of families with teenagers.

What do you do if your family seems scattered to the four winds as the dinner hour approaches? You can hold a family meeting to discuss the issue, you can refuse to serve those who won't come when called, you can demand that people let you know if they will be late for dinner, or you can be a doormat and reheat dinner for the latecomers. I'll give you one guess as to what most mothers do.

When Tastes Differ: Dinners in large families are rarely gourmet affairs, but they do have to be well balanced, fairly simple to prepare, appealing to most young palates, and easy to reheat (especially if you have teenagers). They should also be relatively inexpensive. Stews, casseroles, and pasta are the staples of many large families because they meet many of the above requirements. If you have an older infant or toddler, you can frequently feed him these dishes well mashed up. Many large families, in fact, eschew proprietary baby foods entirely, making their own from whatever is served to the rest of the family that night and pureeing it well.

In most families children have definite preferences for one food over another. This is likely to be more of a problem with toddlers, who don't eat much at any one time anyway. They prefer to snack throughout the day and can go for months refusing to eat anything except chicken and noodles (or some other weird combination). There are times when teenagers can also become rather finicky, although at other times they will devour everything in sight.

A large number of children will eat almost anything, except for the one or two foods that almost make them sick. Then there are children with food allergies and children who are sensitive to additives, sugars, or dyes.

If you are blessed with children who always eat every-thing, you are probably in the minority or are an exceptionally talented cook. If you experience problems from time to time, you might consider implementing some of the following measures:

1. Unless allergic or sensitive, everyone must eat a little of each food. Ease toddlers into this rule.
2. Food must be eaten within a reasonable time span.
3. There is a penalty (be creative here) for saying bad things about the food in front of impressionable younger siblings, such as, "Oh, yuck! Not that junk again," and for hiding uneaten food in such places as under your chair or under your paper napkin in the trash compactor.
4. Parents will make every reasonable attempt to rotate menus so that each child in the family will have a chance to eat his favorite food.
5. No trading food with your siblings unless you have the okay of your parents; also, no bribing a younger member of the family to eat a food you don't want. The corollary to this is not taking another's food for any reason without prior parental authorization.
6. Family members will come to dinner when first called, with no exceptions for really good parts of a TV show, a cute boy on the phone, or a whole lot of homework.

Having Friends Over for Dinner: Large families attract other kids like a magnet. One mother of four related how a little boy in one of her fourth-grade son's classes seemed to spend a lot of his time at her house. Finally she asked him why he never went home. He replied that his parents, affluent career folks, wanted him to know what it was like to have brothers and sisters but didn't want to go to the trouble of providing him with any, so they encouraged his frequent trips to her house to learn about life in a large family.

One of the times you are most apt to have guests is at mealtime. You need to decide how you want to handle this issue. Some families want absolutely no friends at meals. It's expensive and besides, they feel, mealtime is for family members only. Other families limit mealtime visitors. Each child may have a friend over for dinner once a month on a rotating basis. Still other families welcome mealtime visitors, feeling that one or two more won't be a problem and that this courtesy will probably be reciprocated.

There are definite advantages to having your children's friends to meals. It gives you an opportunity to see what type of people your children's friends are. You can ask questions about their families, backgrounds, and opinions without seeming overly inquisitive. And you can learn how they behave in social situations. You may pick up some clues that will help you guide your own children in their relationships with these friends. For example, one mother found out, in casual dinnertime conversation, that her daughter's friend's mother had an alcohol problem. This information allowed her to make some wise decisions about who drove the girls and when. Another parent found out that her son's best friend's mother had lost her job. This mother discreetly supplied the child with food and clothes until his mother obtained another job.

If you do decide to have friends over at mealtime, you should consider serving a casserole or pasta. Both are cheap, and by adding a few extra noodles or a bit more rice or whatever, you can feed a couple of extra children. Be prepared for the child-guest being finicky and requesting that something else be prepared for him—the answer to this request is "No way"—or the guest liking the food and company so much that she asks for seconds and thirds. The answer to this is "Only after everyone else has been served."

Sometimes you will be pleasantly surprised that your children behave better at the table when there is a guest. There are some guests, however, who seem to incite food fights, burping games, or the giggles. When this happens, you have to step in very firmly and quickly. When you have to exclude a trouble-making friend from dinner, discuss the reasons openly with your child. Decide on conditions under which the offensive friend will be reinvited to meals: "When Freddy learns to control his funny face-making at dinner, then he will be invited again" or "If Alice stops saying that my cooking and your little brother are icky, then she can come back."

Don't be afraid to request that friends help with the dishes if this is the rule in your house. Friends must be held to all of the house rules when they come over. And there must be a stated time for the friend to go home after dinner. Unless otherwise agreed upon, his own parents must provide any needed transportation home. An invitation to dinner is not automatically an invitation to spend the night.

At what age should children begin to have friends for meals? A toddler might enjoy having lunch with another toddler, but serious meal sharing usually starts when the children enter grade school and peaks in the middle school years.

You might also want to include these additional rules concerning having friends at dinner: Friends do not come over on school nights and are allowed only when it will not inconvenience the family. Children must give sufficient warning when their friends are coming over.

After Dinner

Dinner may be a frantic period, but there's more to come before you can collapse onto your warm, cozy, perhaps crowded bed. At no time of the day are your managerial skills put to the test more than after dinner.

Most families with children old enough to do dishes have these children help in some way with kitchen cleanup. In others, fathers help. Mother and Father are often stuck with simultaneous kitchen cleanup, baths and bed for the little ones, and helping the older ones with homework.

Babies' needs have priority. If your baby is nursing, you will have to allow twenty or more minutes to feed her, change her, maybe bathe her, and get her to sleep. If she is bottle-fed, perhaps Dad or someone else can get her settled for the night.

Toddlers come next. Sometimes a responsible elder sibling or Dad can help bathe or undress them, read or sing to them, and put them to bed. More often Mom must do this in between other chores. If you have children of preschool and younger ages, you may want to get everyone in bed before you even think about kitchen cleanup.

Let's say you have both older and younger children or only school-age children. Then your main focus will be cleaning up while helping children with their homework. Many parents find that they can clear off the kitchen table and then do the dishes while the children do their homework at the table. If any problems come up, the parent can easily solve them or stop doing the dishes for a minute to oversee the homework already done. Problems arise, however, when one child distracts another or a toddler comes wandering in.

Some children require intense parental direction to complete an assignment. They daydream over their homework, don't understand directions, hide comic books inside their textbooks, draw pictures of houses and battleships on their looseleaf paper, and generally take all night to get one page of work done. To help these children, you practically have to sit right next to them until their assignments are completed. Of course you don't have time to do that, but in these cases, at least at first, you must make time.

One alternative is to take a few minutes to get them set up. Read over their assignments, get out the appropriate books and supplies, open to the correct pages with book-marks, make sure their pencils are sharpened, go over directions with them, and remove all toys and recreational distractions from their study area. Be sure to check on these children every twenty minutes or so, however. Also make sure when they have finished their assignments that they pack everything into their bookbags for the next day. And don't take their word that they are finished, check what they have done against their assignment sheets.

Unlike the above children, the majority of grade schoolers are able to complete their assignments with a minimum of parental input. While most need quiet places to study, some children actually study better with a little background noise—which does not mean TV. Some children even have to be active to study—walking around as they memorize something or playing with a toy such as a Slinky as they read. Just be sure they do not disrupt those who need quiet to learn. Each child has his own optimal learning style, and as long as he is performing well in school and not disturbing others, he should be permitted to study as he feels best.

Keep learning styles in mind when you are helping your children with their homework too. Some children learn best by seeing something done; others learn by touching, hearing, or even smelling. For example, your eldest may have learned her times tables by going around the house shouting, "Six times one is six; six times two is twelve; six times three is eighteen . . ." until she drove everyone crazy. Your second studied his times tables best by having you ask him problems in the car on the way to school: "Okay, Josh, how much is seven times six?" Your third, however, might not understand the whole concept of times tables unless you dust off the old abacus from his nursery school days and demonstrate. Your job as a parent is to figure out how each child learns best and to help him have these learning conditions both at home and in school.

Let's assume you have children who study fairly well on their own. There will nonetheless be those times when they will need special help with a project, a term paper, or a test review. How do you handle those situations? Try to have the child give you a little advance warning if possible. This will allow you to scrape together some extra time— maybe by preparing a really quick dinner or bathing the baby earlier in the day. Find a spot in the house free from the other children and help the child as long as you can between minicrises. This is also a time when fathers and big brothers or sisters can be of immense help. Older siblings often have insight into the learning process that you do not. It might even be worthwhile to take your older child's turn at doing the dishes while she explains long division to a younger child.

Some parents make school calendars for their kitchen walls on which the children record important projects and papers, and when they are due. Parents then know when they will have to make time for a trip to the library, when they might have to drive on a class outing, and when they should allow time to quiz a child on the night before a scheduled test.

Things get even more complex when you have to go out on a school night. Try to anticipate these evenings and serve a dinner that doesn't result in a great number of dishes. Maybe homework and even baths can be worked in before dinner. Get school clothes ready way ahead of time and lay out pajamas if you are usually the one to get them for the kids. Get home as early as possible to be sure things are on track.

Bedtime

First, a little review of sleep physiology. Sleep is composed of several different stages that change and develop as a child grows from infancy to adolescence. In sleep stage one, thoughts are fragmented and discontinuous, and if someone awakened you, you would not be able to quite remember what you were dreaming. The further stages of sleep are divided into two big types, REM (or rapid eye movement) and non-REM sleep. Babies' sleep time is about equally divided between REM and non-REM sleep, but as we get older we spend more time in non-REM sleep. During REM sleep you can see a child's eyes moving under his eyelids. Sleep cycles, which we all have, last about one and a half hours, with periodic "awakenings" during the night, although most of the time we don't remember them.

Unusual things that can also happen during sleep are called parasomnias. A very common example is a night terror. During a night terror a child seems to awaken, may cry incoherently and thrash about, is sweaty and shaky, doesn't respond normally to you, and looks to all the world as if he has just had the worst nightmare ever. In a few minutes he calms down and goes back to sleep, except that he has really been asleep all along! And the next day he will remember nothing about the event that probably almost scared you to death.

Other parasomnias, much rarer than night terrors, are sleepwalking, sleep paralysis, and other forms of automatic sleep behavior that are probably seen more often in adults.

Children have different sleep requirements. Some require relatively little sleep, and others need to sleep a good deal. Some children function best in the morning and like to go to bed early, and others love to be up late at night and would sleep all day if you let them. Some children are awakened by the slightest change in their environment: a small noise or a night-light being turned on. If you have two children with dramatically different sleep personalities who happen to be roommates, you may be in for trouble!

Bedtime Rituals: Bedtime is the homestretch. If you can make it through bedtime, maybe you can sit down and read the newspaper or, if that's too ambitious, collapse on your bed and be asleep in five seconds.

It's important to realize that for the young child bedtime is seen as a time of separation from parents. For this reason young children may approach bedtime with just a little anxiety. Rituals that emphasize closeness and security, and reassure the child of the parents' ongoing presence, serve as a good way to breach the gap from being awake to sleeping. (The presence of siblings through the night can also help.)

Most families have bedtime rituals. In one family with five young children Dad holds the baby until she falls asleep, while Mom bathes and reads to the two preschoolers before tucking them in. In another family with five children all under eleven, there are also rituals, but they work less than perfectly. Says Lynnette, a mother with a frank sense of humor,

> I hate bedtime. Bedtime is a horrible time in our house. If I ever lose it all, it will be at bedtime. That is, the one thing that I have been very strict and consistent on is bedtime. The children are expected to go to bed at 8 P.M., but every night you'd think they had never heard of that rule or they would like it bent a little. It seems as if bedtime is the one thing that gets harder and harder with more children. The older children want to stay up later, but the younger children won't go to bed without the older ones going to bed too. The babies are always so tired and irritable at that time, screaming and needing to be put in bed, while the older children are arguing: "Do I have to go to bed?" Then there are the nights when homework and practicing haven't

been done or the kids want to stay up late because a school report is due, and I have to say no. Once I get them all in bed, someone has to get a drink, brush his teeth, go to the bathroom, or something. One thing that has helped a little is that either my husband or I will lie beside the children for a few minutes each night and talk to them about their day, tell them a story, sing a song, or something like that to calm them down and help them go to sleep. This also gives the children an incentive to get into bed because "lie by me" time only lasts until 8:30. If they waste time getting into bed, then they waste their "lie by me" time. By the time I get the children to bed every night I'm ready for the funny farm. That's how I handle—or survive—bedtime.

Bedtime rituals become less important as children get older. For grade school children rituals are largely replaced by rules, enforced with a greater or lesser degree of success. For example, a mother of five grade school sports-minded children who have lots of other activities admits: "Bedtime is very inconsistent. Our schedules don't always permit homework to be done right after school because of practices and workouts. The older two go to bed when homework is completed, usually 10:30 to 11:00 P.M., the younger three by 9:30 P.M."

Some grade school children can prepare themselves for bedtime, but many still need you to go through the litany: "Did you brush your teeth and take your shower? Are your school clothes all laid out for tomorrow? Did you put all your homework in the bookbag? Did you find your shoes? Are your gym shorts in your bookbag too?"

Most still like to be tucked in, or at least bid good night. If several share a room, you can save time by saying good night en masse, with a special stop at each child's bed or bunk.

What is a good hour for bedtime? It depends on your life-style and on the needs of each child. If the children must do farm chores in the morning, then they will have to be in bed earlier than city children who have soccer practice or choir in the evening. Some children need lots of sleep and others need only a little. As a rule of thumb, grade-school-age children should probably have at least nine hours of sleep on school nights. (There are exceptions in both directions.)

It can be difficult for a child to share a room with a sibling who goes to bed at a much later time, especially if she turns on the light or makes a lot of noise, and the one who goes to bed earlier is a light sleeper. It can also be difficult when a brother or sister who is only a year older has permission to stay up an extra hour or if one occupant is a night person and the other is an early riser.

Parents might consider the following when dealing with different sleep schedules:

Put night owls in with night owls when assigning rooms, if possible. Have a "lights out" time. If someone wants to stay up later, he/she has to get ready for bed in the dark. Have the same bedtime for everyone in the room.

Resistance to Bedtime: There are many reasons for bedtime resistance, and you will probably be more successful in dealing with it if you can figure out what is going on in your children's minds. At times bedtime resistance can reflect serious problems that a child is trying to deal with. Her anxiety may peak at bedtime when activities that normally distract her from her worries cease, and she is alone. If your suspicions are aroused because a child has developed bedtime problems all of a sudden and because other things in the child's life are not going well (for example, a best friend has moved away, grades are falling, or the child seems uncharacteristically sad and irritable lately), you should certainly discuss the problem with your child. If the anxieties can't be resolved, bring up the topic with your physician.

When children are older and choose their bedtimes, their

slightly younger siblings who still have a regulated bedtime can become envious. These younger ones don't have enough insight to realize that their fussiness or inattention is a sign of fatigue. You find yourself having to order them to bed, over their protests that you are being unfair.

If you have considered the situation well and feel that there are good reasons for close-in-age siblings to have different bedtimes, then explain these reasons and continue to enforce your rules. Children need to know that everyone can't be treated "the same" because each child's needs are different, including the need for sleep.

Teenagers can have very erratic sleep patterns predicated upon when tests occur and when term papers are due. They seem to be able to get recharged on four or five hours of sleep for several days, then sleep for almost twenty-four hours to catch up. Some teens sleep all the time, others seem never to sleep.

As a parent you have to keep an eye on the quantity of sleep your children receive. If you feel that they procrastinate about schoolwork and then stay up all night to get it done, look at the quality of the work they do and whether this pattern of procrastination ultimately affects their grades. Some teenagers (and adults) perform better under time stress, and others turn in very poor work when they are fatigued. You may want to discuss with your teenager what sleep and work patterns are best for him. One sixteen-year-old, for example, would stay up almost all night studying for each test and then sleep on the next weekend, and he maintained straight A grades, while his brother, a year older, did assignments and studied each day, and got the same grades.

Common Reasons for Sleep Problems: To solve difficulties in getting to sleep, you need to have a working knowledge of each child's sleep needs and any particular fears or problems that may temporarily disturb their sleep routine. You may also find that there's additional gain for a child who is the only one who can't fall asleep: He may get to stay up alone with Mommy and Daddy. One big problem that parents face occurs when a valid difficulty such as an ear infection turns into a chronic sleep disturbance because the child realizes she can have her parents' undivided attention during the time she is up and the other children are asleep. Even nine-month-olds can figure this one out.

Most children will be asleep within ten or fifteen minutes after being put to bed. If one or more of your children consistently do not fall asleep within a half hour or less, there are several things you should consider.

Are your children going to bed too early? If they get up relatively late, say 8:00 A.M., or if they take one or two naps a day, they may not be ready to sleep at 6:30 or 7:00 P.M., no matter how much you want them to. You need to know how much sleep each child needs because children, like adults, vary widely in their sleep requirements. Allow each child to follow his/her natural sleep inclinations for a while, then figure out how much sleep each child requires. Plan bedtime and naptime to fulfill these personalized sleep requirements. For example, if you find that Steve, three, needs twelve hours of sleep in a twenty-four-hour period, and Jon, four, needs only eleven hours, and they share a room, you could decide to put them to bed at 7:30 P.M. and get them up at 6:30, with a nap only for Steve. Or you could give both a nap, put them to bed a little later, and allow Steve to sleep longer in the morning. The chances are that putting Steve to bed earlier either won't work or will take a lot of effort, but you may want to try that approach.

Are your children worried about being separated from you at night? Nocturnal separation anxieties are very common and may be one reason for many of the delaying tactics we know so well. Fortunately, children in large families seem to suffer less from separation anxiety because there is usually a sibling sharing the room. However, a bad day at nursery school, a scary TV show, or an overheard dispute between you and your mate may trigger a bad night. If a child who usually goes to bed easily seems to be having trouble getting to sleep, you might just want to talk with her about it. If it is a chronic problem, you'll have to dig deeper, maybe combining reassurance and "special time" with firm rules about bedtime. Bedtime rituals work well here.

Do roommates keep their siblings up? Children usually adjust pretty well to sharing a room, but occasionally one child may cause sleep difficulties for another. (Make sure, of course, that the complaints are justified and not a way to get back at a brother or sister.) One child may snore, for example; be sure to check this out with your doctor because respiratory obstruction may become a serious problem. When children share beds, one may be an active sleeper, kicking, pushing, or stealing covers. Roommates may disagree over room temperature, lighting, and so on. You will either have to do some problem-solving with the roommates or change sleeping arrangements.

Are your children staying up for quality time? Some children will fight sleep so they can be with their parents when their brothers and sisters are asleep. You will have to deal with this by enforcing bedtime rules while setting aside other private time for this child, and this can be difficult to do.

Is the problem the result of poor planning? As a child gets older, poor planning can play a role in bedtime problems. As examples: Clare neglects to do her homework early because she was talking on the phone all night, or Tim stays up worrying about the book report and just can't get to sleep. Although bedtime must be more flexible for the older child, you may need to teach such a child some time management skills.

Special Occasions: What about letting children stay up

late for special occasions? Everyone does it, but there is a price to pay. Children with early bedtimes get fussy and droopy even when the event they stay up for is a very exciting one. This orneriness can carry into the next day, when you may have to help them make up lost sleep time. If your children are waiting up for something such as an evening play or a religious service, you can probably expect them to fall asleep in their seats when things get relatively quiet. Be prepared to carry them out.

In comparison to school weekdays, weekend and summer evenings are a delight. Forget baths every so often and let the kids stay a little dirtier than usual. Read and play games. Go to bed early and let the big ones put the little ones to bed. Take an evening walk. These are the best nights of the year. Enjoy!

CHAPTER 5

Chores, TV or Not TV, and Other Dilemmas of Growing Up

SOME day-to-day encounters could become major dilemmas if not planned for properly, and among these are chores, television viewing, and the spread of infection. Large families also have to include special safety ideas in daily living and be prepared for an occasional longer visit from a relative. With a little preplanning, all of these encounters can be made more enjoyable for all.

Chores

"Mom, Debbie didn't do a good job on the dishes last night. You have to make her clean up better. I never leave junk on the plates when I do the dishes, and I'm sick of eating off plates with all that crud on them. If you don't do something about it, I'm going to blast her."

"Mom, Jeffrey won't pick up his toys like you told him, and now he's getting more toys out! I'm not going to help him clean up this mess."

"Dad, I don't see why I have to clean up the garage this time. I did it two months ago, and if Pete and Sam can't keep it clean, they should clean it up alone this time. Anyway, you know what a sloppy job they do."

"Mom, nobody will trade dishes with me tonight, and I have to go to the library (babysit, study, and so forth). Will you make one of those guys help me?"

Do these statements sound familiar? In the large family chores can become weapons of battle in the unending saga of sibling rivalry. If Mom or Dad praises how one child does a chore and forgets to praise another, bedlam can ensue. Your job is to be as fair and evenhanded as you can about chore distribution and "quality assurance." You cannot do more than that.

The Chore List: Few large families would survive without some variety of the chore list. You see it posted on refrigerators, bulletin boards, any place readily accessible to parents when kids start fighting about whose turn it is to do what.

A chore list is a series of assignments to be done on a daily, weekly, or monthly basis to keep the home functioning. These assignments can be done by children of various ages without undue parental supervision. Tasks that many families include in a chore list are dishwashing, lawn maintenance, washing and ironing, vacuuming, dusting, taking out the garbage, cleaning the garage, farm and garden chores, setting the table, and in-house babysitting. You can be creative, though. Families with driving teenagers may include transportation of siblings, car maintenance, and shopping.

How do you decide who gets what chore? Most families divide chores according to the developmental skills of their children, not according to the individual child's likes and dislikes. (Otherwise, all three-year-olds would opt for dishwashing.) Some families allow children to swap chores, and some do not. If you permit children to swap chores, get it in writing: Make the children who are trading chores both write in and initial the changes on the chore list so there will be no dispute later.

Some parents base each child's allowance on the chore list. Others feel the chore list is an obligation to the family, and there should be no monetary reward. Some parents will "forgive" chores when a child has a big test coming up the next day, while others feel a child learns time management by doing his chores and studying for the test too.

Some children are always grumbling about their chores, and others enter into a kind of sibling rivalry over who cuts the grass quickest or who does the dishes best. The bottom line is that chores, if not excessive, do more than just help the family function, they teach work habits and pride in doing a job well and give each child a sense of being important to the family's survival.

Teaching Responsibility: How do you gauge how much responsibility to give an older child? This can be a difficult question because sometimes the answer is to use your own intuition.

Your common sense should tell you that there are some responsibilities you never give any child. A six- or seven-year-old cannot be left completely alone with small babies while you drive off to the grocery store for an hour. An eight-year-old shouldn't be expected to cook dinner for the whole family. A parent shouldn't expect all of an adolescent's free time to be used for household and babysitting chores.

But there is a gray area. Some children are more able to handle responsibility than others; those others, even though they are theoretically old enough for a certain chore, just don't have the maturity. Of course your other children, who had to do that very same chore at an early age, will complain, so you will probably have to come up with an equivalent task that the less mature child can accomplish.

Some children are just not talented in a specific area. For instance, there are teens who are great with babies, and others who couldn't care less. Here again, substitution may be in order. Or you can try training-acclimatization, where you decide on an age-appropriate chore, explain and demonstrate how to do it, and progressively increase the child's responsibility for that chore. In that way you can gauge his success yet not give him too much to handle too early. For example, you can show him how you want the dishes washed, give him the plates one night and the plates and silverware the next, and over time he will work up to tidying the kitchen and doing all the dishes.

Here are some examples of age-appropriate chores:

Two to three: Getting diapers for the baby; polishing (windows, tables); carrying silverware to the table; picking up toys if not too numerous (but with help if there are lots of toys); folding washcloths; feeding animals; helping to weed the garden; keeping the baby amused.

Chores at this age should be fun but frequently must be done over by Mom. The object is to teach, not to accomplish a great deal. When doing chores with a toddler, be sure to work alongside her and give her a task that's short and that she feels she can finish. You want her to experience the thrill of doing something and actually seeing the results. Don't forget to praise her liberally and hug her when she's done.

Four to five: Picking up own toys; setting the table; minding the baby when Mom is on the phone; dusting; animal care; sweeping or vacuuming easy, small areas; clearing the table; helping with bed-making.

At these ages a child can do simple chores a little more completely than the toddler and may "surprise" you by doing a chore on his own. Praise this initiative; it's something you want to encourage as he grows older. You can begin to stress the importance of completing a task, but again, make the task fairly easy so that he has the experience of mastering something.

Six to seven: Straightening up a room; setting and clearing the table; sorting the wash; weeding the garden; helping a younger sibling put away toys. Many children at this age enjoy the feeling of having responsibilities they are able to fulfill. Some, however, do not.

Eight to ten: Weekly cleaning of a room (excluding heavy cleaning); babysitting chores for longer durations of time; full responsibility for animal care; sweeping and vacuuming; taking out the trash; ironing simple garments under supervision; assisting younger siblings with homework; folding and putting away wash.

As you observe a child at these ages doing chores, you may notice a wide range of abilities. You need to tailor chores to abilities. If you notice a child having difficulty performing sequential chores—that is, when you tell him to do three things in a row and he invariably forgets one of them—or having trouble following verbal instructions, you may wish to check with his schoolteacher about whether he shows signs of the same difficulty in school. Many children are labeled "uncooperative" when in fact they have a type of learning disorder involving sequencing. How a child does his chores may give you a helpful clue as to how he processes information.

Eleven to fourteen: Washing; ironing; vacuuming; babysitting; cleaning the car; helping on the farm or in a business (depending on age and local laws); full care of vegetable garden; meal preparation and dishes; careful use of lawnmower and other lawn-care tools; painting.

A child at these ages, if well coordinated, can do almost

any reasonable chore. He also will probably be more eager to do the job right than an older sibling who just wants to get the chore over with. If the child of these ages is the oldest (or even if not), be careful not to overburden her with work even if she seems eager.

Fifteen and up: Although children of these ages can do just about everything you can, they often don't want to and may revert to doing a chore quickly and poorly, just to get it done. Or they may do it very well, tempting you to give extra chores. In dealing with a teen, you need to have patience. He has chores that must be done expediently and satisfactorily, but he should have a way of scheduling them or of trading with another sibling when an important social event pops up.

Making Chores Work: Here are some general approaches that parents have found successful in handing out chores:

1. Make chores age-appropriate.
2. Post a chore list on a weekly or monthly basis.
3. Rotate chores where possible.
4. Allow chore exchanges or substitutions only when documented.
5. Set penalties for failure to do chores responsibly, and enforce them. (Penalties must be reasonable, such as the chore being done twice by the sibling whose turn has been taken and completed by another at the parent's request.)
6. The corollary rule to number 5 is that if a child does a chore in an obviously careless manner, have him do it again.
7. Make a list in advance of acceptable excuses for not doing chores, such as being ill with a fever or being invited to Switzerland. (Being invited to a friend's house does not usually count as a valid reason.)

8. If a child has genuine difficulty doing a chore, you have two alternatives: You can teach him how, or you can reassign him to do something more appropriate to his skills.

9. Give praise when deserved and try to make the praise specific; for example, "Joey, the lawn really looks nice. I like the way you hand-trimmed all the nooks and crannies you couldn't reach with the mower."

10. Don't be too critical if a child is genuinely trying. Help him to do better in a positive way; for example, "Daniel, the dishes are nice and clean. But remember, it's important to clean off the table and the stove as well as you cleaned the dishes."

11. Be aware that children go through "chore stages." A sixteen-year-old may have been a big help at ten, but now he has to be forced to work and does a sloppy job to boot. While understanding that this is normal behavior, you must enforce minimal task standards.

Ask parents of large families about allowances, and you get a whole spectrum of responses.

"I give allowances if they realize they have to earn it," says Dawn, mother of five. "If they don't do the work, they don't get paid."

"We feel the children should have money so they can learn to deal with it in a respectful way," states Helen, who has four children.

Sara, whose oldest (of six) is just eight, says, "We haven't started yet. We plan to start allowances at age eleven or twelve."

Linda's oldest is only seven, but she says, "I'd rather they earned their own money."

Mary, with five children, says she feels she should be

giving her children a regular allowance, but she keeps on forgetting to.

Christie, mother of seven, says, "We don't have a consistent allowance. We pay the older girls for babysitting, and the children earn money for doing special jobs above and beyond their regular chores."

Another mother is philosophically opposed to allowances because she feels the children owe the family a certain amount of help and shouldn't be paid for it.

Sue, mother of seven, probably summarizes the attitudes of most parents when she comments, "We don't give allowances, mainly because we aren't organized enough to keep track and do it on a regular basis but also because we really don't feel they are necessary. We don't think children need a regular income or spending money until they are old enough to earn it outside the home, babysitting, mowing lawns, pet sitting, and so forth. If the kids need money for an event, then we give it to them if we approve of the need—not for buying such things as candy and toys. Birthday money is spendable or savable, depending on the child's age or desires."

Parents who give allowances do so to teach about money. They generally start when they feel their children understand how money works and can make appropriate decisions about its use. Sometimes the allowance is large enough to cover the cost of clothing and extras, but sometimes it is just a token sum.

In most large families the work necessary to keep track of who gets what sum for what purpose and when is just too difficult. Besides, allowances add to sibling rivalry. Of course, you can always pay for chores or just give a flat rate to everybody, but the bottom line is that most parents of large families do not give regular allowances and really don't believe they're necessary. They prefer to pay for chores done and skip the bookwork. It simplifies life.

Television Viewing

If you don't have a TV, congratulations. But often kids with no TV spend a lot of time watching the TVs of their friends. If you do have a TV, who controls it in your family? Do you have one over which you exert absolute control? If you can actually fully control TV usage, either your children are all under two and have not yet mastered the fine motor control necessary to turn it on, or you could be in the running to be the next Margaret Thatcher.

Or perhaps you allow TV viewing at specific times, with a fair understanding of the appropriateness of the show's content. This is probably the most realistic approach to TV usage.

On the other hand, you may have given up entirely and either bought a dozen TVs (two for each room in the house) or let your kids fight to the death over which show to watch, while you hide in a locked bathroom.

The issue of TV viewing is one our grandmothers, with their large families, did not have to face. And yet it can have a major developmental impact on your children and can spawn many a fight.

What are the good things about TV? Well, it can save your sanity by serving as a babysitter, but you must not use it in this capacity too often. Some educational programs can be outstanding and can help a child in school or can lead to further family discussions about science, the arts, history, and so on. Today, a great deal of political campaigning is done on TV, and children can become better-informed citizens by watching candidates and talking about their ideas afterward. And let's face it, a certain amount of TV "literacy" oils the social wheels for your children.

What's so bad about TV then? For one thing, TV has taken the place of the real world for many children. It is easier for a child to plop down in front of the TV with a bag of chips than to read a book or take the trouble to round up the neighbor kids for a game of ball. If you're not a particularly great ball player, it's a good escape from having to play with kids who are better than you are . . . and might just tease you. TV requires no effort toward social interaction. Even toddlers are finding cartoons a good replacement for the imaginative play they need so much at this stage of their development. "Sesame Street" may teach letter recognition, but it just cannot teach three-dimensional problem-solving!

Once, a very chunky seven-year-old boy was brought into my office for an exam. Most pediatricians nowadays will want to know about TV and snack habits when they see an obese child, for we all recognize that the seeds of coronary disease are sown in childhood. When I asked his harried mother, who was simultaneously trying to nurse a fussy infant, control a toddler, and give her son's medical history, she said that he did watch a lot of TV. I asked the seven-year-old whether he disliked being outside. He replied that whenever he was outside and tried to run with the other kids, he started to cough and couldn't keep up. He got so discouraged that now he just stayed indoors, watched TV, and ate, finally becoming too fat to even try to keep up with the other kids.

This child had exercise-induced asthma; he could not run without wheezing and therefore got no exercise. His wheezing was easily controlled with a little medication before he went out to play, and he slowly slimmed down and returned to playing with his friends outside.

In addition to preventing children from developing other skills, TV can actually reinforce beliefs and values that are directly opposed to yours. Certain philosophies and beliefs presented on even fairly responsible programs can contradict those espoused by you. If you don't see the particular shows and don't pick up on and discuss the nuances presented, your children may accept as correct some ethical values you find quite objectionable. For example, premarital sex and casual sex are presented as the norm on many sitcoms, and many of us prefer to have our children consider sex in a different way.

We are often told to monitor all our children's TV viewing. This may be impossible to do in a large family because your time is taken up with too many other things. Anyway, children are often far cleverer than we are and can come up with many ways to get to see what they want. One family of eight learned this the hard way. Their nine-year-old son's friend spent Friday night visiting. The next day they received an irate call from the child's mother asking how her young son could have been permitted to watch *Animal House* on TV. It turned out that the kids had sneaked downstairs at 3:00 A.M. to watch the movie on cable TV and had thought it was a pretty great movie! Of course, this little episode was never repeated, but then, the friend was never allowed to visit again either.

Let's assume you have only one TV for child viewing. The following rules may help to minimize arguments, make sure viewing time isn't excessive, and keep children away from shows you find morally, emotionally, or aesthetically objectionable.

1. Limit the total number of hours viewed per day. Two hours or less is generally plenty for a school day.
2. Restrict any shows whose contents you find objectionable.
3. Make sure everyone's homework is completed before anyone is permitted to turn on the TV. (This rule is practically guaranteed to cause a few quarrels at first. Stick with it!)
4. Chores must supersede TV until and unless children can prove their responsibility in always getting chores done.

5. Dad's or Mom's TV choices generally take precedence.

6. When two or more children want to watch different shows on the same TV at the same time, you have several choices, of which the least satisfactory is letting them fight it out. Consider one of these solutions, to be agreed to by your whole family ahead of time: the most educational show wins; there is a vote, with the majority ruling; the TV goes off; parent arbitrarily decides; take turns (the trouble with this one is everyone thinks it is his/ her turn); assign each child a day of the week to be in charge; the Solomon solution: threaten to chop the TV in half or thirds or eighths; any other creative, fair solution you can come up with.

7. Poor school grades or insufficient exercise or independent reading is a cause for temporary TV suspension. The reality of life in a large family is that it is difficult to restrict one child's viewing without restricting the others' too. You may have to limit everyone's TV time until the errant child is back on track. But that's okay.

Parents must always be vigilant not to allow the TV to substitute for them emotionally or physically, but they can also be allowed to use it occasionally to distract their children when they need a little time for themselves.

The Roving Virus

Have you ever heard of the "youngest child syndrome"? It describes the frequent infections the youngest children in a large family often seem to get. Older brothers and sisters bring home all sorts of germs and viruses. Little children, who have never been exposed before, catch them right away and get much sicker than their older siblings.

The good news is that these children build up immunity and often will be healthier when they are older. The bad news is that there's not much you can do to prevent the spread of infection in the large household. Most infections spread by touch and by cough and sneeze. (A few are spread only through intimate contact, of course, and these present risks to spouses but generally not to children.) With a large family it's almost impossible to isolate children effectively from one another. The best thing you can do is be sure all your children are immunized on time and spot and care for infections early. If one child has a strep throat, be on the lookout for others who may have early signs. Tell them to let you know if they start to have symptoms.

For some infections there are no effective treatments or vaccinations. If chicken pox gets into your household, you'll just have to grin and bear it. If you are pregnant, be sure to let your doctor know when an infection that hits your household is one you haven't had. Sometimes extraordinary treatments can be used for a person at special risk, and your doctor can advise you if these are indicated.

Be sure to keep good family medical records—a chore but these documents become very important over the years as it becomes harder to remember which child had what illnesses, allergies, and vaccinations. Baby books often have spaces for this information. Be sure you have one for each child.

There are a few serious infections, such as certain types of meningitis, that call for preventive treatment of certain family members and contacts. If a family member is stricken with a serious infection, ask your doctor whether the illness fits into this category.

Safety Tips

Several years ago, after putting all of my children in our station wagon at my daughter's nursery school, I went over to another car for a second to chat. Then I came back, got into my own car, and drove off. It was only when I reached home that everyone realized we had left my daughter at school. While I was talking she had slipped out to get a sip of water and hadn't made it back in time. I hadn't bothered to count the children again and never realized she was gone. I drove back and found a very tearful little girl, who hasn't yet forgotten the incident.

In addition to the usual childproofing done by all parents, such as putting plastic plugs in the electric outlets and locking away all medicines and poisonous materials, here are some special safety tips for families with several children:

1. Teach older children about toddler safety measures so they don't do something inadvertently such as leaving a door open through which a two-year-old could get to a busy street or a swimming pool. I recall a city toddler who fell out an open second-story window and died twelve hours later.
2. Establish a "buddy system" when you go anywhere, even to the store. That way an older child can keep an eye on a younger one and can alert you to problems. This is especially important if you go someplace new, such as an amusement park, where a little one could easily wander off.
3. Let your children know that they aren't tattling if they inform you about a safety violation—such as an old refrigerator, with its doors still attached, left out on the street.
4. Be especially alert to safety problems when you

are visiting, under stress, or distracted. That's
when accidents are likely to happen.
5. Be aware of where all your children are at all times.
Do a mental roll call from time to time.

House Guests

For most children, having grandparents (or aunts, uncles,
and other relatives) come to visit is a special treat. For
parents it is sometimes a mixed blessing. If the visitors come
from large families themselves, love children, and know
just how to pitch in and be helpful without getting in the
way, and if you as parents have good relationships with
your "relations," these visits will be memorable. But if the
grandparents are disturbed by noise, are frail or insensitive,
need attention themselves, or tend to be critical or disap-
proving of your family, their visits may be less than pleasurable.

Sometimes conflicts that parents have had with their own
parents will resurface during these visits. Sometimes old
conflicts are washed away or put aside by the joy of seeing
grandchildren. Sometimes relations between parents and
grandparents are fine and always have been, but it turns
out that Grandma likes Paul better than Margaret, and
Grandpa prefers playing with the baby to playing with
toddler Mike. So Margaret and Mike are unhappy. Occasionally there is simply not enough room for everybody!

Most parents are able to take a long-range view when
dealing with visiting relatives. The relationship between
grandchildren and grandparents can be a very special one,
giving children a sense of security in the continuity of the
generations, allowing them the opportunity to have extra
attention, and creating memories for the future. (Aunts,
uncles, and cousins can do much the same.) For most par-

ents it is worth putting up with a little inconvenience because the benefits are so great.

Assuming there is good will all around, there are a few things you can do to make Grandma/Grandpa/Uncle Jeff's visit a happy time for everyone:

1. If possible, plan the invitation for a time that is convenient for you as well as for them. You can't be a good hostess/host if a big project is due at work or you're involved in the Girl Scout cookie drive—unless Grandma and Grandpa are the kind of people who pitch right in and help.

2. A time-limited invitation works best for many families. Then you can plan better how to make the most of the visit and are less likely to feel overburdened.

3. Know your relatives. Expect that they will be pretty much as they have always been and prepare yourself mentally for them. If Mom has always been critical of your housekeeping, she probably will continue to be. But you can let it roll off your back by expecting it and by appreciating what a great job she is doing teaching your daughter how to sew or reading to the preschoolers.

4. Nip problems in the bud. Most grandparents are sensitive to the need to show each grandchild equal amounts of affection, and many have a wisdom and tact born of years of experience. But grandparents are also human and might have preferences among your children. If you notice that this is the case, take Grandpa aside and tell him. Most grandparents, once aware, will do their best to distribute their attention equally.

5. Praise grandparents when they are especially helpful with the children or with household chores. They also need to know they are appreciated.

6. Enforce household rules but add some flexibility. Grandparents often like to give their grandchildren treats and sweets, but you may be afraid that this will spoil them—or at least spoil their dinner. If you feel strongly, you can ask Grandma ahead of time not to do it, but if it doesn't bother you too much, let Grandma go ahead and feed them cookies a half hour before dinner. She's only here a few days, and it's unlikely that your children's one-time dietary indiscretions will have a permanent effect on their health.

7. Encourage grandparents to recount well-loved family stories (and get them on tape if you can). Older children especially love to hear them. They are invaluable to a child's sense of identity and they are fun!

CHAPTER
6

Discipline

WHAT'S the toughest part about being a parent (aside from making enough money to feed everyone, that is)? Many people agree that disciplining their children is their biggest headache.

Discipline is not limited to punishing children when they've clearly done something wrong. Rather, it covers the whole spectrum of teaching children how to get along with others and how to be responsible human beings who live up to their potential. Good discipline takes time and a lot of energy, and it should be individualized to the needs of the child.

The first child is more likely to respond to a simple

talking-to. For far more than half of "senior offspring," a discussion is all that is ever needed. In fact, 6 percent of firstborns are so cooperative they aren't disciplined at all. If a verbal reprimand doesn't do the trick, the next best method for a firstborn seems to be taking away privileges or grounding him if he's old enough, and if he's not, isolating or giving him time-out. Ten percent of young firstborns get an occasional whack on the behind.

Second children are a bit more complex. Ten percent never need discipline, and another 10 percent are always in hot water. For these latter children, no disciplinary method seems to work well. One mother of seven, when asked what disciplinary approach worked best for her "bubbly, flighty, disorganized" teenage daughter, replied, "I haven't found one yet. Consequences, if I can think of the right ones, have sometimes worked for the past year or so. Before that, nothing worked." Contrast this child with another girl the same age from a family of six: "Just a look or seeing that you're upset is all that's required, she wants so much to please."

Discussion is also used a lot with second children, but a larger percentage need isolation, grounding, or withholding of privileges.

Third children are much like second children in their responses to different methods. A few more get a spanking or are isolated, but they are also a little younger overall. Talking a problem out is still the favorite method of discipline, even if the child is quite young. Some parents have come up with innovative methods of discipline for third children, probably because they've had practice with older siblings. One mother likes "making her teenage daughter write about persons, feelings, and behavior. She was very willing, until this year, to behave. The problem now is mouthing off, so writing seems the best way to deal with this so far." Another mother complains, "There is no good method. Rachel can make you laugh no matter what she's done and get away with murder! But when I speak with her, she will cooperate with almost anything."

Fourth children, like the oldest child, are most often just talked to. A considerable number don't ever require discipline at all. Young ones are spanked or isolated. Parents also like to use positive reinforcement for this cohort and for their younger siblings.

The older the child in the family, the less concerned parents seem to be about discipline. Discussion continues to be the favorite method overall for all children, and other methods are used only for extreme circumstances. One explanation for this phenomenon may be that by the fourth, fifth, and sixth child, the "house rules" are pretty well known by everyone, and older siblings clue in their younger brothers and sisters. There may not be such a need for parental discipline in the very large family.

A small subgroup of children are very difficult to discipline. They don't respond well to discussion, and sometimes even physical discipline has no effect. Some of these children are bright but a bit disorganized, some have a temper problem, and a couple have learning disorders as the root cause. One or two are so bright they challenge their parents' disciplinary attempts. Luckily, only about one in twenty children seems to present a serious problem for his/her parents.

Let me tell you a story about a small boy, about three years old. This child was becoming more and more of a disciplinary problem as each week passed, and his mother was at her wit's end. She thought the reason for his disobedience was that he was sandwiched in between two brothers and now had a new sister to contend with too. She tried to be understanding, but having to go back to work two months after her daughter was born didn't improve her patience any.

One day everything came to a head. The little boy was sitting on the kitchen floor, playing with some toys, and his mother came along and asked him to pick them up. He didn't budge. She made the request again, explaining why she wanted it done. No response. Furious now, she ran over to the child, grabbed his arm, and twirled him around in frustration. The look on his face when she did this was not fear or anger, it was absolute surprise. He had not heard a thing she had said!

The little boy had had a severe ear infection a while back, and his ears were full of thick gluey material. What his mother had been interpreting as defiance was actually a profound hearing loss.

I was that mother. As a trained pediatrician I should have realized much sooner what was happening. As a tired working mother, I didn't. My son underwent surgery soon after and has been a most attentive and reasonable child ever since, but the lesson I learned will stay with me forever. Discipline means teaching. In order to teach, we have to send an effective message, but even more important, our children have to be capable of receiving the message. That's why it's so much tougher to get kids to obey when they're tired or hungry or overexcited.

Why do we discipline our children? One big reason is that we want them to get along with others. They have to learn and follow the rules of society so that they'll fit in, and we must teach them those rules. As an example, we generally teach our children to say, "Hello, Ms. Jones," not "Hello, Sally." In Japan the etiquette for speaking with elders is even more exacting. But if the children of either culture don't know and follow correct forms of address, they are judged to be impolite and may even be socially ostracized. So we parents discipline, or teach, our children how to address others in a way that is acceptable in our own culture, and we correct them until they do it properly. It's a part of our job as parents.

We also discipline our children to avoid physical harm. While children have an instinctual fear of heights, we have to teach them a fear of swimming pools, poisons, and hot stoves. Sometimes these lessons must be taught with emphasis because there may be only one opportunity.

A third reason to maintain discipline in the large family is that with many children the parent must keep order at all times because it is easy for any situation to degenerate into chaos. If a parent sees a problem starting, he or she must take rapid disciplinary steps.

Discipline must be age-appropriate; infraction-appropriate—"make the punishment fit the crime"; child-appropriate, using the method that brings the best results with the child in question; and done with the desire to help the child, not to get back at him.

In order to be good disciplinarians for a large family, you and your spouse need to decide on a general approach to discipline, and you should discuss important disciplinary issues as they arise. You need a clear idea of your disciplinary goals, and you must focus on how to accomplish these in each case. (Needless to say, once parents have decided together on the "how-to" of discipline, they need to support each other in front of the children. If they don't, the whole process falls apart.)

Mary and Mark faced such a tough issue when their normally obedient eighth grader, Brent, failed to turn in a term paper and got his first D. He had already been accepted at the high school of his choice and wasn't in the mood to do anything that required effort. The class ski trip was coming up, and Brent had been looking forward to it for two years. Mary and Mark probably would have excused a poor grade, but Brent had also lied to them about turning in the paper. They decided, with much reluctance, not to permit Brent to go on the trip.

Brent himself, although deeply disappointed, agreed that the combination of poor grades and lying made this a reasonable punishment. He never repeated the behavior, and neither did his younger siblings, who were very impressed with what had happened to Brent when he lied to his parents.

Individualizing Your Methods

In a family of two children, especially when they are fairly close in age, the rules must be pretty much the same for both. But in the large family it's just about impossible to discipline everyone the same. What is effective for one child may not work at all with another, who may either be at a different developmental stage or respond better to methods that are different from ones used for his siblings. Since the function of discipline is to teach, almost all parents of large families tailor their methods to each child.

Take Terry's family of five, for example. Jennifer, the oldest at almost fourteen, has good self-discipline. Terry says that "talking with her about the situation has worked since she was a baby. It is not necessary to discipline her in other ways." But Jeremy, just a year younger, needs a different approach. Terry prefers "denying him a much-loved activity or privilege and talking with him. He protests, argues, and two weeks later sees the light. We need to let him cool off for a couple of hours when he's mad."

Philip, ten, is an exceptionally bright child. To discipline him Terry prefers "talking to him about it quietly and reasonably and gently." Christopher, eight, is disciplined still differently: "I have to send him to his room for 'thinking' time. Then it's effective to talk to him," says Terry. "I have to deny him a privilege at the same time or sometimes he repeats the offense."

And for the youngest, Kathryn, six, Terry and her husband try "talking to her about the situation. If she's angry or frustrated, she has to go to her room and cool off for a few minutes. She responds well then to cuddling and talking about it."

If Terry had only two children, she'd probably discipline them pretty much the same, but with five, if a child complains that he's being treated differently from another child, Terry can point out that all the children are disciplined differently according to what works best for each personality and character type.

Personality Types

Perhaps one or more of your children have variations of the following personality types:

The Macho Kid: Mike is the second child of five, and at twelve years of age he's a real extrovert. He has many interests, including sports, nature study, and being with people. His mom says he is a gifted student but one who "tends to slide if left to his own devices." Mike's mom and dad generally believe in talking out a problem, asking why something was done and what should have been done instead. But Mike is

> more hot-tempered than the others, so a cooling-off period is necessary before we talk things out. I have learned that he needs that time, then I talk to him; then I bite my tongue while he tells me I'm wrong, and then I watch him change his mind two hours to two days later. I can't push him at the time, yet he always comes around. He is the only one I really have to handle differently. If I push, he becomes rude, I fling out punishments, and the situation rapidly deteriorates.

This wise mother has intuited several things in dealing with her hot-tempered, somewhat aggressive son. If she feeds into his anger, she might end up giving punishments she didn't mean to. And since it would be a mistake to give punishments and then fail to carry them through, she exercises restraint to avoid making things worse. She also knows that when her son's temper improves, he is able to see more clearly and eventually gets the message his mother is trying to send.

If you have a child with traits like Mike's, you might consider these ideas when dealing with him:

1. Know exactly what you want to accomplish with discipline.
2. Realize that the message may take time to be received and accepted.
3. Control your own temper.
4. Allow "time-out" for this child to cool down before a confrontation over an issue, especially if your child looks as if he's so agitated that he won't be able to discuss anything logically.
5. Use touch and eye contact in a nonthreatening way to reinforce your message, especially if the child is young.

The Very Responsible Child: David, eldest of four, is a shy and introverted adolescent, but he has the makings of an exceptional human being. According to his mother, he has always had "a special way with children which is very difficult to describe; it has manifested itself in dealing with the handicapped." David started doing volunteer work with handicapped youngsters as a part of a high school program, and he now plans to make this his vocation.

Needless to say, David's behavior seldom has to be corrected. On those rare occasions when a problem arises his mother says, "we just point out to David what has been done wrong and let him tell us how he plans to correct it. Punishment is seldom used because he doesn't need it."

Brigham is much younger than David—he's only six—and is the fourth in a family of seven children. Brigham's mother describes him as a good-natured, easily pleased child who is single-minded, a hard worker, and diligent. She says, "I can't remember having to discipline Brigham. He is hardly ever in trouble and seldom involved in squabbles."

The very responsible child does a lot of self-monitoring and internalizes discipline at an early age. He's rarely motivated by fear of punishment. Rather, he doesn't want to disappoint himself by doing something contrary to his own conception of good behavior. Children who have this precocious ethical maturity aren't necessarily goody-two-shoes types either. Often they're nice, friendly kids who were happy, easy babies. They get along well with other children but can be fairly sensitive to criticism. If you have a child like this, consider yourself blessed. You can discuss disciplinary issues with this child and allow her to come up with ways of correcting things. When this child does something wrong, you might find yourself reassuring her that everyone can make a mistake. Chances are that she'll be a lot harder on herself than you are.

The Legalist: This is the child who can quote how three years ago, under like circumstances, a sibling was given a much less severe reprimand for a theoretically similar offense. He seems to keep records on each one of his siblings and the exact nature of their infractions since they were born. He will admit to guilt for a wrongdoing only if you can prove that you previously warned him about this particular behavior . . . and give details on when, where, and before what witnesses.

Jason's mother has figured out how to deal with this because Jason is such a child. The oldest of ten, he's analytic, self-motivated, and a leader. His mother "sets the rules, with natural consequences." When she "reconstructs the whole picture, he follows."

For this type of child, usually a gifted logical thinker, consider the following methods:

1. Be logical yourself. Outline all rules and regulations, the reasons for their enactment, and the natural consequences of infractions.
2. When he has done something wrong, walk him through his behavior and point out why it was wrong. Discuss possible modes of restitution.
3. Avoid emotional responses to misbehavior.
4. Remember, even little children who enjoy cause-and-effect-type thinking can benefit from disciplinary measures explained to them as outlined above.

The Brooding Child: This child seems to have shaky self-esteem, and when you punish him, he feels singled out and harshly judged. He also seems to have a long memory. Philip was such a child. One of the middle children in a large family, he wasn't able to take a reprimand and bounce back. He interpreted every little criticism as an indication that he wasn't loved.

Philip's parents found that a disciplinary technique based on boosting his self-image worked best. When Philip left his toys all over the floor, his mother would come over, hug him, and tell him that he was a great guy and now his toys needed to be put away. When he got into a fight with his little brother, his dad intervened with, "Okay, big guy, you're such a strong fellow that we want you to stop this fight," at the same time scooping up little brother. And when Philip did something right, the whole family commented on it.

If you have a child like this, you should mix your discipline with a lot of love and reassurance. Praise those qualities that will help him to do what he has been told to do, so he will actually be building up his own self-confidence when he obeys your directions. Be firm, but choose words that will not challenge his sense of himself, such as "stupid," "lazy," or "stuck-up."

The Defiant Child: Sometimes a child with a strong independent streak or normally responsive to verbal discipline but determined when he feels he is right will defy a parent. If the child is still quite young, isolation works well. Confrontation can be a test of wills, even with a two-year-old.

When the child is a teenager, the stakes are higher. You as a parent must be sure that the offense for which you are disciplining your child is an important one and that you are being fair and honest with your child. You must know that you are acting in the child's best interest. For example, if you know that your teen is hanging out with a drug-using crowd (and remember that alcohol is also a drug), you have no choice but to force a confrontation to protect him. If, on the other hand, your daughter insists on wearing pants instead of a dress to the church youth group outing, this is not an issue for a major confrontation.

Cecelia made a wise but difficult decision in confronting her daughter over a boyfriend. As Cecelia tells the story, her daughter, fourteen, was seeing a young man four years older than she was. Cecelia and her husband felt their strong-willed teen was just too young for this type of relationship. An angry confrontation followed between mother and daughter. Cecelia added,

> Much to our surprise, when the air cleared, our daughter broke off the relationship with her friend. We worked through the problem over a period of time. When we asked her why she thought we desired the breakup, she said she didn't know. To her mind there was nothing wrong. With her inexperience of human nature, she could not see the pitfalls ahead. We, the parents, had to play the heavies.

Now that she is eighteen and a half, she says she can understand somewhat the concern we felt. She does see this young man occasionally in the group of friends she has made. When asked why she hasn't dated him, she states it is a mutual agreement between them, that seeing each other in their respective group is enough for now.

Cecelia acted forcefully in what she felt was her daughter's best interests, and she acted out of love. She didn't expect her daughter to thank her because sometimes it can take decades for a child to mature enough to recognize why parents did what they did.

If you have a child like Cecelia's, the following ideas should be helpful:

1. Be very clear in your own mind that your requests are reasonable and in the best interests of your child.
2. Have the courage to take a stand even if it means your child will be angry.
3. Explain your reasoning.
4. Be consistent, logical, and firm.
5. Think through what steps you will take to enforce your directives if and when the child continues to defy you.
6. If your child has complied with your wishes, don't embarrass him by going over and over what he did wrong or how you always know best; in other words, don't gloat, even a little.

The Impulsive Child: A child who is impulsive doesn't seem to be able to monitor his or her own behavior or to anticipate the logical consequences of an act. These children are very tough to discipline and often respond poorly to whatever method parents try.

There are many reasons for impulsiveness, and sometimes a good medical evaluation can be helpful. Children with attention deficit disorder, or "hyperactivity," are usually impulsive and can be almost impossible to discipline. Jeremy was such a child, and his parents often resorted to spanking, grounding, or time-outs. Currently he is under the care of a therapist, and special disciplinary techniques are being worked out. Jeremy's mother is worried about having to use different techniques with Jeremy and with the other three children, all of whom are considerably easier to discipline. She says, "Having so many different techniques makes it difficult to remember who belongs to what and also makes the children feel that we are unfair to them."

Children with learning disorders can also appear to be impulsive and difficult to discipline, depending on the nature of the learning problem. For instance, some children are unable to recognize emotions in others. Your child obeys you best when he sees a very angry or determined look on your face and your body tensed and ready for action. A child who cannot read these body-language clues will be far less inclined to do what you say now! This same inability to read other people's body language may get such a child into trouble with other children.

As a result, discipline problems and impulsiveness should also alert you to look for communicative and learning disorders. Your physician and school psychologist should be able to help you get the proper testing done.

Patricia doesn't have an attention deficit, and she is an A to B student in school. But her personality is "bubbly, flighty, disorganized . . . distractible," and her mother, Sue, hasn't found a good disciplinary technique yet for this young adolescent. (Sue, it should be added, is a very creative disciplinarian who is quite successful with her other six children.)

Sue feels that one reason for her daughter's failure to respond easily to discipline may be traced to allergies. (Remember, allergies can cause chronic discomfort, irritability, and decreased hearing in a few children.)

Sue says,

> Our second child and oldest daughter, Patricia, was affected by allergies in several ways: rashes, stomach problems, and behavior (I believe). When she was young, she had an attention span of about thirty seconds, it seemed. Kindergarten was very difficult for her because of her behavior—she couldn't sit still. She also was still wetting the bed at night, with no daytime accidents. She almost fit into the category of the hyperactive child, but not quite. I happened to see a doctor on TV talk about milk allergies. I got his book and it described her to a T. I took her off milk, and her behavior changed drastically for the better —temporarily. Finally I decided to have her tested for allergies, and it turned out she was allergic to lots of things. I did more reading, talked to pediatricians, and decided upon diet and medication instead of shots. We still "manage" the allergies, but she is lots better and we have only seasonal bouts.

It's important to realize that many children have allergies, and the great majority of these children aren't difficult to discipline at all. Certainly any "impulsive" child should have his hearing and vision tested. His impulsiveness could be due to an inability to pick up visual or auditory clues.

Some impulsiveness may even turn out to be due to medical conditions that have yet to be understood. Whatever the cause, impulsive children are often a disciplinary, fairness, and safety challenge to parents of a large family.

If you have a child like this, consider the following actions:

1. Bring this child to your physician for a thorough checkup, including hearing and vision testing.

2. Keep a diary of good and bad days, and see if you notice any behavioral trends.
3. Talk to the child's teacher to see if behavior in school is also impulsive or chaotic.
4. If there are problems of any type at school, request that your child have in-depth testing. This should be done through the school system at no cost to you, and the results will be available to you and to your physician if you wish.
5. Above all, keep this child out of situations where his impulsiveness could get him into serious trouble; for example, don't leave medications around and don't give him a skateboard for his birthday.

Age-Appropriateness

The infant and toddler must be protected from harm and introduced to proper social behavior. Children under two or three are too young for complicated forms of discipline. Parents have a duty to provide an environment where it's hard to do "naughty" things, which to the toddler are not naughty at all, of course. He's just exploring his world.

An example of making the environment safe would be putting plastic outlet guards in all your electric outlets. The child who puts his finger in an outlet is being curious, exactly what he should be at age eighteen months or thereabouts. But his behavior is so dangerous to him that you have to let him know in no uncertain terms that he is never to do it again. To avoid that kind of confrontation as well as the risk of physical harm, protect the outlets beforehand with guards.

You can probably think of many times when safety-proofing your house and car not only saved your children from physical harm but decreased the need for discipline too.

No parent needs to be told that a child's understanding of right and wrong evolves as he grows. You probably have children at different developmental levels, so in addition to making your discipline appropriate to the personality of each child, you should also consider her age and ability to comprehend. Two-year-olds need discipline to occur right after the infraction so they can understand why they are being reprimanded. If you wait until twenty minutes after your toddler has spilled flour all over the floor to put her in her room, she won't see the relationship between what she did and being temporarily isolated. You'll confuse her without teaching her anything. On the other hand, adolescents are starting to think in an abstract manner, so discussing the impact that irresponsible behavior has on them and others may be (for some) a very effective technique. (Many excellent books deal with age-appropriate disciplinary methods. You can consult these for the individual child.)

Since you have several children, you will want to explain to your other children that when you discipline by age for the same infraction, you aren't playing favorites.

Inappropriate Methods

Although severe, Brent's punishment was appropriate. What kind of punishment isn't appropriate?

There are two main kinds of punishment that parents should never use. The first is punishment that diminishes a child's self-esteem. You've heard the old saying about "catching more flies with honey," haven't you? Well, the flip side is that if you make a child believe he is bad, more than likely he will act bad. So you must let the child know that it is his behavior that displeases you, while you continue to love him. You can remind the child that you would not discipline him if you didn't love him. It's often easier to look the other way, but a good parent recognizes that constructive discipline is part of the job description.

Discipline should not be degrading to a child. Among other things this means that you should try to discipline in private, not in front of sisters and brothers.

And talk to your child about why you are disciplining him. He needs to know what he did wrong in order to do better next time. One method is to ask him if he understands why he is being sent to his room or why he is grounded from the movies next Saturday. By asking you are showing respect for him as an individual, and you open a dialogue that can give you the opportunity for further teaching. Of course you may have one of those children who say, "I don't know," but at least you tried.

The second form of discipline that you must use with great care is physical punishment.

Dotty, pregnant with her third child, was taking her two-year-old daughter for a walk near a very busy street. Maya suddenly broke loose and ran for the street at the same time that a big truck came lumbering toward them. Dottie wasn't agile enough to run fast, so all she could do was watch the scene in horror.

Luckily, the truck driver saw the toddler in time and managed to stop just inches from hitting her. By this time Dottie had waddled out into the street, where she grabbed her toddler and "walloped the tar out of her rear end." Maya never ran into the street again.

Physical discipline was called for in this case. When the safety of a young child is at stake, it is not inappropriate to choose that part of the anatomy which is cushioned to make one's impression. But this is one of the few occasions when physical discipline is appropriate. Other forms are generally not only less risky but also more effective.

Keep these caveats in mind when considering physical discipline:

1. Use it only in cases where a child's physical well-being is at stake.
2. Never overuse it; the child will begin to think that he is bad or that physical violence is okay.
3. Make sure that you are in control when administering it.
4. Do no harm; use the padded part of a child's anatomy that conforms to the contour of your hand.
5. Explain why you spanked the child: "If you hit your little brother with that hammer, he could get very hurt."
6. Never use methods that could injure your child.

Another pitfall is holding back from appropriate discipline when it is clearly called for. If your child has willingly and deliberately done something wrong, she needs and deserves appropriate, loving discipline. A failure to set reasonable limits will send the kind of message to your other children that you probably don't want to send them.

Group Punishment

You have a splitting headache, your husband will be at work late tonight, and a dispute over a toy has accelerated into a riot with all the children taking sides. You have no idea how the whole thing started, and even if you asked, you probably wouldn't be able to make any sense of the answers anyway. This is definitely a situation that calls for group discipline, which is the method to use when you don't care who was at fault, you just want it to stop, *now*!

Group discipline is applied in those situations when you are in imminent danger of losing your sanity, your hearing, or both. Be prepared to hear choruses of "it's not fair" from all sides in the dispute. Don't listen. You are not attempting to be fair. Don't give a second thought to their little psyches either. Send them all summarily to their rooms, and if two of them happen to share a room, send one of them to the bathroom.

If group discipline is necessary while driving, tell your brood that you will stop in the middle of the freeway and there will be a Sig-alert. (For those of you unfamiliar with Sig-alerts, they are horrible traffic snafus reported on all local news stations.) Say that Mom or Dad will be taken to jail, where he or she can get some rest and quiet. This method has never failed me!

Is group discipline fair? No. Is it practical? Yes. Use it when you are at the end of your rope.

Authority of Older Siblings

Older siblings discipline younger ones all the time in the large family. You, the parent, need to give your older children very clear guidelines about what is appropriate discipline and what is harassment. Chances are, your older children will have already picked up guidelines about discipline from you.

In guiding older children to discipline siblings correctly, take into account the ages and maturity of all the children. Consider under what circumstances you will permit siblings to discipline one another; for example, when an older sibling is babysitting for you, she has to be able to correct the little ones. Also, think about what kind of discipline you will permit. Don't allow an older child to use physical discipline except in a life-threatening situation. Check afterward to be sure that your older child did indeed use his authority with wisdom. And if an older child does apply discipline too harshly or unwisely, be sure you address the issue right away and tell him how to do better next time.

If you have an older child whose maturity does not reflect

his age, do *not* allow him to discipline siblings. The stakes are too high.

When Strangers Intrude

Brittany was seated at a table with an elderly woman during the church pancake breakfast. Her three young ones were running around the table while she tried to feed the baby. The elderly woman finally couldn't stand the confusion any longer and said sharply to the children, "You youngsters sit down this instant and be quiet while your mother feeds your baby sister." How would you respond if you were Brittany? With a thank-you to the woman for restoring control? With an angry remark that she should mind her own business? With silence? The best response in this case would be a noncommittal smile.

We parents consider the discipline of our children to be our exclusive prerogative. And indeed it is, as long as we do not allow our children to infringe on the rights of others. Some folks are especially sensitive to the noise and confusion children create (as we probably were before we had our own), so we need to be reasonably considerate of their needs—but not to the point where they undermine our authority as parents.

The Cooperation of Relatives

When relatives discipline our children, the situation gets a bit stickier. Some general rules:

Explain to relatives how you discipline and get their cooperation.

Tell your children before a visit how they should behave at the relative's home and how the rules may be different there.

Don't permit physical discipline of your children except for dangerous situations.

In your house, politely ask relatives to respect your methods of discipline.

If relatives have problems with the way you discipline your children, the spouse whose relatives they are should deal with them.

Listen respectfully to concerns that relatives may have and act on them only if they make sense to you and your spouse.

Sibling Interactions

ONE evening last week four of our children came to us complaining of the behavior of a fifth, who they felt was being too bossy. A sixth child, with tears in his eyes, valiantly supported his "bossy" brother. The seventh, having often needed the good will of the "bossy" one in the past, remained neutral. The above scenario is a good example of sibling alliances. Every large family is familiar with them.

How Sibling Alliances Work

The large family has within it a blend of personalities, ages, likes and dislikes, and often sexes. Children seeking out playmates will become friends with other siblings, and children having a dispute will seek support for their viewpoint from other brothers and sisters. What you end up with is a virtual United Nations, with alliances and friendships changing as frequently as they do among world powers.

After observing fifty families and focusing on the oldest child, we discovered that 40 percent got along very well with their next younger sibling but 44 percent did not hit it off well with number two. Thirty percent each liked or disliked the third sibling in line. The fourth, fifth, and later siblings were liked as opposed to being disliked by the oldest in a ratio of four to one. Sixty-two percent of oldest children preferred friendships with like-sex siblings, while 42 percent fought more with these same siblings. The reason for the overlap was that some children found their same-sex siblings to be their best friends one day and their worst enemies the next. On the other hand, 46 percent liked their opposite-sex siblings, and an equal percent didn't.

The bottom line is that long-term sibling friendships are based on the interests and personalities of each child in a large family. In addition, though, there are day-to-day and month-to-month variations in the way brothers and sisters get along that almost defy interpretation. Parents need to remember that the more children in the family, the more combinations of likes and dislikes among them and the greater the complexity of their relationships.

The following suggestions may help in dealing with sibling alliances:

1. Recognize that these alliances are pervasive.
2. Keep mental notes about who pals off with whom in different situations.
3. Demand that all the children treat one another with fairness, regardless of who is "friends" with whom.

4. Do not allow alliances to sway your decisions as a parent.

5. Intrafamilial friendships are all right and probably can't be prevented, but you as a parent need to make sure that one child isn't always excluded. If you sense this may be happening, you need to talk about it with all the children.

6. When one of your children is constantly harassed or excluded by the others, think about why this is happening. Is this child having problems elsewhere, such as in school? (Some children with communicative and attention deficit disorders have trouble getting along with others.) Is this child perceived by the other children as your favorite? Or, conversely, are you not giving this child attention so that he is acting out in order to get it? Is this child just naturally bossy? Sit down with the child and see how he/she feels about the situation. Only when you have identified the problem can you devise methods to correct it.

7. When alliances fluctuate, you probably don't have too much of a problem. But if two factions are always at each other's throats or if physical struggles occur, you have a more serious situation, one that probably calls for a family council and strictly enforced rules.

Special Relationships

Have you ever wondered why your eight-year-old daughter wants you to drive her across town to play with her best friend when there's a perfectly good eight-year-old girl living right next door that she hardly even says hello to? Or why some of your children always seem to get along so well with each other, while others just rub each other the wrong way?

It is the rare family (although I've heard such families do exist) where siblings love one another equally all the time. In most families children develop special friendships with certain of their siblings and, in many cases, a mild ongoing antipathy toward others. Parents generally feel a little guilty about this, wondering if somehow they caused it, but actually it is quite normal for a child to prefer one of his brothers or sisters over another. It is unclear why these preferences arise. It sometimes seems that the personalities of the children have more to do with it than do their age and sex.

Almost every family can tell exactly which children get along with which others. Lynn, for example, has five children, ages ten, eight, six, two, and one. The six-year-old is the only girl. Lynn says of her children:

> The ten-year-old gets along best with the babies and worst with the eight-year-old (competition), and then with his sister. The ten-year-old and the eight-year-old are always at odds but occasionally are the best of buddies. The eight-year-old loves the babies and is best with the one-year-old. He and his sister get along. The six-year-old (girl) is best with the two-year-old and next best with the baby. She has always gotten along with the eight-year-old but not so well with the ten-year-old. The two-year-old gets along best with his sister. He adores her. She is like a second mom. I think the baby and the two-year-old will be good friends.

Although certain sibling pairings are strong, they can also change over time. This often happens when one child leaves for college and the balance in the family changes to adjust to the absence.

Sometimes quiet or even cantankerous children, as they approach the top of the heap (that is, as older brothers and sisters leave the nest), will surprise you with their ability to turn into good leaders. They just have never before had a chance to show what they can do!

You may also have noticed that the whole tenor of the family can change when one brother or sister isn't present. That one child may have set the tone for a certain kind of behavior or may have been so dominant that he could always get his brothers and sisters to do what he wanted. When he's away, even for a day, the other children have a chance to assert themselves. A child who is very excitable may keep everyone agitated a good deal of the time. When he's gone, the rest of the children become easier to manage. Or things might become much more chaotic because the "organizer" has gone, leaving the parents wishing she were still at home because she makes sure all the others keep the house straightened.

Then, too, siblings who have never much cared for each other may discover a common interest, such as baseball or ice skating, and all of a sudden they are the best of friends. Unfortunately, the reverse can happen too: Good sibling friends can fall out as they enter puberty and compete, or develop along different paths. But not to worry. Years later, they often find each other again.

When Somebody Gets Left Out

As parents you cannot force your children to "love" all their siblings equally, but you can insist that they treat each other fairly.

Has this scene ever occurred in your house? Amy, six and a half, and Vanessa, nine, are playing Barbie dolls in the family room. It's raining outside, and you have lots of housework to catch up on. Beth, your eight-year-old, comes in whining, "Mommy, Vanessa and Amy won't let me play with them." How do you respond?

Go in to the family room and tell the two girls that either they let Beth play with them or you will make everyone go to their room?

Tell Beth to stop bugging the other girls and let them play in peace?

Ask Beth if she would like to have a friend over to play with her, and then get in your car and drive across town to get her best friend?

Find a project, such as polishing furniture or baking brownies, for Beth to work on with you (and slowing you down in the process)?

Tell Beth to solve the problem herself and give her some practical suggestions?

There's no one right answer to the above scenario. Beth's exclusion may really be only a temporary problem and reflect the fact that your other two girls are so engrossed in a play story which would have to be changed if Beth joined them. If you know this to be the case, you may decide to take Beth under your wing for a little while until the other girls reach a point in their play when she can join.

You may have a rule in your family that nobody gets left out when they want to play, and decide you must enforce the rule in this situation. Or maybe you've observed that any two of the girls play just fine together, but when the third joins, there's always trouble. Or this scenario may represent a real personality clash between the girls. Vanessa and Amy might be sibling friends and enjoy playing alone together. Beth may be looked upon as a rival or too pushy, or maybe she just doesn't have their sense of imagination and she's no fun to play with.

If you as a parent sense that the last possibility is the most likely one, you need to look at the situation from a long-range point of view. You want the girls to get along together, but you also recognize that their personalities are very different. In that case your best approach may be to go over to Vanessa and Amy and say something like, "I know you girls really enjoy playing together, and it's hard for you to let Beth in right now." (You are acknowledging their feelings.) One of the girls will probably sense what you are going to ask and interrupt with a statement such as, "But Mom, Beth will ruin our game" or "Mom, Beth's so bossy when she plays Barbies" . . . or something worse. You can then repeat, "Yes, I know you feel Beth is bossy (or will ruin your game, or whatever), but for just a moment I want you to think about how she feels. You will have to let her play with you for fifteen minutes. Then maybe she can help me." Turning to Beth, "Beth, Amy and Vanessa don't want you to be bossy in this game." If you're lucky, the kids will become so engrossed in their game that they will forget about the fifteen-minute time limit. If you're not lucky, they'll start fighting in five minutes.

But if this is a long-range problem, you may not want to deal with it incident by incident. You may want to anticipate when problems will arise and prepare for them. For example, knowing the day before that you will be very busy and that the girls will all be indoors together, you may plan ahead of time to have a friend over to play with Beth. You may also want to make her aware of her tendency to be bossy, being careful not to threaten her self-esteem. She cannot change her basic personality, nor would you want her to, but you can give her techniques to help her get along better with her siblings and others. You could say, "Beth, I have an idea that you're going to be a real leader someday. That's terrific! But right now it's important that you let Vanessa and Amy make some decisions when you are playing games. Even when you know the best way, ask them what they think you all should do. Sometimes let them do what they want, even when you feel your way is better. That way you'll be teaching them to be leaders like you." (And when you see Beth acting on your advice, be sure you hug her and praise her.)

When Siblings Don't Get Along

Parents of large families are usually aware of the differences in personality between their children and realize that these differences are innate. Even so, when two children never seem to get along, parents feel bad. It helps to know that there are certain children in many families who just have very different ways of looking at the world. They would never pick each other out of a crowd as friends, and even in the intimate structure of the family, they remain distant to each other. They may either avoid each other or fight frequently. Their relationship may change as they get older, or it may not.

When you have such children, you cannot force them to enjoy each other's company. You can be sure, however, that you do not contribute subtly to the problem by paying more attention to one than the other. If you're sure that's not the case, then let them know that you love them both and expect them to respect and cooperate with each other in the family. You will not support one over the other, but it's okay for them to be different from each other and even to prefer not to spend much time together. You will respect their individuality and ask that they have the same attitude toward each other.

Whatever the circumstances, parents need to make very clear what kinds of fraternal behavior they will and will not tolerate. For instance, a parent may say to her children, "Frances and Jenny, I know you two haven't been getting along too well for the last couple of months. You don't have to play with each other, but I will not permit either of you to try to get the smaller children to gang up on the other." Or, "Mike and Tom, no matter how much you guys can't stand each other, we will not tolerate any physical confrontations. If you feel as though you're getting close to throwing a punch, tell one of us or go out and ride your bike." Or, "Jenny, when Erica's friend is over, you don't say mean things about Erica to her. And don't tell the little ones to, either!"

If you find, however, that one of your children seems to be on the outs with all the others a good deal of the time, that child may have a more serious problem. She could have a communicative disorder, a physical problem such as poor hearing, trouble understanding how to make friends, too much stress in her life, or even a serious depression or substance abuse problem. Almost certainly she'll have poor self-esteem.

As a first step you will want to talk to this child's teacher to see if there are problems at school, and to your doctor to investigate the need for medical or psychological intervention. Don't forget to talk to your child, if he is old enough, to get his perspective. You may say something like, "We've noticed that it's been hard for you to get along with your brothers and sisters. The teacher says you have a similar problem with others at school. Can you tell me a little about it?"

If you're dealing with a very serious problem, such as drug or alcohol abuse or adolescent depression—especially if your child is a teenager who doesn't want to share with his parents—you will need professional intervention right from the beginning.

Jealousy

When you have your second baby, you are mentally prepared for your firstborn's jealousy. You have practically memorized all sorts of strategies to deal with it. You even swap tales with your friends about how you plan to fight the green-eyed monster in your family. But you don't really appreciate how complex jealousy can be until you've had your third baby.

When the third arrives, the first is sometimes secretly thrilled that number two will now know what it feels like not to be the baby anymore. On the other hand, the first now has two rivals instead of one. The second child, who has never had the stage all to himself anyway, may be more upset with his older sibling, who by this time has probably decided to get attention through exploiting his position as the oldest.

But how much of a problem your family will have with jealousy also depends greatly on each of your children's personalities. Some domineering first children practically demand their share and more of attention from everyone. Others never get over the loss they felt when other siblings were born.

Nine-year-old Russ did both. His mother says that he "claims he would love to be an only child," and though he's smart, bossy, and plays the "oldest" role to the hilt, he still requires a good deal of time with Mom and Dad.

But most children fall into neither of the above categories. By the time the third child comes they have given up expecting to be the sole focus of their parents' attention. They have devised their own strategies to deal with feelings of envy, and they begin to see some of the benefits in having brothers and sisters, such as full-time playmates, someone else to share the blame when something goes wrong, and being able to play more creative games.

When the fourth or fifth child comes along, envy is not much of an issue anymore. Older children sometimes take it upon themselves to give the next youngest special attention so he/she will not feel left out. Everyone realizes that the pie is pretty well sliced up and no one is getting a big piece.

The times when you do see jealousy in the large family, however, tend to be situation-specific. For example, a family may contain three children of one sex and a fourth of the opposite sex. The three may feel that their brother or sister is being specially treated because the rules are slightly different for him or her, or because he or she always has new clothes while they get hand-me-downs. Or perhaps the oldest child is given authority that the second oldest would like to challenge. One child might be talented, and the parents may decide to spend extra money and time in nourishing this talent. Or a parent and child may share a special interest. Sometimes the other children can even be jealous of a handicapped or emotionally fragile child who needs more parental attention.

Although jealousy isn't a big issue in most large families, here are some things parents can do to keep it that way:

Find a special quality in each child and let that child know how much you appreciate that quality.

Learn to spot jealousy early and give the jealous child an extra hug or a few moments alone with you, even if it's only driving to the gas station.

Praise the children when they are getting along well.

If you have a child who needs more time than the others, explain the circumstances to all the other children. They may even want to help out.

Consider the situation carefully and perhaps hold a family conference before making a decision to allocate scarce family resources or time to one child.

Remember that jealousy can have many faces depending on the ages, sex, and personalities of the involved children. A teenager jealous of the attention a kindergartner receives may tease and criticize her or even attempt to discipline her physically. A four-year-old could try to dump her new brother out of his stroller or seek approval by being excessively sweet to the baby.

There is such a thing as group jealousy, which goes something like this: "Mom, you never yell at the little kids like you used to yell at us. They get away with murder, and you don't even care!" Or, "Dad, it's not fair! The boys get to do whatever they want whenever they want, but just let us (the daughters) come in five minutes late and we're grounded."

When faced with group jealousy, examine the allegations. Are you really easier on the little ones? If so, why? Is it because you've learned how to parent better or you're more relaxed? Or is it because you're more tired than you were when the first bunch were little, and you're taking the easiest way out? Once you understand what you're doing and why, you can either explain your reasons to the jealous bunch or change, if you feel that's called for.

Special Privileges

When one child in a two-child family is given something the other isn't given, parents can always say, "Well, dear, she's older (or younger) than you." For obvious reasons that excuse seldom holds water in the large family, so parents are stuck with explaining one of the bedrock principles of raising a large family: You can and must treat all of your children fairly, but you cannot and should not treat each of them identically. The reason is obvious: Children are remarkably different in their needs, interests, and aptitudes, and what's good parenting for one child may fail miserably with another. If you feel that one child needs or deserves a special privilege, go ahead and grant it, and let the others know their turns will come.

Be forewarned that some children keep track of special privileges. They'll inform you that Greg got to do something special twenty-three times in the last two years, and Tiffany had fifteen special things. They, of course, were overlooked entirely. (You may suggest to this child that he pursue a career in accounting.)

You could do what one mother of seven does. When a child complains that a sibling is especially favored, she informs the child that it's because she loves the sibling more. (She does this with all her children.) The children have heard this so many times that they realize Mom doesn't mean it literally. But strangers don't, and this mother has gotten a good many horrified looks in supermarkets and other public places.

Favoritism

It's natural to find yourself drawn to one child more than another. There are all sorts of reasons: You may share an interest or hobby with a child. She may be especially sensitive to your problems or have a sense of humor just like yours, and make you laugh when you feel down. She may be very intelligent, and you have a commitment to her academic success. He may always be getting himself into difficulties, so you feel you have to give him extra attention. But as a parent you have to be very careful not to let your preferences get out of hand. Favoritism is one of the few "mortal sins" parents can commit.

First of all, you have to be aware of how you feel about each of your children. If there really is one who stands out, ask yourself if the other children are aware of it. Here is one way you can tell: When the children say, "Mom (or

Dad), you always let Suzie . . ." is the same child's name always mentioned, regardless of which sibling is doing the complaining?

One mother never noticed how much attention she was giving to her thirteen-year-old daughter until she realized that all the other children perceived this child as her favorite.

If you notice that one child is special to you, don't curtail the relationship with this child; rather, upgrade your relationship with your other children. Find something special in each of the others to praise. If, say, Mark and Lisa grumble because they think you like Joel, your firstborn scholar and athlete, the best, you might make a special effort to praise Mark's ability to make friends, telling him often how lucky you are to have such an outgoing, likable child. Lisa, your only daughter, may be involved in special projects with you (and this includes girls' soccer as well as cooking). Remember: Children never tire of hearing about their special good qualities, and every child has some area in which he or she can be your "favorite."

How to Avoid Fights

An offshoot of jealousy and sibling alliances is fighting. Because everyone often has a stake in everyone else's business, a one-on-one fight will occasionally erupt into a family conflagration. Let's say Dick and Jane are having an argument. Mary comes along and supports Dick. Ann hears interesting noises and rushes to Jane's defense. Then a few more join in. You, the parent, now have a full-scale war on your hands. If it gets physical, and it sometimes does, you have an even bigger problem.

Luckily, these are uncommon events in most families. Most older children and teenagers are smart enough to know that physical fights don't pay off. If a fight is in the offing, however, you must intervene with decisiveness when the potential conflagration is still at the brushfire stage. The authority and tacit power that a father commands can be especially important here. It must be made very clear that physical fighting will never be tolerated between older children. A child who thinks that a particular situation might lead to blows has the responsibility of leaving that situation immediately. Penalties for fighting sometimes have to be quite strict, in the interests of the physical and emotional safety of all the children.

In order to avoid most fights altogether, you should recognize and try to prevent circumstances that lead to fighting, such as the following:

An adolescent has suffered a loss of self-esteem and is angry at himself. This child is especially likely to start a fight and not care about the consequences. Take him aside before problems arise and let him discuss his frustrations and disappointments. Then he won't have to take them out on others.

One child has a big accomplishment and the others feel left out (the Cain phenomenon). Take some time out to notice something special about the jealous ones.

Everybody is under stress, is tired, or is hungry. (You know what the Old Lady Who Lived in the Shoe did under similar circumstances: She fed her kids and put them to bed. But don't whip them as she did!)

The weather has been bad, and the kids have cabin fever. Exercise them.

The family is coping with a difficult problem; for example, Grandpa is sick and Dad has had to leave for a few days to be with him. This is a toughie. Children need to know what's happening. Do something to break the tension, such as going out to dinner where you can talk over everyone's feelings.

If you don't permit fighting when the children are little, there's less of a chance it will occur when the children get older and more difficult to manage. The saying, "As the twig is bent, so grows the tree," wasn't invented by the parents of an only child.

If fighting does occur, have significant consequences for everyone involved. If a fight is already in progress, the combatants must be physically separated, and fairly tough punishments for all involved must be enforced, such as not going to a special party or cleaning the cellar completely with an inspection afterward. Do not attempt to judge who was right and wrong unless there was a blatant act of unprovoked hostility on one child's part. The very fact that fighting isn't permitted is enough to trigger consequences for everybody involved.

(One mother suggests that if all else fails, you can lock yourself in the bathroom with a good book and let them kill one another.)

Teasing

Teasing is a common, very disruptive problem. Second children perhaps tease a little more often than others.

Parents have two problems in dealing with teasing. The teasee needs to be protected and comforted, and the teaser, besides being reprimanded when the act takes place, needs attention too. Children tease when they are frustrated, tired, hungry, or feeling insecure or unloved. When one child is always the teaser, the parent should take that child aside and find out how he's feeling about himself and about the way he's treated by the family. Sometimes a little TLC goes a long way. The teaser could be given lots of praise when he does something nice for the teasee. He might even be assigned to help care for his potential "victim," under close supervision, of course.

When a child teases just one sibling, such as the next down the line, he's probably working through a specific jealousy. If a child teases all his siblings, look for a problem with self-esteem. When they all tease one another, the parents may be unconsciously modeling this behavior. Teasing done with good humor and love is not much of a problem, but when there's an underlying current of bitterness, you need to take a good hard look at how your family is getting along.

Tattling—a Secret Weapon for Crowd Control?

Parents of several children have one method of keeping tabs on their young that the single-child parent does not: the tattler, your secret weapon.

Most children tattle to get back at a sibling or to control brothers and sisters. Some families have one principal informant who makes a career of censoring the behavior of all her brothers and sisters.

But occasionally children are really concerned about a brother or sister, and are trusting the parents to intervene in a situation that could injure someone. A brother or sister might be hurting another child, stealing or lying, or using alcohol or drugs, and the parents are not aware. When siblings report on this kind of behavior, they need to be told they showed good judgment in letting their parents know what was going on, and the complaint should be investigated immediately (even when the parent finds it painful to do so).

One parent actually took each of her children aside and explained the difference between tattling about minor things that parents don't need to know, such as what boy a sister has a crush on, and informing a parent about something that could potentially cause harm, such as sneaking out to meet a boy. She stressed that if there were doubts, it was better to inform the parent, who would then respect the informant's confidentiality if at all possible.

Property Rights

You're cooking dinner, the baby is hungry, and your husband has just called to say he has to work late. As if things weren't bad enough already, your seven- and nine-year-old sons suddenly fight themselves into the kitchen clutching different wings of a G.I. Joe plane. "It's my property," says the oldest. "I got it for Christmas." "But I had it first, and you never even play with it at all. You just don't want me to have it," the second one retorts.

It would be better to bite your tongue than to say something as obvious and rational as "Why don't you boys play together with the plane? It'll be more fun that way." The only way to handle this kind of argument is to prepare for it ahead of time, and this comes under the heading of sibling property rights.

Families handle this type of problem in one of three ways. The first is the "socialist" approach: Toys and other goodies belong to everyone equally. In a dispute whoever has something first, regardless of ownership, keeps possession. The second, or "capitalist" approach, gives possession to the one who can prove ownership of the item, regardless of who started using it first. The third approach, a compromise, gives absolute possession of certain sacred items, such as a prized bracelet or a collector's doll, to the actual owner. Other items, such as everyday dolls, are retained by the child who began playing with them first.

Whatever approach you choose, decide upon it ahead of

time and make sure all the children are aware of this family rule. It'll save you a few gray hairs. Remember that the second and third approaches teach respect for the property of others and therefore may be wiser than the first.

Respect for Individual Rights

Since most children in large families don't have their own rooms and sometimes even share beds, it's hard to arrange private space and time for them. You might want to establish special times and places where each child can do what he wants and not infringe upon others' rights. Here are some suggestions:

A music hour, when your teenagers can play their tapes loudly and other family members won't complain.

Large plastic containers, where special possessions can be kept and to which brothers and sisters are not allowed access.

Friend days, assigned days when a child can have one friend over, and the other children will leave this child and her friend alone.

Daddy or Mommy time, a special hour or half hour that one particular parent and child will spend together.

"Me toys," a few toys totally under the control of one child.

You can probably think of other ways to reinforce respect for individual rights while still promoting family cooperation.

When Siblings Parent Siblings

Lynnette has four boys, with a girl in the middle. She relies a lot on her two oldest boys, ages ten and eight. "The older children can be and usually are a big help with the two little boys. They run errands, hold, bathe, feed, and help dress them, and lots of other little things like that. The oldest son can help tend his younger brothers and sister for short periods of time with a neighbor checking in on them. (The neighbor is physically there but not doing the actual child care.) The biggest help, I think, comes from silent support. They are each other's best supporter and friend when the chips are down and they really need each other."

Kathy, whose eight children have profoundly different interests and talents, says, "It is always amazing to me that children are capable of so much compassion at such a young age. Our children when as young as one year old have shown love to another when he was hurt. They are always there to help."

Says Linda, the mother of five, "The older ones help the younger ones with things that they are physically unable to do. If the younger one allows it, the older will also sometimes teach certain skills—doing a puzzle, letter recognition, and so forth."

Large families have "chains of command" that allow them to function even when Mom and Dad are not there or are occupied. Older sisters and brothers take over some tasks normally done by the parents in the one- or two-child family. What tasks they take over depends on their ages, interests, and the needs of the family at the time. For instance, a six-year-old may be asked to keep an eye on the four- and two-year-olds while Mommy folds the laundry in another room. Or a nineteen-year-old may be in charge of her younger brothers and sisters while Mom and

Dad spend their anniversary in a hotel on the other side of town.

We recently did a pilot study at the University of Southern California School of Medicine, focusing on communication patterns in large and small families. In brief, what we found was that, although parents interacted more with their children in the small family, the overall type and quality of interactions for each child was approximately equal in both small and large families. Siblings in the large families took up the slack. Why is this important? Because most of what children learn comes through physical and verbal interaction with others.

Older siblings "parent" younger siblings. In some very large families, groups of children are further broken down into "subfamilies" with their own structures. Sound confusing? Let's see how this would work. In a family with eight children, four teenagers and four children under twelve, any one teen can and does at times assume responsibility for one or more of the younger ones. But sometimes the four teens go out together. They are used to having the oldest brother, nineteen, be in charge. He's been watching over them since they were all in nursery school and he was in first grade, so he is their natural leader when they are away from home together.

Now let's return to the home where the little ones are playing. The eleven-year-old sister is the oldest of the little ones. Since the teenagers are gone for the day, she assumes leadership with relish. Mom and Dad are hard at work with chores, so she will watch the littler ones, discipline them when they fight over a toy, and open and cook a jar of spaghetti for them at lunchtime. If there is something she can't handle, she'll go to a parent or to an older sister when the teens arrive home.

It may sound as if kids in the large family have a lot of responsibility, and they do. As long as parents are careful not to overburden their children, this responsibility might actually be good for them. The best way to learn is to teach, and children in large families have many opportunities to do that.

In playing a parental role, children first have to learn such a role from their own parents. They have to master the whys and hows of a task themselves before they can teach a younger child. And they learn empathy in trying to help younger siblings who are having difficulty doing something or who are hurt or discouraged.

Almost every large family has one child who is far less interested than the others in caring for his siblings. If this occurs in your family, just try to work around it. Such a child may shine in other areas and will probably have to be given only minimal child-care duties.

The following are guidelines for allowing siblings to care for siblings:

1. Know each of your children and how they interact together.
2. Spread responsibility as evenly as possible; don't allow one child to spend all his/her free time doing child care while others don't do any.
3. Boys as well as girls can look after their siblings.
4. Children under age twelve (fourteen, by law, in some states) should not be left alone for long periods with sole responsibility for their siblings.
5. Never leave children under eight or nine alone with younger brothers and sisters even for a short time.
6. Provide backup in the form of a neighbor, a telephone number where you are reachable, and so forth.
7. Give children guidelines for what they can and can't do while you are busy or away; for example,

the eight-year-old is not permitted to use the stove.

8. Have a "disaster plan" for fires and other emergencies that the children can implement even if you are not there.

9. If you have infants and/or toddlers, they should be left only with an older teen. (If you are in another part of the house, of course, younger children can watch babies.)

10. When one of your children has a hard time with child care (always fights with his charges, for example, or doesn't have good judgment), don't risk leaving him/her alone with the children; give that child another duty instead.

11. Some combinations of kids just don't work well together. If you have such a combination in your family, don't leave them alone together.

12. As a general rule, friends should not be visiting when a teen has heavy-duty babysitting to do; they can be too distracting. You know your own child and whether this applies.

Babysitting

Isn't it wonderful when one of your children finally becomes old enough to watch the others when you go to the store or even out for the evening? You probably haven't had such a feeling of freedom since the day you first passed your driving test.

How do you know when this magic moment has arrived? Children become competent babysitters at different ages. You need to know the capabilities of each of your children, taking into consideration the number and ages of the children being cared for and the physical dangers in the environment. If you have a baby, a couple of toddlers, and a backyard pool, it may be unwise to leave a twelve-year-old completely on her own for any length of time. On the other hand, the twelve-year-old may do fine with seven- and eight-year-olds who are pool-safe. Our theoretical twelve-year-old may also have trouble with a ten- and an eleven-year-old who are always fighting or who challenge his authority.

Remember, some states have laws against leaving children alone who are below a certain age. (Usually the cutoff age is fourteen, but check your local situation.)

The wise parent is sensitive to the needs of the babysitter as well as the well-being of those being cared for. No matter how willing a child may be, limit the number of hours per week that he must devote to sibling care. If you need him for an emergency above and beyond those hours, consider paying him. Make sure your babysitter has enough time to do schoolwork, socialize, and have fun. It's also prudent not to permit friends to visit when your adolescent is sitting for you.

Adolescents from large families are often asked to babysit for other families who know they have had experience with small children. Most parents are happy to allow their teenager to babysit if they know the other family or have friends who do, and if the circumstances seem appropriate and safe.

The following might be considered reasonable rules for your babysitting teenager:

1. The family must be known to you, directly or indirectly, that is, through a friend.
2. Generally, no sitting on school nights.
3. Your teenager must be brought home at the agreed-upon time after babysitting (except for a valid emergency, in which case your child should

phone you), or no more babysitting for that family.

4. Your teenager may not bring a friend with her/ him unless the other family has given permission. That friend may not be of the opposite sex.

5. You must know the address and telephone number of the family, and the number and ages of the children where your teen is sitting.

6. Teens need to clear babysitting jobs with you first.

7. If you legitimately need your teen to sit for you, that takes priority. (Some parents pay their child when this happens.)

8. Once a babysitting job has been agreed to, your child is responsible for keeping this commitment or finding an acceptable replacement.

Siblings as Teachers

In Susan's family of seven children, everyone does homework after dinner around the big kitchen table while Susan does dishes and takes care of the baby. If a child has a problem understanding something, he asks his next oldest brother or sister, a grade or two higher. Only when the older siblings cannot help does Mom step in, and this is rare because the kids usually know the material better than she does anyway.

Siblings often teach a younger brother or sister in the large household. This teaching can be through imitation, such as a younger sister trying to fix her hair the same way her big sister does. It can also be formalized, as when a big brother tutors a younger one in math.

When siblings teach one another, lots of good things happen. The older sibling has to understand what he teaches, so he learns the material more thoroughly. The younger sibling has help that oftentimes parents are too busy to give right then and there. The relationship between tutor and student is reinforced, at least for the moment.

You can encourage your children in several ways:

1. Model teaching behavior yourself. Let your children know how important you think learning a new skill is.
2. When you're busy and a child needs assistance, ask an older brother or sister to help.
3. If you notice that an older sibling is trying to teach a younger one something, let the older child know you appreciate her efforts: "Melanie, I really liked how you tried to show Michael how to tie his shoes. If you keep helping him, he'll be able to do it alone one of these days."
4. Use teaching to reinforce the self-esteem of an older child. If Matthew is a poor student but great at basketball, ask him if he'll teach Tommy how to shoot baskets.

Bossiness

If your older child or children assume any kind of responsibility for the younger one(s), sooner or later the older one will be accused of being bossy. It is the rare older child who can manage little ones without occasionally seeming dictatorial.

The closer two or more children are in age, it seems, the more the younger will challenge the authority of the elder. Teenagers seem almost like parents to toddlers, so a four-year-old is hardly likely to fuss if her fifteen-year-old brother asks her to pick up her toys. But if her seven-year-old sister tells her to clean up, she may well challenge the request. This is especially true if the younger child is more aggressive or more of a leader than the older one, or if they are habitual rivals. And some kids really are bossy.

(The truly bossy child needs a one-on-one parental discussion about this particular trait. In the large family, it's not likely to last long.)

How can you, the parent, support the legitimate requests your older children make of the younger ones while discouraging "bossiness"? As a parent you are aware that if an older child is responsible for caring for a younger one or getting a certain task done, such as picking up a shared bedroom, that older child has to have some authority—but that authority must be coupled with good judgment.

You can legitimatize the older child's authority while instructing him in how to use it wisely. This is best done in the presence of both or all the children involved. For example, let's say you want Mark, your nine-year-old, to help Ed and Fred, seven and six, clean up the mess they made in the backyard. You might gather them all together and explain: "Mark is going to be responsible to help you clean up. He knows what has to be done and how to do it. When he asks you to do something, he will make the request very politely, but you will have to obey him. Mark, be sure you're not pushy. If you have problems, see me. Ed and Fred, I'm sure Mark will be considerate and help you, and you'll all do a great job!" If things do go well, a comment on how lucky you are to have children who work as a team will reinforce behavior next time. If things break down, you need to stress the original agreement.

You can model considerate order-giving. Children should be told what their task is and why it needs doing, and they should be given a time frame and helpers. If they are engaged in another activity (but are generally responsible types), you might say, "Claire, the dishes need to be started within the next fifteen minutes. You can have a couple of minutes to finish what you are doing, but then get started because we need to use the table." This kind of modeling usually trickles down to the kids. They are more likely to treat siblings with respect if they are treated that way. Sometimes, of course, we must be arbitrary—and may seem downright mean to our children. But what we do when not under pressure will, it is hoped, be the type of leadership behavior our children exhibit.

The Family as a Team

Chris has a chore list on which is the task of doing the dinner dishes, and the children adhere to the list with a fervor unsurpassed since the Children's Crusade (A.D. 1212). If one child agreed to do another's dishes, the payback was usually double dish duty. That's why she was so surprised when Alan gratuitously, and without being asked, did Billy's dishes the night Billy was sick with stomach flu.

Sue tells the story of the day three of her six little boys were playing in Little League games at the local park. During the game the family discovered that Johnnie, the youngest, had wandered off. Ben, the oldest, suddenly became an awful catcher, and Daniel missed a fly ball; no one could think of anything except their baby brother. When Johnnie was found by his father over by the playground area of the park, Ben remarked with obvious relief, "Thank goodness! Now I can concentrate on the game." And sure enough, everyone's playing immediately improved!

If there is anything that makes parents of a large family feel it's all worth it, it's seeing how siblings care for each other when the chips are down. Any honest parent of a large family will tell you there's a fair amount of teasing and bickering in her household and that it sometimes comes close to driving her up a wall, but most will also tell you that one of the best things about having several children is how often they help and comfort one another and how, when they recognize that one child is having a rough time with the outside world, they do their best to make things better for that child.

Many parents comment on the teamwork involved in making the large family work. They stress that every child, however young, has a job to do and that this job is important to the family as a whole—even if it's just putting the spoons around the table. One mother of ten had a three-year-old son who was very ill in the hospital. His job had been to tidy up the flight of stairs leading to the bedrooms. One day, when his family came to visit him, he asked if anybody missed him. Oh, yes, he was told by one older brother, they sure did: The stairs were so cluttered that no one could get up and down. He had to get well quick and come home and clean them again!

Families have reputations, especially when there are lots of kids at the same school or going to the same dentist or doctor. People will remember an older brother or sister, and have expectations for the younger ones. There is a feeling of pride in being a Guerrero or a Johnson or a Cahill or a Lewkowicz. (Of course, there is also sometimes a feeling of frustration that you are expected to be as good in math as your older brother when you like recess best.) Parents do well to encourage a healthy family pride and sense of teamwork, while simultaneously encouraging the individuality of each child. To build a family team, you should stress that each child is important to the total function of the family and let each child use his own particular talents to assist the family. Let the children know in a nonstressful way that what they do, good and bad, cannot help but reflect on the family as a whole. And talk about your family genealogy so that your children get a sense of their unique family history.

CHAPTER 8

Time for Each Child
and Special Time
for All

WHEN parents were asked what was their biggest worry about having a large family, their overwhelming response was the same as that of thirty-four-year-old Maureen, the mother of five. Maureen, a homemaker whose day starts at 6:00 A.M. and ends at 11:00 P.M., not counting the baby's night feedings, is worried about "providing enough quality time for each child."

No doubt about it, time and attention are the essence of parenting. Children from large families need this attention just as much as children from small families. Parents of large families, realizing this, often feel guilty about not having as much time with each child as the parents of a small family. They are aware that their infants and toddlers are time-intensive, and so the children most likely to be deprived of parental attention are the older ones.

Many parents have observed that one or two of their children are "squeaky wheels," getting more attention from the parents than do their quieter, less demanding brothers and sisters. Somehow, this doesn't seem fair either.

Susan, mother of seven, gave us a good example of how older children, deprived of parental time, can experience unfortunate consequences down the line. Charles, one of her older children, received very little help with schoolwork because she was always so busy with one or another of the younger ones. He was a hard worker, however, and managed to achieve excellent grades throughout his high school years while holding down a part-time job and being active in leadership roles at school. His dream had been to go to an Ivy League college, and he seemed very competitive, except for the vocabulary portion of the Scholastic Aptitude Tests, which was in the mid-five hundreds. When push came to shove, he was rejected, almost certainly due to these scores. (His math S.A.T. score was in the seven hundreds.) Susan was fairly sure that, had Charles been an "only" or one of two children, she would have had time to read more to him when he was little, he would have had a better vocabulary S.A.T. score, and he would have made it into the Ivy League college of his choice.

Time Management

Realizing that it may never be possible to give each child as much time as you would like, how can you make the most of the time you do have for each child?

One way is by prioritizing and making mental or written lists of what has to be accomplished each day. In this way you can decide what is vital, what is urgent, and what would be nice to do if you have time. Some parents keep pocket date books and write in all important dates, such as team soccer pictures, as they are scheduled. They consult these pocket calendars while prioritizing their day.

The tenets of prioritizing are as follows:

Change your attitude. Now that you have three (or more) children, you must stop thinking about how to be the perfect wife/mother/homemaker and start thinking about how you are going to get everyone through the day in one piece.

Learn to do first those things that are essential for the functioning of your household. This applies whether or not you work outside the home. For example, feeding the family is more important than the laundry, which in turn is more necessary than getting the draperies cleaned. Do these chores in their order of importance.

Act on the fact that people's needs are more important than a tidy house or a gourmet dinner. When your toddler wants to read a book, forget about cleaning the bathroom. (Unless it's unsanitary!) If your spouse has had a rough time at work and needs to talk, save the fancy dinner until tomorrow night and throw together some pasta tonight so you both have time together.

Maintain your self-esteem. Don't put yourself down for not having time to be team parent. Ignore your mother's comment that if you didn't have all those children, maybe your life would be easier, your house cleaner, your children better behaved. Compliment yourself on your many accomplishments, even if they seem small. And allow yourself to become a priority when you feel tired or unhappy.

A prioritized list for a mother of five who works part-time might look like this:

6:00 A.M. Get up. Feed children, make beds, put in a load of wash, send kids to school, and leave baby at sitters. Go to work. (Part of daily routine.)

12:30–1:30. Get haircut after work at drop in shop if time permits. (Nonessential.)

1:30–2:30. Pick up baby at sitters; run to grocery store. (Essential—need food for dinner.)

2:30–3:30. Fold and put away laundry while waiting for the children to get home from school. (Essential—laundry cannot be permitted to back up.)

3:30–4:15. Drive the car pool to Little League. (Essential.)

4:15–5:00. Bake cookies that children have been wanting while helping first and third graders with homework. (The former a luxury but the latter important.)

5:00–7:00. Dinner and cleanup. (Essential.)

7:00–8:00. Back-to-school night. (Not quite essential but fairly high priority.)

8:00–8:45. Kids' baths and bedtime. (Absolutely essential.)

8:45–9:45. Do bills, if not too sleepy. (Not essential, but will have to be done sometime soon.)

9:45–10:15. Time with spouse. (Essential; that is, if both of you can stay awake!)

"Windows of Time"

One mother brings her bills to basketball games. Another writes letters to her relatives while watching her nine-year-old's soccer game. A third has mastered the art of doing dishes (but not pots and pans) while on the phone. And a fourth uses dead time in a supermarket line to teach her three-year-old the alphabet from titles on magazines stacked in front of the cash register. These mothers are using the two techniques so valuable to parents of large families: doing two things at once and using windows of time, which are short periods between major duties. For example, the baby has just gone to sleep and the older children don't return from school for another twenty minutes. Instead of wasting this period of time, too short for any major projects, a mother may sew on a few buttons or read to a toddler.

Making the Most of Your Energy

Another timesaving technique for parents (or anyone, for that matter) is learning how to maximize productive periods during the twenty-four-hour day. Notice that I say "twenty-four-hour day." That's because we all have biorhythms that result in periods during the day when we seem to get things done faster than at other times.

Most of us instinctively know our own daily cycles. For instance, Marti, the mother of four, says she is "definitely a morning person. I need lots of sleep and can take late nights for only short periods." And Dona, an employed mother of four, says, "I have a lot of energy in the mornings and usually throughout the day. I poop out totally around 9:00 P.M."

On the other hand, Lucy says she is a "high-energy-level

night person. After everyone [four children] is in bed, I do my best work."

If you know your biorhythms, you can schedule difficult tasks for your energy peaks and get them done a lot more efficiently. You will also know what times of the day are going to be difficult for you and not overburden yourself during these times. When you take advantage of the times of the day that are good for you, you'll feel better and your household will run more smoothly. For example, the woman who gets up full of energy but slows down when the sun goes down may want to prepare dinner in the morning and serve it early in the evening. The nighttime dynamo will want to clean her house or do the bills when the kids are in bed.

Are you a morning or evening person? Find out by answering the following questions:

1. Do you get twice as much accomplished in the morning than in the evening?
2. Do you feel alert and energetic once you're out of bed and on your feet in the morning?
3. Do you sometimes wake up early in the morning without the help of an alarm or before the alarm goes off?
4. Do you start to wilt when the sun goes down, falling asleep the second your head hits the pillow?
5. Do you have trouble keeping awake on those (rare) occasions when you dine out late at a restaurant or go to an evening sports or cultural event?
6. Are you grouchier toward the children at night?

or:

1. Do you need about three hours or four cups of coffee to awaken in the morning?

2. Are you less likely to yell at the children after sundown?
3. Do you do your most creative work after everyone is in bed?
4. Do you sparkle at evening social events?
5. Did you cram all night for tests in high school or college, and invariably got an A?
6. Do your best ideas come to you after the ten o'-clock news?
7. Do you hate people who wake up raring to go at 6:00 A.M.?

Once you're working in tune with your own biorhythms, you'll be astonished at how much you can get done and how much better you'll feel while you're doing it!

List-making

Scratch a mother of twelve, and you'll probably find a human being with organizational skills to rival Lee Iacocca's. The one common trait shared by mothers of three who work in an office all day, mothers with four babies and preschoolers at home, and fathers who drop the kids off at two different schools each morning on the way to work is that they make lists of what they must accomplish by the end of the day. Many of them don't even realize they are doing this because the lists are in their heads, not on paper. But they do tend to think through the upcoming day and devise mental schemes for getting everything done.

Making a list can be a very casual thing and can even be done when you first get up and are trying to gather energy to swing your body into a sitting position. It can be done at night, as you drift off to sleep and are thinking of the next day's schedule and what needs to be done and the most efficient way of doing them. You may also wish to keep a daily schedule book on your person so that all important events are immediately written down and won't be forgotten. This avoids the embarrassment and cost of realizing too late that you forgot the dentist appointment you made for all four kids two months ago.

Group Efforts

You, dear parent of a large family, need to save time wherever you can. For you, time is often more valuable than money.

As we've already discussed in Chapter 4, whenever you can, join a car pool, and if there are none to join, create your own. The same holds true for a play group.

And don't forget the multipurpose shopping trip. It's usually a waste of time and gas to go to just one place or to purchase just one item. You should plan your excursions so that many chores are done at one time. For example, you can pick up the children at school and drop one off at Girl Scouts or a dance music lesson, and another at soccer. From there you can go to the drive-in teller to do some banking. Then onward to the grocery store and the dry cleaners. Your younger children can go with you in most cases. And you've saved time, money, and gas.

Fitting in Emergencies

Little emergencies constantly crop up in everyone's day; they just do so with more frequency in the large family. You know the kind: The car breaks down, a child gets sick, Dad has a business meeting out of town and must be driven to the airport, and your mother-in-law comes to visit for a week. On top of it all, you have a special project due at work or have to write a newsletter for the town council. It's important to be psychologically prepared for these types of emergencies. If you expect them to occur and so factor them into your daily life, they will be less disturbing to you.

You can be prepared for some emergencies. One mother of seven always has extra brownie mix on hand. She can whip up a batch in half an hour for the child who tells her at breakfast that he has to bring snacks for the cub scouts that afternoon. (She also has a case of fruit drinks stashed away for emergencies, in a flavor her kids hate.)

Other emergencies have to be dealt with as they arise, but you can do contingency planning ahead of time. Think about garden-variety emergencies and how you would handle them before they occur. If the car needs urgent repairs, what are your alternatives? Call a friend? Have Dad take the bus to work? Rent a car? Walk? If a child gets sick and you are working outside the home, do you have a reserve babysitter lined up? Can Dad take a mildly ill child to the office? Can you?

And finally, what changes can you make in your schedule to handle emergencies without totally unbalancing your life? Use leftovers for dinner? Reschedule a hairdressing appointment? (Yes, I know many mothers of three or more who get to the beauty shop a couple of times a year.)

This is how one mother of five says she plans for emergencies:

> I try to stay calm and plan ahead. We have a family calendar, and my husband and I each keep a personal planning calendar. Once a week the family gets together and we plan the week and the month as far as we know. This planning keeps me mentally and emotionally calm and my mind uncluttered. I know the essentials are written down, and I don't have to worry about them. I can rearrange them, make excuses, or whatever, if someone breaks an arm, needs to go to the library four days ago, and so forth.

Tips from Mothers

As was mentioned before, parents of three or more children are very concerned about meeting all the needs of each child. Many parents have come up with ingenious ways of spending one-on-one time with each child. Here are some of their methods, which may be adaptable to your family too.

One mother of five (the oldest thirteen) lists what she and her husband do:

> My husband spends time with each child at bedtime, talking to her/him, telling a story, reviewing the day. We've learned what regular "strokes" each child needs and try to provide these daily. We drop whatever we are doing and give attention to an upset child's needs—talking at 2:00 A.M. if necessary. We schedule "dates" with each child—one parent, one child—and make an effort to take care of everything but not to rush. Staying calm and enjoying the time with each child, whether it is reading a book, helping with a project, correcting homework, or overseeing practicing, should all be basically enjoyable. An attitude of "let's get through this quickly" makes for a frantic evening, and there is not enough time to do a fast, sloppy job and have what is known as quality time. The quality time is the homework, car pool, scouts, and practicing time that affords the opportunity to talk, absorb values, laugh, and just be together.

Another mother has five, all under seven, and this is what she does: "Different children come at different times to the supermarket with me or to my husband's study. We don't have a schedule but try to keep an overall view on each having private access to us. I car-pool Rebecca and Rena once a week and often take them alone to the library or somewhere else after dropping their friends off."

A mother of four volunteers in rotation in her children's nursery school and grade school classrooms. Her presence is a special time for each child.

Another mother of five (the oldest seven) takes each child one at a time for shopping and an ice cream.

A mother of seven uses vacation time away from home for meeting the needs of each child.

Another mother makes sick time memorable. If one of her school-age children happens to be home ill, she'll devote the whole day to that child, reading to him or her, doing projects, and so forth. It's a wonder this mother's children don't have the highest absentee rate in school!

And a working mother of seven has "early morning time" for the smaller children. One child at a time will be awakened a half hour ahead of the others for a walk, some reading time, or just to talk.

And birthdays, of course, are a big way of specially celebrating each child.

There are signs that indicate when a child needs more parental time/attention:

1. Your child seems grumpy or "down" all day.
2. He comes home from school or play and is unusually quiet or negative.
3. She says derogatory things about herself or others, such as "I'm such a dummy."
4. There is a change in the usual pattern of behavior; the child who loves sweets refuses chocolate, for instance.
5. He does badly in a test or is the losing pitcher.
6. She expresses inappropriate worry about a situation. (She might really be worried about something else that she has difficulty expressing.)
7. Something bad happens to him; for example, he learns his best friend will be moving to another state next year.

8. All her siblings have had good things happen recently, and she hasn't.
9. A major decision is coming up: where to go to high school, what courses to take.

Besides one-on-one time between the children and the parents there are other occasions when everyone is gathered together. With a little foresight and planning, these events can become particularly memorable.

Dining Out

Children should be taught "dining out" skills, especially children from a large family. Bad table manners are infectious in large families. Children need to learn about how to be seated at a restaurant, how to order from a menu, salad bar etiquette, appropriate conversational tone and volume, and the concept of several successive courses of food. They need to know what utensils are proper to use with soup and appetizers, and how to eat a drumstick or bony fish. (They don't want to have to learn these skills on their first big date!) Since it's socially necessary to know restaurant etiquette, you need to see that your children acquire the necessary exposure. Do not expect, however, to enjoy the meal yourself.

There are several methods of introducing children to restaurants. (McDonald's doesn't count.) You can pretend to have a "restaurant dinner" at home: Create a several-course meal, have the children make menus, and elect the oldest to play the role of waiter or waitress. Break out your best silverware, put flowers on the table, and have everyone get dressed in his/her best clothes. You can then discuss seating, etiquette, different types of food, and how to pass various dishes to others. This approach takes a lot of work and planning, but it is fun for the children and costs much less than the real thing. You won't be embarrassed if the baby spills his soup all over the floor or somebody utters an expletive because someone else just kicked him under the tablecloth.

Another approach is the "special day" method. This involves taking one child at a time out dining, perhaps to celebrate a birthday. You can focus on this child, make her feel special, and in the process teach manners. It's also cheaper than taking everyone out together. Another alternative, if a grandparent or another special relative lives nearby: He or she might enjoy taking one or two children out to dinner once in a while.

Finally, you can bite the bullet and take the whole family out at once. If you elect this method, be prepared to let the baby dump all the sugar on her high-chair tray because it's the only activity that will keep her from getting bored, screaming, and disturbing all the other patrons. Plan on going to the rest room at least as many times as you have children under ten.

If you do take the whole tribe out together, there are some things you can do to minimize the cost and stress, and perhaps even make the occasion a pleasant one:

1. Selectively patronize a "family" restaurant until you can assess your children's dining skills. If the other patrons have children with them, you won't feel so pressured.
2. Choose a time when the restaurant will be relatively uncrowded—perhaps empty.
3. Remember, luncheon dining is usually much less expensive than dinner.
4. Call ahead of time, even if reservations are not required, and let them know when and how many of you to expect, and how many booster chairs and high chairs will be needed. This will give the restaurant time to prepare and expedite service

to you. (You may even be assigned a room of your own.)

5. Inquire about splitting portions if the restaurant doesn't have "kiddie menus."

6. Before you arrive at the restaurant, give the children a rundown on proper restaurant behavior. Emphasize that quiet conversation and manners are mandatory.

7. Bring toys or books to amuse your high-chair-size children so they don't have to amuse themselves with the salt and pepper shakers.

8. If you are nursing an infant, ask about where you can feed her in private should it become necessary. Sometimes restaurant booths and a big blanket are all you need, or the ladies' room may have a chair. It would be easier all around, however, if you nursed the baby at home *before* leaving for the restaurant.

9. When bringing a small infant, choose a time when you know he will be calm or asleep.

10. Seat your children strategically; that is, if Nancy and Joe bicker all the time, have Dad sit between them.

11. Praise children often during the dinner when they behave correctly: "Brian, you passed the butter very politely to Marta when she asked for it."

12. Plan on a big tip for the waiter/waitress if he/she is helpful and patient. You might even want to thank the management if the service and food were especially good.

Birthdays

Parents are constantly on the lookout for ways to give special attention to each of their children without making the other children jealous. Birthdays afford an excellent opportunity. They are, says Bonnie, mother of seven youngsters, "your own special day that you don't have to share."

Birthdays are celebrated in an amazing variety of ways in different households. One mother of four reminisces that in her birth family of seven siblings "birthdays were always special. We picked out our own special dinner and cake, and we didn't have to do dishes!" Another mother of ten averages a family birthday every four weeks or so, although some birthday months overlap. In her household and others, birthday outings occur when children reach eight, and again at twelve. An ambitious mother of five very young children says birthdays are "special. We usually have two parties, one for family and one for friends. I love birthdays!"

In one family of nine, the girls have pajama parties. The mom remembers the year that her nine-year-old daughter invited the distaff side of the entire third grade (twenty-plus kids) and some other friends, all of whom showed up! At 2:00 A.M. one little girl became ill, started throwing up all over the living room, and it turned out that her parents were out of town and had left her in charge of neighbors! When all the children went home the next morning (no one, of course, had slept during the night), there was so deep a layer of trash on the living room floor you couldn't see the rug. This mom says the party was such a hit that her daughter's classmates, now in high school, still talk about it.

While some families focus on birthday parties for friends, other families limit birthday parties to the immediate family. Still others have two or three celebrations: children's parties, school celebrations, and family gatherings. It is lots of work, but parents feel it's one way of reinforcing the specialness of each child. And some families just really enjoy birthdays.

But there are pitfalls. Although the other children know their turn will come, there's likely to be a bit of envy anyway. And parties are very stimulating. Children are more prone to giggles—and tears. If you have your party at home, there's usually a big mess to clean up afterward. Most parents feel that, overall, it's worth it. And many families become quite skillful at party-giving. After all, if you have five kids, you can figure on ninety birthdays by the time everyone turns eighteen.

Parties require a significant amount of advance preparation. Below is a timetable and some hints, gleaned from experience, on giving a do-it-yourself birthday party. You may also consider holding your party at a place that will do all the work for you. Some of the fast-food outlets do this well and quite inexpensively.

Three weeks before blast-off: Have a family discussion about the party. The birthday person has final say, but siblings love to contribute ideas. Decide where the party will be held (local park, your family room, outdoors, and so forth), who is to be invited, whether there will be a theme, such as Halloween if it is an October birthday, School's Out for June, or perhaps a Tom Sawyer, Astronaut, or Dinosaur party. Will Mom, the kids, or a bakery make the cake, and what flavor? Will lunch be served, and if so, what? What activities will be planned? Some families permit each nonbirthday sibling to invite a special friend: Who will that be? What about party favors? Maybe the birthday person would prefer taking one or two friends to a movie or the local amusement park. Then you have to decide if siblings get to go too. Some siblings, born close together, choose to share parties, and there are double decisions to make. On the other hand, twins may want separate parties. (This is more likely if they are different sexes.)

Two weeks before blast-off: Write and send out RSVP invitations or make phone calls if this is easier. Don't send invitations to be delivered at school unless you invite the whole class and the teacher gives out the invitations. Many mothers say that school invitations often don't reach the intended guests' parents. When planning how long a party should last, keep in mind the ages and attention spans of the children you are inviting. For children three and under, invite the parents too. Preschoolers do best with short parties; an hour or ninety minutes is plenty long. You'll be pretty frazzled, too, after spending ninety minutes with a pack of preschoolers. In the primary grades consider a party lasting no more than two hours. When you have a child nine or above, parties can be long or short, with the number of hours the party lasts being inversely related to the number of children you invite. Teenage parties are undertaken by only the most ambitious. They are usually evening parties, planned by the birthday person, and need very close supervision. Consider asking some adult friends to help chaperone. Alcohol in any form is a big mistake and most likely illegal in your state. Consider checking with your neighbors about their feelings if you plan a large party with loud music. Be aware of the problem of party crashers. And good luck!

One week before blast-off: Buy supplies. Discount stores are best. These trips can be great fun for all the kids, but the birthday child gets final say on the purchases. While you are there you might want to buy a small gift for your other children, to be given the day of the party. Be sure you buy an extra prize for the birthday child too. Many a birthday child, although receiving tons of gifts, ends his birthday in tears because he didn't get a prize like the guests did! To cut down on expenses, you may want to buy white paper supplies, which are much cheaper than the decorated ones. Your children can then decorate these at home (with nontoxic colors, such as food coloring or crayons), or the guests can decorate their own plates and cups, with prizes for the best, most original, and so forth.

Twenty-four hours before the party: Unless you live in a small town, save time for phone calls from all the parents who need directions to your home or would like to leave Sammy two extra hours at your house, and so forth. If your house is especially hard to find, you might want to include a map in the invitations. Bake the cake.

The morning of the party: Decorate, hang balloons outside, and go over strategy with all your children. For example, if you are having a party for four-year-olds, you may wish to have an older child be responsible for keeping guests safe—away from the street and the neighbor's pool, and using the jungle gym in your backyard safely. Another older child might be in charge of games and helping to dispense cake and ice cream. Fathers can be a great help with parties, but many dads may claim they don't know what to do, and others hide!

When the children arrive: You'll need an official "greeter" at the door, preferably the host if he/she is old enough. If your party is held in the backyard, post a sign so that latecomers will know where to go. Remember: The most important thing about a party is keeping the children safe, out of mischief, and occupied, in that order. Here's a tip for if and when you run out of things to do: Play some bouncy music on a tape recorder—loud—and give a prize for whoever dances the longest and the most vigorously. If your party is at a park, you'll need to be especially careful to watch all the children unless the park is securely fenced and gated, or parents stay with their children. This is where having a large family comes in handy. You can post your big kids at the perimeter of the party to keep strays in place. An older child can watch his toddler or infant sister, freeing you up for party duty.

If you serve lunch, ask about allergies and kosher or other religious proscriptions when planning the menu. If there are none, pizza and hot dogs (not for small children

—they could choke) are inexpensive and go a long way. Try not to serve soup or other liquids for obvious reasons.

All children know the birthday cake ritual. Candle safety is of utmost importance here. Once the song is sung and the candles are out, have your older kids help get the cake and ice cream to everyone quickly, before they can think to argue about the size of the piece they get or the color it is decorated with.

Present opening can be a tough time for siblings, who often want to help open the gifts. You can put siblings to work handing gifts to the party person, writing down who gave what for reference when thank-you notes are written, and securing gifts after they are opened. Now is the time to give each sibling the gift you bought when purchasing party supplies.

Siblings also come in handy at the end of the party. They can find misplaced shoes, mittens, and children, say good-bye, and help with cleanup.

If all your children are small, consider hiring someone else's older children for your party.

After the party: Everybody is now very tired and fussy, and the house/yard/park is a disaster area. Before tackling cleanup, get everyone who is young enough to take a nap (this does not include you). The older kids can be assigned specific chores.

Several days after the party: Return all the personal items the guests have left behind, have your child write thank-you notes, and start planning the next birthday party.

Congratulations on giving your child a very special memory.

Sleepovers

Some of you may even be brave enough to consider a sleepover. Here are some suggestions:

1. Be sexist. If your son wants a sleepover, tell him they are only for girls. Instead, let his best friend stay overnight for his birthday.
2. Sleepovers work best between the ages of seven and ten. Along about midnight, younger children decide they want their mommies. Older girls decide to call boys they have group crushes on at about midnight.
3. In the interests of peace, make sure that the children invited get along fairly well with one another. Also, it's terrible to be an outsider at a sleepover; for example, if a child knows your daughter from Brownies but all the other girls are friends from school.
4. Expect that at least one parent will be up all night.
5. Discreetly ask all mothers if their children are bedwetters. If so, provide plastic lawn bags to be placed by everyone under their mandatory sleeping bags. (Do *not* use bags made of the type of light plastic that can smother if accidentally moved over the face during sleep.)
6. Make sure you have the phone numbers of all parents.
7. Plan activities for the morning before pickup time. This could be making and decorating pancakes for breakfast or a "treasure hunt" in the backyard.
8. Keep meals simple and have plenty of inexpensive fillers, such as popcorn.
9. Brothers and sisters can help out but should not camp out with the party participants unless invited.
10. Chaperone your TV and telephone. You'd be surprised what can happen late at night if the partygoers are able to use the TV and phone.
11. Get everybody tired with lots of exercise early on

in the party, such as Dance Till You Drop contests. They still won't sleep all night, but they won't have the energy to squabble.

12. Don't invite more children than you have patience (or chairs) for.

Holidays and Family Traditions

What do you think children really enjoy and remember most about the Christmas and Chanukah holidays? The gifts? Well, only in a negative way, meaning that if they don't get enough gifts, they feel slighted. What children care about most are the family traditions. In our country, many customs, including a wild buying frenzy that starts in November and lasts until Christmas Eve, are dictated by Madison Avenue. But the traditions that really count with kids are the ones your family develops on its own.

Emily's family of seven children, all in school now, adopt a disadvantaged family each year. The adopted family has children approximately the same age as theirs, and each child plans a gift for his counterpart. In addition, a big gift is given to the family. One year it was three beds because the adopted family's six children had all been sleeping on a stone slab floor. The day after Emily's children brought the beds over, there was a terrible storm. One of Emily's kids remarked that she was glad they had gotten the bedding to "their" family before the storm broke; now she didn't have to worry that the "adopted" kids would freeze!

For Mike and Lupe, going to Disneyland on Christmas Eve (they live nearby) has become a tradition they wish they had never started. It's just gotten too expensive, but the kids won't hear of stopping it! Long ago, when Mike and Lupe had only five small children and admission prices were lower, they took their group on Christmas Eve because they both had that day off, the place was almost empty, and the kids were so tired out after running around all day that getting them to sleep that night was no problem. Now the oldest are teenagers and pay full fare, two more children have been added to the family, and the cost is prohibitive. But the kids clamor so much to go that their parents work extra for the money to take them. Lupe is convinced that you should never start a family tradition unless you can live with it for the next fifty years.

Many large families are themselves a part of other large families. Having fifty or so relatives in the house at Thanksgiving is one of the high points of the year—unless you have to do all the cooking. Most large clans have developed cooperative plans that permit massive amounts of food to be efficiently prepared and cleaned up afterward.

Christmas, Chanukah, and Thanksgiving are not the only holidays around which traditions are built. For some families the Easter season or another religious holiday is very important. Some families put a lot of emphasis on St. Patrick's or St. Joseph's Day. In one family Valentine's Day is special because Daddy buys a chocolate heart for each of the girls. In another, the Fourth of July means a giant barbecue with all the cousins, and summer can't officially start for the children until this barbecue takes place.

Family traditions are fun, but more than that, they give children a sense of the continuity of life. They are powerfully reassuring in a very uncertain world.

The following are helpful suggestions if you want to start your own family tradition:

Pick a holiday, major or minor, universal or unique to your family (such as the day you became engaged).

Think about an activity you want to do every year for the next twenty-five or fifty years. (One family has started a "Christmas notebook," and each Christmas they all write in special things that have happened to them that year. Imagine how much fun it will be when baby Sara reads, twenty-five years from now, how her parents felt the Christmas they were newlyweds.)

Once you have settled on a tradition, be faithful about doing it. There's nothing more disappointing for a child than to expect an activity will take place because in his memory it always has, and then one year it just stops. One family always had an end-of-summer party. One year Mom decided to go back to school and felt the party would be too much of a hassle. Besides, the children were all teenagers by this time. She was really surprised by the depth of disappointment shown by her "sophisticated" adolescents when the party was discontinued.

Don't overdo. Family traditions should be simple, not exhausting.

Vacations

Imagine your dream family vacation. You and your spouse manage to get two weeks off at the same time. The kids are out of school. Money is no problem. You decide to rent a condo in Hawaii . . . for the children. Their island babysitter is a reliable and enthusiastic Hawaiian Mary Poppins who drives a large minibus and knows all the kiddie tourist traps. You and your spouse have your own condo close enough to the kids to be available some of the time, far enough away from the kids so you can have some romantic moments alone together. The children have promised not to fight or get sick for the entire vacation, and they stick to their promise. The baby also has agreed to forgo putting foreign objects in her mouth, and will not violate any safety codes. The weather is perfect in paradise.

Given the above set of assumptions, what do you think

you would do during your vacation? Most parents of large families that I know of would catch up on their sleep!

Picture the dilemma of the Smith family. They live in a moderate-size city, a couple of hours' drive from either mountain or seaside resorts. Both parents work, so getting vacation time together took luck and preplanning. One summer, when the oldest two were in high school and the last baby was out of diapers, they decided to take their first family vacation ever. They chose the seashore, three hours away. They took two cars because all eight children couldn't fit in one. They rented a condo by the sea where they could prepare their own meals. Even at that, the cost was exorbitant, so they limited their stay to four days and three nights.

The kids had a great time. Of course, there were the usual disagreements on what to do each day, and one child got sick at the zoo, but considering all the things that could have gone wrong and didn't . . .

Mom and Dad, however, were exhausted at the end of the four days. First there was the three-hour drive, one parent to a car. Then all the meals Mom had to cook and the laundry, all full of sand, and shopping for food and hauling kids around, in a city unfamiliar to them. Sleeping in was out of the question. Children who had to be tugged out of bed on school days were up before dawn. The condo was so small that once one child stirred, he awakened everyone. All in all, it was worth the money spent because the children felt it was such fun. But it was not a vacation for the parents.

The Johnsons had a different approach. They figured from the start that the vacation was just for their six kids, not for them. Since they were on a strict budget, their solution was to camp out. In their section of the country there were lots of campgrounds, but they had to be reserved far in advance.

The Johnsons rented a camper from a friend and bought

a tent for the older children. They also bought lots of food, much of it snacks, at an outlet store. Blankets and clothing had to be appropriate for chilly nights, even though it was summer. They planned a Monday through Friday stay.

Things were great the first two days. Of course, Mrs. Johnson spent nearly all of her time cooking, cleaning up, and running after the two-year-old. But Mr. Johnson got in some fishing with the older boys. By day three a few of the kids were bored and spent most of their time in the camper playing Monopoly, the toddler still kept trying to run away, some of the children had made friends with other campers, all the snacks were gone, and things had settled into a routine.

By the time the vacation was over, the kids were filthy, tired, and had great memories. Mom and Dad were also filthy, tired, and glad the kids were happy. They had made plans to spend the following weekend at a local motel . . . without the kids.

What to do on a vacation (if you get one) is a real dilemma for some large families. Relatives who were happy to put you up for a few days when there was just you, your spouse, and a cute little baby blanch at the thought of turning their house over to three or four active kids. Staying at home and catching up on repairs is an option that the kids won't like much. "Vacationing" at home, where you actually make up in advance an itinerary of all the local sights you plan to see, may please them more.

Vacationing away involves considerably more planning and expense. Some large families have summer homes. This sounds like an awfully expensive proposition but might prove less costly in the long run. Time-sharing may also be an option, depending on your family's finances and ability to travel. Some less costly options you may want to explore months in advance are house swapping for a prearranged period, camping out, renting a house for a few weeks, or house sitting.

No matter where you vacation (except, of course, at home), you will have to get there and back. Most vacation trips will be by car, some by airplane, and a few by bus or train. Most trips will take at least an hour or two; some may take considerably longer. How are you going to keep all the children quiet and amused, and prevent them from killing each other, while in transit? This is the part of the trip that demands the best planning of all, and some tips culled from other families may be helpful:

Plan your trip far ahead of time: This planning should include where you will go, how you will get there, which children you will take if you don't take them all and who will babysit those left behind, and how much you can spend. Make camping, train, and plane reservations early. (When making hotel reservations, tell the registration desk how many children you have. Don't assume their advertisement that children can stay for free in their parents' room means your brood of six can.)

Realistically map out an itinerary: If you have an infant, toddler, or overactive child, there will be frequent pit stops. Allow at least an hour for each meal. Don't plan on traveling more than about four hundred miles a day, less if you're traveling through heavily urbanized areas. Plan traveling time so as not to get caught in rush hour. Think about who will drive, who will navigate, and how often drivers will switch.

A word here about children who are difficult to travel with:

Nursing infants will demand frequent stops. It is unsafe to remove your baby from her infant car seat to nurse while the vehicle is moving.

Toddlers get restless and fuss often. Luckily, they are generally easily distracted from their fussing, and they usually sleep a lot.

Both infants and toddlers require frequent diaper changes.

If you have a child who gets carsick, see your physician well before the trip. Medications are quite helpful here.

Children with poor self-quieting abilities, whatever their ages, travel poorly. These children are upset by changes in their environment, such as heat, cold, noise, or vibrations. Their attention spans may be short. They wriggle and fight in the car. They may, in fact, be a bit anxious about leaving the security of home. Many also have a poor concept of time. This means that when you say to Frankie, "Don't worry. We'll be there in half an hour," he is not reassured because he has no concept of how long half an hour is. If you have one of these children, you need to discuss the trip itself with him beforehand so he knows what to expect. He also will need to get out of the car and run around periodically.

Get your car in good working order: This includes making sure the car has enough seat belts and child carriers for everyone. You want to avoid at all costs a breakdown on a freeway a million miles from anywhere, with three or four kids fighting in the backseat.

Plan who does what the night before and the day of the trip: This will aid you in getting started with time to spare. You may wish to make individual assignments so each child has responsibility for some aspect of the trip. Consider making a picnic lunch for the trip.

Equip your car properly: Some suggestions:

Kleenex, paper towels, a first-aid kit.

Nutritious, nonmessy snacks. Stay away from sweets.

Consider nondrippable fruits and vegetables, such as apples, carrots (for older children), and bananas; cereal bars, crackers, cheese sticks, sliced meats, or beef jerky (for older children). For drinks there are self-contained boxes of fruit juice with straws that fit snugly and virtually eliminate spillage. Babies may need a cooler for bottles, or jars of baby food and soft biscuits.

A tape recorder and lots of sing-along children's tapes. You may also bring some blank tapes and record in the car.

One or more coed changes of clothing and shoes. Jogging suits are great because they can stretch to fit almost any child in an emergency. Don't forget lots of diapers for the baby.

Versatile toys, such as crayons, paper, coloring books and storybooks, small dolls, and squeaky toys and keys, for babies and toddlers.

A special kit, kept out of the way of the children, in which you put a sewing kit, scissors, pocketknife, needed medications, loose coins, safety pins, extra car and house keys, maps, and other miscellaneous necessities.

Maintain discipline during the car trip and when you get to your destination: Car safety demands that children do not fight and distract the driver. The children must understand that any breach in conduct will result in an immediate pull over to the side of the road, and if serious enough, may even abort the vacation. They need to be told that this is done for their safety.

Good behavior will also be required when all arrive at their destination, until the baggage is unloaded and the tent pitched, or whatever.

Maintain your sense of humor: Murphy's Law also applies to family vacations!

Rules for vacations:

1. Watch small children closely. Accidents occur more frequently away from familiar surroundings.
2. Consider the ages, interests, sleep-wake cycles, and feeding times of your children when sightseeing.
3. Plan for contingencies such as illness or the need to use an unfamiliar babysitter.
4. Inspect your vacation site carefully for safety hazards when you first arrive.
5. If you rent a car, ask in advance for car seats.
6. Use sun block, sunglasses, and hats liberally if your children are fair-skinned.
7. Assign each older child a younger one for whom he is responsible (the buddy system).
8. When conflicts arise over where to go or what to do, parents must dictate.
9. If you are leaving teenagers at home, identify a responsible adult they must check in with (a friend or neighbor), and be sure this adult has your written permission to consent to emergency medical care for your children.
10. Expect occasional expressions of boredom from your children. This does not mean they are not enjoying themselves.
11. Grab some time alone with your spouse, even if it's only sitting around the campfire when the children are asleep.

CHAPTER

9

Personalities and Successful Learning

DO you believe that firstborns are highly responsible superachievers? And secondborns are very social little beings whose existence has been all but forgotten by their parents? And the baby of the family is an overindulged con artist? Do you think that children from large families have lower intelligence levels just because they were born into a large family? That "onlies" have an intellectual advantage over children from large families so there's no use even trying to outdistance them? Do you ever feel faintly guilty, as though you have done an injustice to your children and may be preventing them from reaching their full potential, just because you had several of them?

If you have worried about any of these things, join the group. Most of us have read and heard about the effect that birth order has on a person's life. We've also been told that children from large families don't do as well in school as only children or duos. (Some people think that all this propaganda is really "social birth control," a way of getting parents to believe that if they have too many children, they will actually be sabotaging their children's chances for success.)

Well, the good news is that "it ain't necessarily so." Most of the studies comparing the school performance of children from large and small families were done long ago, when families really were different. In those days not as much was known about birth control, so having a large family wasn't the choice it is today. Some of the families that were studied were "dysfunctional," a sociological word meaning they didn't have their act together.

But nowadays in big families where the children are planned and where parents are doing a good job of raising them (functional families), we find that academic and social achievement may actually be higher than average. And the most important determinant of a child's pattern of behavior is not so much his birth order as his own inborn personality.

Of course, birth order does still have some impact on each child, but the larger the family, the more diluted the birth order effect. I'd like to tell you about some of the things we noted in looking at two hundred and ninety-six children from healthy, strong families of varied ethnic, religious, and economic backgrounds.

Personality

When you take that tiny bundle home from the hospital, you immediately begin to see little traits that mark her as a distinct person. All this happens long before you have had a chance to mold her personality in any way. You instinctively know that personality is part of the package you get at birth. You can work with a child's personality to make the best of her talents and take the rough edges off her behavior, but you can't make a child who is very sensitive to her environment into one who doesn't notice her surroundings, just as you can't make an aggressive type into a Milquetoast (though you can teach him how to treat others fairly).

Many "experts" feel that birth order fixes personality in some mysterious way. Not a few parents are really bothered by this suggestion, sometimes to the point of limiting their family size so they don't have a "middle child" or having another child for the "only son" with two sisters.

How about it? Does birth order have as profound an effect on personality as some people fear it might? We looked at this question in large families by having parents give mini-profiles of all their children. Past research has shown that observant parents are quite good at appraising their children. After all, they're with them the most. And parents of many children have a basis for comparison too. This is what we found.

Firstborns: First children are the most reliable and conscientious. They also tend to be more reserved and reflective than others in the birth order. That kind of fits: Oldest children are naturally given more responsibility than others, and they learn by practice. Similarly, the oldest is usually eager to please and is sensitive to others. Many eldest children are described by their parents as kind, compassionate, unselfish, and, of course, mature. More firstborns than any other in the birth order are goal-oriented and self-motivated.

So far, firstborns fit the classic description of the older child in small families, and this birth order probably is the one most likely to behave the same regardless of family size. However, the eldest children in large families also generally do a fair amount of "parenting" of brothers and sisters. Firstborn children in small families don't get this opportunity. Perhaps this is the reason that firstborns in large families have a lot of nurturing qualities. A handful of firstborns are temperamental, aggressive, and argumentative. Another subset are sensitive, moody loners. Three in twenty have characteristics usually seen in the baby of the family: laid-back, impish, and happy-go-lucky, sometimes even rebellious. And a few (about one in twenty firstborns) drive their parents crazy because they fail to plan ahead, are disorganized and unmotivated, or seem uncooperative and callous.

Secondborns: Secondborns in large families have many of the traits of eldest children, with a few intriguing exceptions. They're less likely to be goal-oriented and hard-working and more likely to be sloppy and lazy. Close to one in five is described as moody and insecure. Twice as many secondborns as firstborns are quiet, shy loners. This is also the only one in the birth order where several parents specifically mention their child's competitiveness. Many second children are said to be feisty, strong-willed, and persistent.

So far, second children are perceived as having more problem traits than firstborns. Yet they are also more likely to be friendly and people-oriented in spite of the shy ones in their ranks. More than any others in the birth order, they are likely to possess an artistic temperament and be imaginative, creative, and dramatic.

Thirdborns: Third children are the most likely of all to feel misunderstood and to need lots of parental reassurance. They are also the most likely, believe it or not, to have a social conscience, to feel for the underdog, and to show compassion to others. They are rarely quiet and shy, and are much more likely to be argumentative and out-spoken. Though they can be either leaders or followers, they are often quite determined and persistent, though not generally as goal-oriented as their older siblings.

Fourthborns: Perhaps one third of the fourthborns in large families are youngest children. Fourthborns provide a real contrast from oldest children but are just slightly different from third children. (Some traits seem to increase as birth order does.) Fourthborns are the most likely to be funny, easygoing, and sometimes mischievous clowns. However, one in five is just the opposite: quiet, shy, or even melancholic. Fourths are also the ones in the birth order most likely to show determination, persistence, and even a streak of stubbornness. Just as many are independent and self-confident as are anxious and worried about making mistakes. A fair number can be outspoken and volatile at times. Many are physically energetic and viva-cious.

Very few parents described their fourths as exceptionally reliable or conscientious. This may reflect the fact that fourths are not too likely to be put in charge of other children and don't have the chance to develop these first- and secondborn virtues. In fact, about one in twenty fourths is seen as callous, aloof, and uncooperative.

Higher Birth Orders: As we get to fifth, sixth, and seventh children and beyond, birth-order-associated person-ality traits fall off rapidly. It's as though in families this large, the individual personalities of each child come out more. Children don't have to behave in a certain way be-cause of where they are in the lineup. There are fewer preassigned roles. One cluster of traits is seen a lot in these children, however: They tend to be even-tempered and outgoing, kind and caring. A fair number are also goal-oriented, like their eldest siblings. All in all, most parents see their high birth order kids as nice guys!

Common Trends

Some personality traits seem to go along with being in a large family. Generally, these kids enjoy their friendships a good deal, they've learned how to take turns, and they don't expect everything to be always perfect. (And a good thing they don't, because a day when everything goes without a hitch is very rare in the large family.)

Some things can be said about the impact of birth order in the large family:

1. Individual personalities are a good deal more important than birth order when there are a number of children in the family.
2. The personality characteristics most likely to change with birth order are those involved with the leadership role. Oldest children tend to be slightly more responsible and goal-oriented, and the nadir is reached with the fourth child, who is the most fun-loving and easygoing.
3. Second children often have many of the leadership traits of the eldest in large families. After all, they are second in command.
4. Third children, being pivotal children, are generally most in need of attention from Mom and Dad. (No more one-on-one when you have three children.)
5. When there are four or more children in a family, all bets are off. Children of higher birth orders are less and less affected by their birth order.

Lastly, a little story. My son and I were talking about a family with two sons, about four years apart, who followed classic birth order rules. The elder was supergifted. He was the kind of person you were delighted your children had as a friend. The second son was also remarkable, but in a different way. This son was mightily pursued by the opposite sex. I heard rumors that his telephone never rested. True, he was quite good-looking, but he apparently had a charisma that was the envy of every other adolescent male.

My son said he had figured out the reason that this family had produced a superachieving firstborn and a supersocial secondborn. "That family," Bill said, "is parent-controlled. The boys do everything with their parents. Our family is kid-controlled. You people are just too busy to give us 'quality time' so we have our own system among us kids to be sure things go right." (I'm not sure I liked the implications there, but I remembered that this son is a teenager and as such has a deep-seated need to tell us how we blew it. But hey, we try!)

There is a germ of truth in Bill's observations. The small family focuses more on parental expectations. In the large family parental expectations are there, all right, but usually not as strictly imposed, so the child in a large family is a little freer to follow his own internal compass and less likely to have a personality based strictly on his birth order.

If you're like most parents of large families, you're fascinated by the variety of personalities and experiences your children provide you. You can go from your Lamaze class to Mommy and Me swimming lessons, followed by a chat with your son's Little League coach, and top off the evening at a fund-raiser for your daughter's high school.

But how about your children? How is their development affected by growing up in a large family? If you worry that your child's development will be harmed by growing up with several siblings, you're not alone. But the good news is that there are lots of things you can do in the course of your day to teach your children the same skills that parents with more time and fewer children do. First, a quick review of what these skills are.

CLINICAL LINGUISTIC AND AUDITORY MILESTONE SCALE

MEAN AGE IN MONTHS	SEQUENTIAL MILESTONES
0.25	Alerting (R)*
1.25	Social smile (R)*
1.6	Cooing (E)
4.0	Orients to voice (R)*
4.0	Ah-goo (E)
4.4	Razzing (E)
5.0	Orients to bell I (R)*
6.3	Babbling (E)
7.0	Orients to bell II (R)*
7.7	Dada/Mama indiscriminately (E)
8.6	Gesture (R)
9.0	Orients to bell III (R)*; understands the word "no" (R)
10.8	Dada/Mama discriminately (E)
11.1	1-step command with gesture (R)*
11.3	1st word (E)
12.2	Immature jargoning (E)
12.4	2nd word (E)
13.2	3rd word*
14.7	4 to 6 words (E)
16.5	Mature jargoning (E)
16.7	Pointing to 5 body parts (R)*
16.9	7 to 20 words (E)
19.2	2-word combinations (E) (incomplete sentences)
20.6	3-word sentences (E) (noun + indiscriminate pronoun and verb)
20.9	50-word vocabulary

Mean Age in Months	Sequential Milestones
24	Pronouns (I, me, you) indiscriminately (E)
30	Pronouns (I, me, you) discriminately (E)
36	All pronouns discriminately (E)
36	250-word vocabulary (E)
36	Plurals (E)
36	3-word sentences (E)

Source: Adapted from chart in "Marking the Milestones of Language Development," by Arnold J. Capute, M.D., M.P.H., Bruce K. Shapiro, M.D., and Frederick B. Palmer, M.D., *Contemporary Pediatrics* 4 (April 1987):26–29, originally published in *Developmental Medicine and Child Neurology* 28 (1986):762–71.

*Responses that can be elicited directly rather than reported by the parent.
(R) = receptive language
(E) = expressive language

Communication

Learning a language actually starts in the womb. The fetus can respond to loud sounds by the fifth month of pregnancy. (The Bible contains a dramatic account of this phenomenon. When Mary goes to visit her cousin Elizabeth, the unborn John the Baptist leaps in his mother Elizabeth's womb at the sound of Mary's voice.)

Language has two components: receptive and expressive. This means that in order to communicate a child must first hear and interpret a sound or word, and then he must produce a sound or word in response (this latter skill is called expressive language). Besides verbal language we also have another form of communication: body language. Most little babies become good at body language early. (Sometimes failure to communicate with parents by cuddling and hugging is the first sign of a serious condition called autism.)

All normal babies, regardless of the language their parents speak, follow a fairly uniform path in the development of language skills. Premature babies may be a few weeks behind.

Building Vocabulary: Normal children from large families are no different from those in small families in learning language skills. Children in large families may have a less extensive vocabulary and sometimes use body language more. Here's where parents and siblings come in. Children add to the number of words they know by being spoken to and read to, and by having their questions answered. You, the parent, must set the example that your older children will follow in communicating with their younger siblings. Here are some methods:

When a child uses body language instead of words to ask for something, tell him the words he needs to request what he wants. For example, a sixteen-month-old may point at the pitcher of orange juice on the table to indicate that he wants some. Instead of pouring it for him in silence, say, as you pour, "Alex, I can see that you are trying to tell me you are thirsty and want some orange juice. Can you say for me, 'Please, orange juice?'" Instruct your older children to teach Alex words when he points too. But don't withhold the juice until he says the words!

Use new vocabulary with a child but define the new words by using words she already knows. You may say to a three-year-old who is dressing up in her party clothes, "Goodness, Crystal, you look so stylish. That word 'stylish' means that your clothes look so nice on you."

Read often to your children and explain new words or try to have the children guess what the words mean as you go along. A book such as *Go, Dog, Go*, a classic by P. D. Eastman (Random House, 1961), is great to explain prepositions defining position to toddlers. As you read, you can say, "Now point to 'up' in our room, Karen. And Paul, can you show me 'under' our chair?" Have the children take turns answering your questions as you read.

Sing children's songs in the car. They build vocabulary and they're fun. Each child can suggest a song to be sung in succession.

Listen respectfully when your children tell you things. This can be a real challenge in a large family where you have to hold two or three conversations at once. When all the children absolutely have to talk at the same time, you can intervene and say, "Peter was talking to me first, and then I want to hear what Danny and Rhona have to say. Peter, go ahead." Even if a child wants to tell you something when you are reading the paper, try to take the time if you can.

Play word games, such as Scrabble, with older children if and when you get the time.

Take kids to the library regularly. Get excited when they use new words. Encourage short story writing and praise the compositions your children write in third and fourth grade.

Movement/Motor Skills

Sitting, walking, and throwing a ball are all motor skills that come to most children quite automatically. A child will learn to do these things in a bare-bones environment, but he may not be encouraged to use his fine and gross motor skills to solve problems and acquire new abilities.

Some children seem to be better coordinated from birth. They climb jungle gyms almost as soon as they can walk and are on a two-wheeler at age four. But their parents still have to provide access to the bike or playground equipment, and need to supervise their children's safety. Other children will require more active teaching by their parents.

Some youngsters, so-called clumsy children, are a subset who "perform fine and/or gross motor tasks in an immature, disorganized, erratic, slow, irregular, or inconsistent fashion," according to Lawrence T. Taft, M.D., and Ellis I. Barowski, Ph.D., writing in *Pediatrics in Review*, vol. 10. These children sometimes have trouble in infancy with feeding, sucking, and swallowing. As toddlers they may drool a lot and later run into trouble in nursery school performing such tasks as using a scissors and coloring. Parents who have a child like this need to be especially involved in teaching the motor skills that their other children have learned automatically. For example, you may have to take extra time to allow your child to button one or two buttons each day until he gets the hang of it. Dad or an older brother may want to practice a particular sport skill, such as throwing a basketball, over and over with him so he won't be embarrassed in school. With much practice these children do get better.

Clumsy children either fall through the cracks in a large family or are given a lot of support from their siblings and do better than they would in a small family.

If you think you have such a child, the following steps are helpful:

1. Talk to your doctor. Some simple office tests may help define the problem.
2. Devise methods that will allow your child to repeat

a specific task until she masters it. This may mean breaking a task down into its simple parts and practicing each of these parts separately. For example, teach dressing skills slowly, focusing on one skill for several days to several weeks, and finally combining them all.

3. Look for sports that your child can do more easily. One child didn't want to be in Little League as his brothers had been because he was afraid he wouldn't be able to get out of the way of the ball fast enough and it would hit him. Soccer was a lot easier for this child. Swimming, horseback riding (though expensive), and track are some other possibilities.

4. Discuss the topic with your child's teacher so that he/she is more patient if your child has trouble writing or coloring neatly, making "projects," or if she sometimes bumps into things in the classroom.

5. Be alert to your child's self-esteem. He may feel bad when his younger brother does better at sports than he does or when other kids choose this brother to be on their team instead of him. Later on he may have trouble making friends in school because he isn't good at sports. You may want to help him find other outlets or show him how to improve his athletic skills to an acceptable level even though he'll never be the team's star player.

6. Encourage siblings to help this child. Older brothers can be great family coaches—and be sure to tell them how much you appreciate their help.

7. If your child is clumsy, don't encourage her to retreat indoors to the TV with a bowl of junk food as company. She needs exercise even more than your other children. You don't want to add lack of social experience and possibly obesity to her problem.

Learning Time

Perhaps you're an at-home mother or father who has decided to be with your children while they're small because you feel you can teach them better than anyone else in the world. Or maybe you are employed outside the home and are making the effort to save special time for each child which you plan to devote exclusively to his/her intellectual needs. Whatever your situation, your first step will be to find some extra time in your schedule. For some ideas on how to do this, see Chapter 8.

Once you have managed to eke out a few minutes from your busy day to more formally "teach" your children, you're probably wondering what to teach them. Actually, to "teach" a child means to be with him and to explain the world to him. You can do this through just about any activity that interests your child, keeping in mind that a child's interests and span of attention vary with his age and personality. Your own enthusiasm and delight in your child and his developing mind and curiosity are of critical importance. Below are some ideas:

Two months through one year: Walks are great for the very young baby—maybe place her in a front pack so you can talk to her about what she is seeing. Of course she won't understand your words, but a pattern of communication will be started that can be built on. Your emotions, as you express them through your words, are important to her. You can say to her, "Look at those beautiful flowers, Elizabeth. Those are Mommy's favorite. Do you want to smell them?" Or, "Look at the trucks, Sara. They're big and they travel on streets. They make a lot of noise, don't they?" Mothers and fathers frequently know, almost instinctively, what to say to their young babies. Just go ahead and do it.

If it's cold outside, just rock her or show her bright

simple toys and talk about them. The most important thing is your delight at being with this baby. That sense of being loved will prepare her best for all of the learning that will take place in her future.

Picture books are great for the baby six months and above. Illustrations should be simple, in bright colors, of faces or common objects that your baby may recognize. Of course, your baby can't follow a story line, so don't bother to read. Instead, ask questions or make comments about the objects in the book. For example: "Oh, look at that pretty red balloon! It's round! Yesterday, at Josh's party, he had a pretty red balloon, and a blue one too!"

Playing with toys or peek-a-boo or dancing together to really lively music or exercising are all lots of fun for the baby under a year. Keep up a running conversation with him too. Your delight in him is what is most important. (And this doesn't even have to be scheduled. You can show that delight all the time.)

One to two: Keep "learning time" short. This little one doesn't have a very long attention span. Walks are great, but be prepared to spend most of the time watching a column of ants troop across a section of sidewalk or a crow peck seeds out of your newly planted lawn. Actually, these are very important activities for the young toddler. You can help by commenting on things such as how slowly the ants travel, not at all as fast as she can walk, or how high the crow flies, much higher than she can reach. This introduces her to concepts such as high and low, up and down, big and small in a way that is relevant to her interests at the time.

Picture books are still great. They can even have a story line, but you will need to stop often to ask questions and make comments about what both of you are reading. For example, "Goldilocks seems very hungry. Do you think she ate her breakfast at home? What did you eat for breakfast?" Or, "The cars in this book are different colors. See, there's a green one and there's a yellow one. But I like the red one best. Point to the one you like best."

Toys are fun. You can have a block-stacking contest. Or push around cars, discussing how fast they go, and what colors they are.

Most of all, do something that is fun for your child and for you. Don't force him into an activity that is too advanced or that he doesn't like. Remember, he learns by touch, smell, sight, hearing, and taste. Baking cookies and having him use the cookie press with you and count the number of cookies he has made may not seem terribly educational—it might also make a big mess—but it uses all his senses. And it's far more educational and fun for the toddler than teaching him to parrot cue cards with "dog" and "cat" on them.

Three years: Learning time with a three-year-old can be a lot of fun. She is fairly verbal, and you can toss ideas around with her and get some feedback. "If we put water into the freezer, what would happen to it?" Or, "Do you like the springtime more, when the flowers start to bloom, as in this picture, or do you like the winter when it's cold and snowy, as in this other picture?"

Learning time can be a trip to the store, counting trucks on the way. Or baking cupcakes or sweeping the floor. And at this age, if you take a walk, you both might actually get somewhere.

Four years: Your own sense of creativity is the limit when you're dealing with a four-year-old. If you are enthusiastic and explain things in simple terms, you can introduce many concepts to him. He won't understand them completely, of course, but then all learning is a matter of repetition. Each time a child is reintroduced to a concept, he grows to understand it on a slightly deeper level.

The four-year-old can be fascinated by projects such as putting a potato in water and watching it sprout roots.

This can lead to a discussion about how roots are like the mouths of plants—they let the plant drink water from the soil. Or he can make icing and color it with different food colors while you make the cupcakes. That way he can learn about the primary colors and how, for example, you can make purple from red and blue. (That's if you don't mind eating purple and green cupcakes, of course!)

Group Instruction

Let's say you can't make time for one-on-one interaction with each child. Don't despair! Group learning can be good too. Set aside about fifteen minutes between chores, have a special place where everyone won't be too distracted, hold the baby on your lap, and get out the books, blocks, or cookie mix. Or take a walk with your caravan in tow. The goals you have are to interact verbally with each child and to get him or her thinking, at whatever level he or she is able to. For example, a storybook can have pretty, touchable pictures for the six-month-old and a simple story line for the two-year-old, who can also be munching a snack. The four-year-old can "read" a page to the others, especially if she has heard this story many times before. You can ask questions, which is the best way to get children to think. For example, "Why do you think bunnies have such fuzzy warm fur?" Or, "Why do trucks go on roads?" If you're doing "group time," the most important thing is to do it regularly so that the children come to expect it . . . but keep it short.

Learning Styles

The children in this family represent some of the many learning styles that parents may encounter: Terri, age fourteen, does all her homework and even her chores with her

Walkman blaring in her ears. One of her four brothers, who is in honors and advanced placement classes in high school, will get up at four in the morning to write his papers and do his studying. It's the only time he can have absolute quiet.

A fifth grade brother is easily distracted from homework and needs constant prodding to get back on track. He does all his work directly under a parent's eye. Another child, a very bright and compulsive first grader, works so slowly that his teacher despairs of his ever completing his workbook. He is an absolute perfectionist about everything. Another sister had a terrible time learning colors and later on was significantly behind her first grade class in learning to read. Both times she seemed to have a burst of learning energy and caught up with her classmates practically overnight.

Most of us think that the best way to learn is by sitting upright at a desk in a quiet, well-lighted room, sharpened pencils at the ready and with plenty of time to complete assignments. And the majority of children and adults do learn best this way. But a significant minority will do their best work under quite different circumstances. Some children need activity to learn, so they walk around as they memorize their spelling words. Some children have good visual memories, so they'll need to write out those same spelling words and see them on paper. Another group may ask a parent or sibling to "quiz" them on the words because they learn best by hearing and repeating.

Perhaps you have even noticed that one of your toddlers seems to get a good deal of information through touch and manipulation. Another may be visually oriented. Still a third may like to ask questions. Of course, all toddlers will demonstrate all of these styles of learning, but some are more efficient or interested in one particular mode.

Which of us in high school hasn't had a friend who

waited until the last minute to do reports and always seemed to pull an A, while another friend would start working on projects as soon as they were assigned?

How to Determine Learning Styles

Figuring out each child's learning style is a hard but important task for you. You often have to manipulate the environment so that each child's learning style can be accommodated. Jane needs quiet, John needs noise, and Jim needs parental help. You have to find a way to meet these conflicting needs, perhaps by staggering homework times or making one bedroom a "quiet zone," or doing dishes as Jim works at the kitchen table.

The best way to start figuring out how each of your children learns best is by observing him or her closely during infancy and toddlerhood and listening carefully to what nursery school teachers and others have to say. Does your child spend a lot of time observing before he tries something? Does he love body movement and activity? Is he upset by changes in his environment? Does she like to touch things? Does she ask for stories? Does he enjoy working with peers? How has he differed from your others as toddlers? (You might want to keep a learning journal for each of your children.)

As each child enters school, ask the teacher what she has observed about how this child learns best, and share your own observations. Listen to how the child constructs his sentences, look at him at play, and notice how he goes about solving play problems.

As your child gets older he will be able to tell you how he learns best. If he gets good grades when he does homework while listening to background music, he may need this noise to help him memorize. If his grades are poor, however, then you know the music is a distraction. If the child is a computer nut, consider using the family computer to teach spelling facts (there are programs for this and for other homework tasks). The procrastinator may need restrictions until a project is completed, and these may have to be instituted as soon as the project is assigned. The "all nighter" who does his best work under pressure and has the grades to prove it will not need these constrictions.

When Everyone's Learning Style Is Different

Now comes the tough part: How do you accommodate several different learning styles under one roof?

If your house is large enough, separate children physically when they do their studying so that the one who is easily distracted and the one who likes to walk or hear background music don't disturb each other.

Stagger study hours so that each child's needs can be accommodated.

Help each child to use his best learning techniques. Make one child write out her spelling list the night before the exam. Quiz another orally. Have a third tape and play back the speech she has to give in class tomorrow.

Explain to each child why you permit different study methods for your different children. Joan needs to realize that past experience has taught you that she must do all her papers as soon as they are assigned, while Vito doesn't need that kind of supervision. You are interested in each child doing things the way that works best for him or her. Since no two people learn exactly the same way, as a parent you must help each child to succeed in the way that is best for him.

Remember that learning is not confined to the classroom. You can make use of different learning styles in daily life too. You can teach one child to count by planting seeds with him, another by having her crack eggs into a bowl for the family's scrambled egg breakfast.

10

High-Maintenance Children

SOME children are low-maintenance children. They are like fine-tuned cars, happily purring along, always fairly cheerful. They don't have problems that they can't fix themselves. Teachers like them, friends swarm about them, the coach calls them real team players. You feed them, clothe them, and say hello to them every morning. You could raise a dozen of this type of child with one hand tied behind your back.

But, of course, no one gets a dozen of this type of child. We all have our share of high-maintenance children too, and these are the ones we'll focus on here.

The Needy Child

Lets face it. Some kids are tougher to parent than others. They require a lot more time and a much more creative approach. Some children will present a temporary problem, such as experiencing difficulty when switching from one school to another, and will be very unhappy for a few months. Or a favorite grandchild becomes depressed when a grandparent dies. The depression could take the form of naughty behavior, sadness, or sometimes even self-destructive activity. These situations and others like them are a challenge to your parenting abilities and may even require professional counseling, but they eventually will be worked through.

There is another group of children who seem to need special attention all the time. They often start out as fussy or colicky babies who have trouble getting into a routine. They may be very sensitive to their environment, crying when they become the slightest bit hot or cold, or when they're exposed to motion or noise. Sometimes they are poor feeders, because they are a bit deficient in the fine-tuned coordination they need to nurse efficiently. Their sleep patterns can be frustrating.

When such a baby is your third one, you usually have enough experience to recognize that you're a capable mother or father but that this baby is just needier. If the baby is your first, however, you could feel pretty shaky about your parenting skills.

As needy kids grow to be toddlers they may have trouble in the sandbox with other children, either being too aggressive or not knowing how to make contact with others their age.

In kindergarten, parents are often told that these children are immature and are pressured to hold them back. In certain cases this may be wise, but often it's the worst thing you could do. Needy children often don't improve with age alone; they improve with sensitive guidance. Holding them back may make them feel even worse about themselves.

Which brings us to the most important issue in dealing with needy children: their self-esteem. Kids who require more parenting realize that life is a little tougher for them than for other children, and they don't quite know why. Sometimes they grow to dislike the way they are. Parents must struggle daily to let these children know they are loved and their talents are appreciated. Sure, Sally gets straight A's and was elected to student council and Jeff was chosen for the all-star team. But your needy child draws beautiful pictures, and you love him so much for the special gift he made on Mother's Day.

These kids often require extra hugs and listening time. You can put another child off for a few minutes while you make a phone call and he will not be crushed, whereas the needy child may feel as though you are rejecting him if you don't hear him out right away.

A subgroup of needy children has learning disorders. These kids have normal intelligence but have difficulty handling certain types of information, leading to all sorts of problems in school and with friends. If you think your child may have a problem taking in, understanding, or giving back information, run to the school district psychologist and demand comprehensive testing. Most school districts do an excellent job, and there are effective methods for teaching kids with specific learning disorders that can make a lot of difference for your child.

Some of the behaviors that alert parents to an especially needy child are as follows:

1. He has always had trouble making friends. Either he's too aggressive, he's shy, or he just doesn't know how to approach another child.

2. He seems to "fly off the handle" easily, and his needs must be met immediately. He's been this way since babyhood.
3. He can't tolerate hunger, fatigue, thirst, heat, cold, or perhaps motion.
4. He has trouble keeping to a schedule and has to be walked through such simple things as getting up and getting dressed for school.
5. He's impulsive and can't seem to think ahead and recognize a dangerous situation.
6. He needs constant reassurance and attention to feel loved.
7. He's been irregular all his life, including problems with sleeping, fears, toilet training, types of foods, and new places or new activities.
8. He's clumsy or perhaps unfocused.
9. He's terribly afraid of new situations or challenges and seems to have almost no confidence in his own ability.
10. He needs advance warning about upcoming events.

It's okay to parent the needy child more than the others. Sometimes you can also enlist the help of your other children. When they are on the family team helping their "needy" brother or sister, they're far less likely to feel jealous.

Peter had been a difficult baby. In the middle of six children, he was a sensitive infant and afterward had lots of trouble making friends in nursery school. Primary school was a disaster until his parents asked two older brothers to help out. They taught him basketball, took him places with them, and generally reassured him that he was a great guy. Peter's personality didn't change, of course. He continued to be clumsy and to have only a couple of friends, but he did learn how to play a fair game of basketball and started to do better in school. As his self-confidence improved, he started reaching out to his younger siblings to teach them things. And he discovered a previously unsuspected talent for writing stories.

When you have a needy child, you can assist him/her in the following ways:

Give him extra hugs and more eye contact.

Work on supporting self-esteem by finding what he is good at and encouraging it.

Praise him when he does things on his own; encourage autonomy little by little.

Invite friends over for him and observe how he interacts with them.

If he is impulsive, you need to be extra concerned about his safety.

Keep in close contact with his teachers so you know what's happening in his life at school.

Teach him ways of helping himself, such as writing a timed schedule of what he has to do in the morning and then giving him a big, easy-to-read clock. And don't feel bad about giving him extra attention.

Since he may not do well with last-minute surprises, tell him very early when something will be happening so he has time to get used to it.

Try to foresee his physical needs; for example, if you'll be away from home for a while, take a snack along for him.

Make sure he gets his rest.

Make a big deal of his birthday, school play, and any other event that is special for him.

Be available when he needs you. Don't put him off.

Get him tested if you think he could have allergies, poor hearing, a learning problem, or something along those lines.

Enlist the support of the other children.

The Gifted Child

Needy children are not the only ones who demand a lot of parental cultivation. Gifted kids are often high-maintenance kids too. Nearly 50 percent of large families have one or more children who are gifted athletically, scholastically, and/or in the arts.

Almost everyone would agree by now that giftedness is not just a high IQ. Sometimes it's the ability to lead others with wisdom and common sense. Or it could be, as it was for Beethoven, a talent for music. George Washington Carver's agricultural talents changed and diversified Southern farming, and Jim Thorpe's genius was to become the world's greatest all-around athlete in 1912.

Parents of three or more children face two main problems with their gifted children: First, you have to identify these children as gifted, and then you have to decide how much of the family's resources should be allotted to your gifted child.

One wise mother said that all her children were gifted in something; she just had to figure out what it was and nourish it.

Giftedness will often manifest itself in early childhood. Drew amazed his father as a toddler when they played kickball together. He would line his right foot up ahead of time so that he would be ready to kick the ball back to his dad. He figured out how to do this all by himself; he had never been shown how.

At eight he learned to play the trumpet, winning his school's music award at graduation from high school. But that's not all. Drew became an Eagle Scout at thirteen. He was student council president of his high school, maintained a 3.9 GPA in advanced courses, and won several scholarships to college in addition to being active in his church. And his dad says that Drew was the only one of his ten children who had to be told to stop studying at 1:30 A.M.

Drew is a typical multigifted child. His ability to plan ahead, his coordination, and his problem-solving skills were evident very early in life, and along with these natural talents he was willing to put in hard work to do his best.

Katy is also multitalented. Her mother remembers that she was always self-motivated and could grasp concepts quickly. At six or so, when her mother mentioned that a twenty-year-old woman had a forty-two-year-old husband, Katy piped up that the husband was twenty-two years older than his wife.

Katy is now a junior in high school. She works as a nanny three hours a day after school, but she still gets excellent grades, taking advanced courses. She has an active social life, plays on her school's athletic teams, and takes tennis lessons. She's held leadership positions at school and is an entrepreneur who has made and sold tote bags to classmates. How does she do all this? Her mother says she plans each day and doesn't know how her friends can get along without a daily calendar. She's demanding of the family's time and resources, self-motivated, asks intelligent questions, and is able to do things on her own. In fact, she'll spend this summer with a family in Spain. (And Katy has had role modeling in leadership skills. Her mother was just elected the Junior League president in her town.)

Some children aren't multigifted but have talent in a particular area. Jon was never outstanding in languages; he hardly talked at all until he was two. His gift was for the sciences. He took astronomy classes while in third grade and tutored his classmates in math because mathematical concepts just seemed to come naturally to him. He collected science prizes and a scholarship in high school, and is majoring in engineering in college. He plans to get his doctorate in this area.

Deanne is also an excellent student, but her real love and talent are in ballet. Romeo, at eleven, is a computer whiz. In fact, when he needs to be punished, his parents just take away computer access for a while. And Kenneth, a GATE student (Gifted and Talented Education), loves dramatics and acting, and is already, at ten, a good public speaker. Then there's Maria, who has always been artistically creative and now designs stationery. David, a very intelligent teen, has a special gift for working with the disabled and is studying for credentials in this area at a top university.

What all of these children have in common besides coming from large families is a passion for learning a skill or subject, and the motivation to accomplish it.

Here are some of the traits that may indicate your young child is gifted:

1. As a baby he lets you know his needs.
2. As a toddler she's very interested in the world around her. She'll concentrate on watching an ant crawl across the sidewalk for hours.
3. He's able to problem-solve even as a baby or toddler. This skill requires thinking ahead and planning.
4. She has a sense of humor.
5. He shows good coordination and balance.
6. She's rhythmical and tries to make music or dance to it.
7. He's creative, using toys such as building blocks in clever ways.

8. You can discipline her just by explaining why something is wrong.
9. He shows concern for others and has a sense of fair play.
10. She asks good questions.
11. He's persistent and knows how to reach his goals.
12. As a toddler she understands the concept of quantity.
13. He talks well, using advanced sentence structure.
14. Other children listen to and follow her, often as early as preschool.
15. His judgment is usually sound, and he's not about to take risks until he's thought the situation through.
16. She can get very interested in something and will try to learn all she can about it.
17. He can take things apart and figure out how to put them back together.
18. People instinctively like her; her self-esteem is high.

The Gifted Parent

Parenting the gifted is tough work. You have to give them time to discuss things with you and to ask questions. You'll find yourself going to the encyclopedia or the library a lot more frequently if you're the parent of a gifted child. You may have to provide lessons or instructions that can cost a great deal. You have the feeling that the giftedness could be lost if you don't do your part to nourish it.

And yet you have other children who have just as much of a right to develop their own talents as the gifted one. Is it fair to pay for expensive lessons for one child but not the others because you know she'll be able to get more out of them? At the same time, is it fair to refuse to send a gifted child to an expensive school and deny him the opportunity to progress as far as he can? These are questions that can cause great anguish for the parents of the gifted.

Even more anguishing is the gifted child who is not living up to his potential. Kids who are not terribly gifted but who are self-starters often do better than smarter children who don't seem to care. Parents of these smarter children search and search for the trigger that will get their kids going.

In several large families with two gifted kids, one will play down his talents, apparently to establish a separate identity from his sibling or to avoid competition. But sometimes the answer is even more complex than this. Sometimes a gifted underachiever actually has a subtle learning problem that gets overlooked. If you think you have a child with this kind of problem preventing him from being his best, it doesn't hurt to have him tested.

Remember that we are a very competitive society. We value productivity, sometimes at the expense of other talents. Giftedness may be defined very differently in another society. If one of your children happens to be a gifted original thinker—for example, he might show great compassion for people less fortunate and spend a lot of time helping others, or he might have an intuitive respect and caring for living things—you need to give support to his talent, even if society doesn't.

It's unusual and probably not practical for a large family, unless it is very wealthy, to focus all of its resources on one child. (That's probably why Olympic competitors in individual sports that require years of expensive training are usually from small families.) But when talents are of an academic nature, parents can help more without compromising the other children. There is what is known as the "gifted parent." Gifted children seldom spring unaided from nowhere. Most gifted children have parents who give them lots of encouragement and just enough autonomy. These parents encourage their kids to ask lots of questions about everything. Very early, when a child seems interested in something, the gifted parent will relate all he knows about it, and if that's not enough, he will get out a library book or set up an in-home experiment to let the child see how something works. The gifted parent praises his/her children for making good observations or for solving a problem and responds to requests for help. But the gifted parent doesn't force-feed information; you won't find him/her making a three-year-old learn to read if that child shows no interest.

On the other hand, if the three-year-old shows interest in the concept of quantities, this parent will go out and buy an abacus and show him how to use it. These parents get excited about their child's emerging interests, not because they want to get the child into the most prestigious school but because they feel that learning is the most rewarding activity in one's life. They have their own interests, too, and they share these with the children. A mother who is a talented seamstress may show her children how to sew. The father interested in astronomy will set up the telescope in the backyard and show the children the rings of Saturn.

And they respect their children's talents, whatever they may be. They also limit TV and give their children the silent message that passivity is not a virtue. They start their children thinking about the future and what kinds of jobs are out there. They encourage work but not to the point where it interferes with studies. They care about their children's spiritual and emotional development.

A gifted parent is exactly what a gifted child needs. In fact, it's what every child needs because every child, as that wise mother contended, is gifted in something.

Here are some of the things you can do to support the natural giftedness in your children:

Have lots of different things to see and do in the house.

Be enthusiastic about everything your children attempt.

Read to the children often.

Go to the library regularly.

Ask your children questions to help them think logically and creatively.

Observe your children to see what their strengths and interests are.

Share your interests with them.

Take time from chores to listen to your children.

Share observations with their teachers.

Introduce them to the different occupations they may have as adults.

Encourage independence and teach them how to do things so they can function independently.

Take them to museums and zoos. Try to bring as much of the outside world to them as possible.

Encourage them to accept reasonable challenges.

Let them read as much as they want but regulate TV strictly.

Give them chores and teach them how to manage their time well.

Help them stay physically fit.

Make sure they know you love them and support their interests.

Coping with a Major Problem

In my survey of large families there were many who at one time or another had to deal with problems of a fairly serious nature. It's reasonable to assume that large families will have more problems than small families.

The most common problems encountered were medical ones, and the most common medical problem involved speech and/or hearing. However, almost 25 percent of the families had a child with an identifiable learning problem, and 20 percent had dealt with an emotional problem. A full 44 percent identified one or more children as being in need of more parenting and love than the other children. Other identified problems were even more serious.

What was most impressive about all of these families was their courage and bonding. As a group they tended to face situations honestly and to take action early when they saw problems developing. For example, a family with a teenage alcoholic confronted him and had him hospitalized. While he was in rehab, they visited constantly, wrote, and let him know how much he meant to them.

In another family an adolescent girl (one of sixteen) started hanging around with a bad crowd. Though she wasn't using drugs, her parents feared it was only a matter of time. One evening she left for a party without parental permission. Her father found out where she was, went there, confronted her angrily before all her friends (greatly embarrassing her), and took her home. That was the end of her association with this group.

A third family lost a toddler in an accident. It was, and still is, a great tragedy for them, but they now generously help others who must deal with similar losses.

Another family had to deal with severe depression in a child whose close cousin had died accidentally. They arranged for counseling to help him get over his grief.

Many families have had children who were bedwetters,

who were born with birth defects such as cleft lip and palate, and mental retardation, or who had allergies and asthma, vision difficulties, behavior problems—you name it. Their collective courage and faith in dealing with these problems are amazing.

(It's important to note that each parent encountering a serious problem also has to deal with his own grief and anger. None of the above parents faced their situations without significant insecurity, self-doubt, and soul-searching.)

Banding Together

Children in large families tend to band together when one of them is having trouble. It could be over something as simple as a fight at school. One of the few times my children got in trouble at school was their involvement in a fight. My oldest was the object of an orange-throwing attack in eighth grade, and his slightly younger brothers attacked the attackers. No one gave John a rough time after that.

Most children have a strong sense of family loyalty. If they feel that a sibling is in trouble, they do their best to help him. Sometimes helping means getting a bandage for a cut knee or teaching a little one how to swing a bat. Sometimes it means a lot more—which brings us to the story of Janice and her family.

Janice had a premonition in high school that she would have a handicapped child, and she remembers telling her friends so. However, her first three children, Jessica, Joanna, and Erica, were all healthy. When she gave birth to Heather, she remembers the doctor checking the baby's head. Late that evening, after her husband had gone home, the doctor stopped by her room; after inquiring about her other children's head sizes at birth, he told her that the baby needed to be examined further the next morning. He then gently explained that something might possibly be wrong, but he wasn't sure. He referred Heather to a pediatric neurologist.

Janice began to notice that Heather didn't make eye contact as she nursed; rather, her eyes looked glazed. A C.T. scan (a special X ray) revealed that part of her brain had failed to develop normally, and she was both blind and developmentally delayed.

Most mothers would have been bitter and angry. Janice was not. Of course she felt sad that Heather would not be able to see and run and play, but Janice was determined to help her child achieve whatever potential she could. It helped that Heather was and is a sweet, loving, and happy child. Janice's husband did have trouble talking about Heather's problems at first, and this was hard on Janice, but now the whole family has been brought closer in their attempt to love Heather as much as they can.

Heather's older siblings are always willing to help out. They are sensitive to the needs of other handicapped youngsters because of their sister. Since Heather attends a special school every day, the other children do have time with their parents. Now there is also a healthy baby boy in the family.

Janice feels that her children have grown in understanding and compassion as a result of caring for Heather. She also feels that the parents' attitude is all-important. The children saw that their parents loved Heather, handicaps and all, so they too were able to see Heather as a kind of blessing. They knew that just as their parents stood by Heather, they would be there for them, too, no matter what.

Heather will probably never be able to sit or speak; it is doubtful she'll get much beyond her current four-month level of development. But her problems have not divided the family, they have brought everyone closer together.

(Sometimes keeping a handicapped child at home is not

in a family's best interest. Parents should not feel guilty if they decide a child will receive better care elsewhere. The important thing is not to forget that the child is a member of the family and for everyone to give him as much love as possible, even across the miles.)

Should your family have problems, it's important to realize that you are not alone and to utilize whatever resources are available for your situation. Don't hesitate to speak with your physician, nurse, or clergyman. These individuals often know of community resources that you do not know exist.

Talk with others, too. Social bonds are all important in times of stress. (Janice was grateful that the grandparents on both sides were very supportive.) Keep the children informed in a way they can understand. Sometimes difficult situations help children learn to cope better with their own future problems.

CHAPTER 11

The Working Mom

BY now everyone is familiar with the statistics which show that over 50 percent of mothers with children under six are employed outside the home. The percentage is even higher for mothers of children under eighteen.

But what about mothers of large families? Surely the working mothers are the ones with only one or two children, while mothers with more children stay at home. Unfortunately, statistics on working motherhood are broken down by age of the youngest child and not by number of children, so exact figures are difficult to obtain. But my research indicates that the mothers of large families are just as likely to work as are mothers with small families. The difference lies in *how* they work. They often will choose unusual work hours. By working nighttime shifts, for example, they have more time to spend with their families, but they also have less time to sleep. They also take advantage of jobs available during school hours. Some work weekends when their husbands can take over with the children, and many work at home for pay or own their own businesses. Not a few work in a family enterprise.

Why do they work? For the money, most often. It takes a large income to provide for the basic needs of several children. This frequently means that both spouses must contribute financially.

Some women have had careers prior to becoming mothers. They work to keep their skills, realizing that if their husbands became incapacitated, they could provide. They work because they know that their children will grow up, and with an ongoing career, they will be able to allow their children the freedom to separate when the time comes. Not a few women find great pleasure in work. Though they love their children, they would go crazy being home all the time.

Finances

As financial conditions in this country now stand, and with an even higher tax obligation predictable in the future as our country is called upon to support an ever-growing number of senior citizens, only very affluent large families can afford a spouse who does not generate some income. How and when this income is generated is something each family must decide for itself.

Some of the questions a family must ask itself are best done in the context of a longitudinal plan. They include the following:

1. How many children are in the family now or are planned?
2. What are the future educational goals for these children?
3. What income does the working spouse(s) generate after taxes?
4. What is the future income potential of the working spouse(s)?
5. What are the family's beliefs about having a parent at home full-time, especially when the children are of preschool age?
6. What effect will a career interruption have on the temporarily nonemployed spouse?
7. Is part-time work an option in either spouse's field?
8. Does the family feel one spouse should work extra so the other can stay home?
9. Do the spouses work in a joint venture (such as a family farm or business) that would allow flexibility?
10. What cost-cutting activities (vegetable garden, sewing children's clothes, and so forth) can be implemented to allow a spouse to stay home?
11. Will the cost of having a spouse employed when the children are young outweigh the benefits? (This includes the emotional cost as well as such items as babysitting, wardrobe, and transportation.)
12. What about investments?
13. Should one spouse be acquiring career skills (such as taking night courses at the local college) while the children are little so that he/she can generate a better income upon returning to work? Or for a future career change?
14. Can one spouse work at home while caring for the children?

15. Most important of all, what are the emotional
    feelings of each partner about work? For exam-
    ple, a husband may feel his wife should be home
    with the children; he might even feel insecure
    when she is in the work force. On the other hand,
    he might feel that she has an obligation to help
    him shoulder the financial burden. He might even
    feel both these things at the same time! The wife
    may be devastated at the thought of leaving her
    babies with someone else, or she may feel the
    need to be with adults at work. She also may
    have both feelings at the same time.

16. If the family is indeed well off enough to allow
    one spouse to stay home all the time, are there
    nonfinancial reasons that both spouses should
    work? What effect will this have on the children?
    Are there reliable caregivers?

Flexible Schedules

Let's say your family has decided that both parents have
to earn money to make ends meet. How can you make
things as easy as possible for your children and yourselves?

One option is the flexible schedule. This can work in
several ways. One parent can go to work early and get off
early, the other the reverse. Then the late parent would be
responsible for getting the children off to school or to the
babysitter, and the other for picking them up and starting
dinner.

Or one parent can work nights and the other days. Some
night workers might even do a double shift a few times a
week and have the rest of their time free for the family.
This kind of schedule is really tough, though, and not for
everyone.

In some families one parent will work weekends, the

other weekdays. Or one parent will do some of his/her work at home. Or one parent will work only part-time. The options are endless but are definitely dependent on the type of job you both have.

If you think your job allows for some degree of flexibility, you might want to propose a flexible schedule to your boss. Don't mention your children's needs, though (unless your boss has a dozen children herself). Instead, concentrate on the advantages to the boss or the company. This is what Marty did when her fourth child was born. She worked at a university, teaching, designing curricula, scheduling, and even doing some research. She convinced her boss to let her do some work at home by pointing out that she would have more time to work if she didn't commute every day. The quality of the work she produced at home was good, and everyone was happy.

Working at Home for Pay

Bonnie and her husband, a truck driver, knew they would have a tough time providing for their six children if Bonnie stayed at home. But things would be even tougher if Bonnie went back to work. Her husband could be gone for days on long hauls, and then who would be a backup for the kids? Their solution was a very practical one: Bonnie would become a child-care provider. She took some classes at the local junior college, got licensed for six children, bought toys at local garage sales, and was off and running. She's been doing this type of work for several years now and has a waiting list. The work keeps her young and happy because she loves little children and her youngest are now in grade school. She also feels she's really making a difference in some children's lives.

As in any business, there are drawbacks. It's hard for

Bonnie to plan any time off. Also, one or two parents have been irresponsible, picking up their children late all the time or "forgetting" to pay her for weeks on end. With most parents, however, she has a good relationship. (She can now afford to drop the unreliable parents.) She shares information about their child with them each morning and evening, and is often asked for advice on child-rearing problems.

Working at home is a financial option for many families that need extra income yet feel strongly about having a parent at home when the children are small. This kind of work also offers tax advantages in some cases. The major problem, of course, is having time to work uninterrupted.

If you are thinking of setting up a business in your home, here are some practical considerations: What ages are your children? If you have three in diapers, you will not be able to have long, uninterrupted blocks of time. You may be able to do something such as child care but only for older children or one or two more toddlers. You must be careful not to so overburden yourself that you cannot give quality care to your own children, much less someone else's. You may wish to consider piecework, cake decorating, or gourmet cooking, which you could work into your schedule more easily.

If your children are older or you have only one in diapers, your options are wider. You may have some special skill or hobby that could become a paying enterprise. Dotty, a mother of three, is an R.N. who chose to remain home with her children. She had always helped her dad with carpentry when she was a child and as an adult became expert at woodworking. At home she turns out beautiful handcrafted wood products that are sold at local establishments. Someone skilled at sewing could start a costume-making home business. A good cook could have her products sold in a local "mom and pop" store. A teacher could tutor. Anyone whose children are addicted to the Berenstain Bears (from a series of books by Jan and Stan Berenstain published by Random House) knows that Mama Bear has opened up a home-based quilting business.

What are your particular skills? If you have training in a service area such as cosmetology, you may be able to purchase secondhand equipment and do this work at home. Physicians, dentists, psychologists, and financial counselors who have a big house, especially those who practice in a rural area, can often convert rooms into an office suite and have someone watch the children while they see patients or clients in an adjacent room. Music teachers traditionally teach in their homes. You may even want to have gourmet cooking or language classes in your home if these are your special talents. And, of course, writing can be done at home too. For those who don't have special training, telephone soliciting, a tough job, can be done at home.

What are the needs in your community? You'll need to do a little market research here. If your community has many two-income families, day care may be desperately needed. Perhaps your community has a large elderly population. These senior citizens may be interested in subscribing to a lunch service, or their relatives far away may wish to invest in a daily telephone contact service you could run from your home.

Consider the legal aspects of a home-based business. Whatever you decide to do, check local ordinances for zoning and licensing requirements. If you have a family attorney or tax accountant, a consultation may be helpful. And if people will be in your home, be sure to check with your insurance agent. Your local Better Business Bureau may be helpful too. Sound complicated? It can be, but it will be an education for you too.

Home Business

Now comes the hardest part of all. How do you make time to work at home free from constant interruption?

First of all, you and your spouse must agree that your work is important. Some men may feel threatened when their wives begin to work and minimize the value of that work. Children can quickly pick up on this attitude. A frank discussion will frequently help a man to examine and correct an attitude he may not even realize he has. (A reverse situation is also possible in families where the wife is the principal breadwinner.)

Then you must take a good look at your day and figure out when you can do your work with the least stress to the rest of the family. If you have three children in pre-school and grade school and do craftwork at home, school mornings may be ideal. But you will have to arrange other times to do your housework. Or maybe you have an infant who sleeps in the afternoon, and you can snatch a couple of hours to work as she sleeps, before the other children get home from school. You might wish to tutor between the hours of 3:00 and 5:00 P.M. when your older children can watch the younger ones. If you write or do illustrations or sew, and are a "morning person," get up an hour or two before the family and work then. If you work best at night, stay up a couple of hours after the children are tucked in. (A word of caution here: Be sure to save some time for your love life!) Perhaps Dad can take over on weekends while you work at home. Maybe a play group will help. Whatever time you set aside, keep that time sacred. Nothing except a major emergency should interfere.

Rules are needed that are fully understood by all the children: They are not to interrupt. If they come and ask for a glass of orange juice or for help with homework, you may feel guilty when you tell them to get it themselves or to wait until after dinner, but you need to be very definite from the beginning about not tolerating minor interruptions. If you have older children, enlist their help. While you are busy, they are in charge of the little things you usually do. And when you do get cooperation, give praise—lots of it. Stress how much the children are helping the family by being good while you work. Let them know you are proud of them. And let your spouse know too.

And give yourself a pat on the back. You're making the sacrifice not only of additional work but of doing it under adverse conditions so you can be with your family. Your family is lucky to have a parent like you. Lastly, make sure you are paid what you are worth and on time, and plan how to use that money wisely. Since you are probably working because you need the money for a particular purpose, the last part should be easy.

Child Care

Everyone seems to have horror stories about child care. One woman recounted how she heard a discussion between two young mothers in the maternity ward after they had had their babies. One was apparently worried about how she would make ends meet. The other suggested that she do child care in her home. "You can buy a big playpen and stick all the kids in it," the second mother said. "That's what I do. Then when they're hungry, just toss in some bottles. It's practically no work at all!"

Another mother recounted how she went to great lengths to check references on a new babysitter. All were excellent, yet upon returning home on the first day she was greeted at the door by her four children who told her that the babysitter was in the backyard with "her friends." Sure enough, there she found the sitter, the sitter's married lover, and the lover's two-year-old son. Though the sitter insisted she had not been derelict in her duty, she was fired that evening.

But for every horror story you hear there is a corresponding success story. One woman told how much her son benefited from being in a large family setting with children of all ages. His siblings were so much older that he was almost like an only child, but his excellent day-care situation made up for his isolated position in his own family. The experience was that much more important for him because he tended to be shy and needed the experience of learning how to get along with other children.

In another family a grandfather watched the youngest child, and the bond that grew between grandfather and grandson helped ease the pain the grandfather had felt after his wife died.

How can you be sure that your day-care experience will be a success story? You're one step ahead of the game already when you have three or more children. Your children can all be together for at least part of the day, the continuity of the family will be preserved even when you're not there, and the older ones can make sure that the little ones are getting their share of attention.

Let's look at what types of care are available and how you can check on the quality of that care.

You might choose to have someone come to your home. This has many advantages: You don't have to pay by the child. Your children will be in a familiar environment. If a child gets sick, you probably won't have to lose a day's work. Your babysitter may even do some of the housework.

There are also disadvantages: When you come home, the house will probably be a mess. Home care can be costly. If the babysitter gets sick or quits suddenly, you are in trouble unless you have backup. But probably most important, it is hard to find a person who is well qualified.

Older people often have trouble caring for three or four children. It just requires too much energy. Young people, just starting careers, are likely to be looking for more challenging positions with room for advancement. You may wish to have an *au pair*, but these young ladies are usually in the country for only a year or less. You also do not get to interview them prior to their arrival.

Some people have been very successful in finding exactly the right babysitter or nanny. When you have an extra room with a TV, a car for the sitter's use, and offer a good salary, you definitely improve your chances. Most of us cannot offer these amenities, and therefore a daytime sitter, rather than a live-in, is more appropriate.

You might consider looking for a mother who has raised her own children and enjoyed it. She now may want to continue being with children, but this time someone else's. Or you might want to find a college student, or even two who can work in shifts. They often need the money and have time and latitude in scheduling classes. Students majoring in early childhood education or related fields sometimes get work-study credit. Perhaps you would like to hire a recent immigrant. Many families have found them to be talented, reliable, and very loving with the children.

How do you find such caregivers? Networking is the best way. Let all your friends and neighbors know what kind of a person you are looking for. Your minister, priest, or rabbi often knows of people in the congregation who would be excellent. You might consider advertising in local papers and getting in touch with college employment services. (Many people feel it's better not to advertise in major newspapers.) Interview many applicants before making a decision and check all references thoroughly. Ask the people listed as references exactly what their relationship with the prospective babysitter has been and whether they would hire her or him to care for their children. Use your intuition too. If everything checks out but you have a bad feeling about the person, don't hire her (or him?).

Make sure you observe all prospective candidates with your children. Leave the room for a moment and see what happens. If you come back and find the sitter playing with the children, that's a good sign. But if she has grabbed a magazine or is staring at the television and ignoring the children, forget her!

Once you have found someone you feel is good, have her come for a few days before you start working. You can teach her your routines and see how she handles the household and children. You may also want to make sure she has had a recent test for tuberculosis; all workers in day-care centers are required to have these tests in most states.

Another option for the large family is family day care. Most states license these homes, so their quality is somewhat standardized, but no one can regulate the personality of the mother and father giving the care. You'll want to look for ones who are warm and cheerful, who really seem to enjoy the work. You can observe how attentive they are to the children already in their care. Do they interrupt a conversation with you to pick up a fussing baby or to answer a toddler's question? That's a good sign. Do they focus their attention on their biological children, favoring them at the expense of the others? That's bad. What are their motivations for doing this type of work? Do they see their work as important, as more than just a way of making money? Does the mothering style click with yours? And what does your intuition say?

Look at several day-care homes so that you will have standards of comparison. You can find them the same way you look for a home-based babysitter. Some communities also have child-care referral services you can call for a list of references. Some day-care mothers advertise in a local paper or community bulletin board.

Once you find a home you really like, check with the parents whose children are or have been there. If everything seems fine, have your children go for brief periods before you actually start to work. Stop in a few times when you are not expected and observe your children. Do they seem happy? Clean? Do they tell you they've had fun doing things? Or do they talk about all the TV shows they've seen all day? Does your sitter communicate with you about how the children have spent their day? Does she offer helpful observations? Does she tell you when they fall or bump themselves? Does this happen often?

When you feel you have found a good day-care home for your children, you must do your part. Let the sitter know how you can be reached at all times, and give her the phone numbers of your doctor, dentist, and a friend or relative. Let her have a copy of your children's immunization records, and let her know about any allergies or chronic medical problems the children may have. Give her a note stating that she has the authority to consent for medical and dental care in an emergency when you cannot be reached. Pick up your children promptly. Pay the sitter on time. Let her know when the children have a cold, are tired, or are in a bad mood. And if you think she is doing a good job, tell her so. She'll be a better child-care mom if she knows her efforts are appreciated.

Here are some things to take note of when investigating a day-care home:

1. Safety features
2. Cleanliness—of the children as well as the facility
3. Caretaker-child ratio
4. Toys, crafts, and play structures available
5. Size of the play area in the house and yard
6. Food preparation area
7. Bathrooms and diaper-changing areas

8. Waste disposal and sinks to wash hands
9. Neighborhood

Your third option is a relative or friend. Sometimes this works out very well; sometimes it does not. Grandparents often feel obliged to care for their grandchildren but can get very weary as they age. Some families may choose to have one young child stay with a grandparent and the others go to an after-school program to avoid overburdening the grandparents. Siblings will sometimes take care of each other's children. Some families have their older teens watch younger siblings after school. If you do this, be sure the older teens are not kept out of extracurricular activities they are interested in. (If relatives become your babysitters, be sure to be sensitive to their needs and feelings and let them know how much their help means.)

Lastly, there is the day-care center. This option can get very expensive when you have three or four children. Day-care centers also vary considerably in their resources, the quality of their teachers, and the staff-child ratio. If you are fortunate enough to have a day-care center where you work, this arrangement can be almost ideal because you can visit your children on breaks or during the lunch hour.

Check out day-care centers just as you would investigate a child-care home. Avoid centers with rigid rules that prevent you from dropping in when you wish. Look at the training and the personalities of staff members. Ask about health and sanitary issues. Does the staff wash hands in between diapering babies? Do they dispose of diapers properly? Do they have some knowledge of first aid and emergency plans for fire evacuation and other disasters? Is food stored and prepared properly? Is the staff knowledgeable about normal child development? How do they handle a fight between two children? How do they share responsibility for supervision of children? Most of all, talk to parents who have children there. If they're not happy, chances are you won't be.

Also to be considered is the issue of backup. Whatever arrangements you have made, there will come a time when problems arise: One of your children will have a bout of conjunctivitis and be excluded from day care; the baby-sitter will get the flu; or your day-care mother will go to the hospital to have her baby. Working mothers must expect these challenges from time to time and should plan for them in advance. It helps to have a backup friend or to set aside some vacation time to be used for such emergencies.

Housework

As an employed mother with a large family, your greatest challenge is behaving at work as though you are childless while at the same time giving your home and family the level of care you would give if you didn't have an outside job. The key issue here is, of course, time.

The unwritten rules in most workplaces are that you don't talk about children or personal concerns on company time, and certainly not in front of the boss, and you don't take time off for family duties except in emergencies. In some business establishments, when a child is ill, the parent will call in and say that he/she (the parent) is sick. It sounds better.

And you never come to work with baby food on your jacket.

Then, when you get home, things get reversed. The children don't want to hear about the difficulty your company is having filling orders on time or how you wish your school could get a new principal. The moment you get in the door, they will probably be all over you. Never mind what all those articles say about working parents having a half hour to unwind after work. Most kids will not let you do that. And even if they did, you probably couldn't stand the guilt. For the parent with several children, coming home from work generally means jumping into the household chaos with both feet.

So here you are, home from a tiring day at work. You have dinner to fix, a household to tidy up, maybe some wash, possibly a cub scout meeting that night. How do you get everything done?

The answer is **to streamline your schedule.** You need to know what really needs to get done and how to do it in the easiest manner possible. For most employed parents this means setting up a mental (or written) weekly schedule and scrutinizing it for "windows of time" where you can fit things in, as we've already discussed in Chapter 8. For example, you may find it convenient to do your shopping on your way home from work. Or you may want to cook a casserole on Saturday so that dinner will be ready when you get home late from the staff meeting on Tuesday night.

Cut back on frills: You don't need to bake your own cookies for the school bake sale. Buy them. Don't purchase clothes that need ironing. One mother of seven decided that making beds was too much of a hassle so she got a bunch of quilts for all the beds and uses just the quilts and fitted sheets.

Delegate: The children can be responsible for daily chores on a rotating basis so that no one is overburdened. Little ones can get in training by doing little things, such as being responsible for their own toys and setting the table. Or they may entertain a baby brother under your supervision so you can fix dinner.

Do your biggest chores when you're freshest: If you get really tired at night, get up early and start dinner so that it will be ready to pop in the oven when you get home. If you're a night owl, do the dishes and wash when the kids are tucked in.

Fragment your tasks: No one said you have to start and complete a task all at once. You may want to put a load of wash in the washer at night, switch it to the dryer before work, then fold it when you get home in the afternoon. Or peel the vegetables for dinner in the morning before work and leave them in the refrigerator. Or leave your mending by the phone and do it every time you are making a call.

Lower your expectations: Chances are your spouse won't notice a little dust under the sofa. The kids don't care at all if the refrigerator isn't cleaned every month. But spouse and children do care if you're so pressed for time that you're not there for them physically and emotionally when they need you.

If you can afford it, make the investment in household help: The daily chores are probably best handled by you, especially if you can interact with your family as you work, but the cleaning woman or service can do the heavy stuff that can be such a burden: the floor scrubbing or window washing or whatever you especially hate to do.

Guilt

Why is the kindergarten play always held in the middle of the day? Why do all the schools your children attend schedule their back-to-school nights for the exact same date? Why are Little League games and T-ball games held at the same time on fields across town from each other? The answer is: to make working parents with several children feel guilty, of course!

If you are a working parent with several children, you have to learn to live with guilt. You are in a demographic minority. Working couples usually have only one or two children. Mothers of large families are generally thought to be in the kind of situation portrayed by Mrs. Brady of the "Brady Bunch." As one teacher-mother of six said, "I hate Mrs. Brady [the character]. There she sits, with Alice to do all the tough work, and all she has to do is help the kids with their problems and go shopping. She doesn't have to work all day and then come home and make dinner!"

As a working parent with a large family, you have a very tough job. You are, in essence, two people: You must do all the things that any parent with several children has to do (and they aren't any easier to raise just because their parents work), and you must be an employee (or boss) who pulls his/her own weight. Guilt is usually a debilitating emotion, so remember: All you can do is the best you can.

Also, let your children know what a terrific parent you are, then maybe you will have the experience that Carol did. She was an employed parent with five children. Her work seldom allowed her the liberty of attending the many functions her children's schools scheduled during the day, so she modeled positive values for her daughters. She let them know that her position at work required skill and benefited many people in their community. One day, to Carol's amusement, this paid off. She overheard her eight-year-old telling an only child friend whose mother attended every function dressed in designer clothes, and who had been teasing her daughter about Carol's absences, "You know, Sarah, that my mother can't come to the school bazaar. She has very important things to do at her job, and she can't play all day like your mom."

Fatigue

How do you function when you don't get enough sleep? If you're like most people, you'll find you can handle an occasional late night if you have the next day to recuperate.

But if you are working and have a large family, sleep deprivation is not episodic, it's chronic! You may notice that you become less efficient when you get really behind on your sleep. Tasks take longer to perform, which eventually leads to even more sleep loss. You are also more prone to getting the flu or another illness, or having an accident. (Even our immune systems demand sleep to function.) And everyone knows that sleep loss wreaks havoc with one's romantic life, even in marriage.

To a certain extent, not getting enough sleep is something you have to live with as a working mother, but you can ameliorate the effects of fatigue in several ways. Find out the minimum amount of sleep it takes to make you function normally. Some people need only four hours a night, though they are rare. Most people need six or seven hours. A few people, who for some unknown reason tend to be artistic or creative, need nine or even ten hours.

Once you have figured out, by trial and error, how much sleep you can get by on, try to get it. If this is temporarily impossible (new baby or other situation), then retrain yourself to function on less sleep. As medical students and interns we were expected to work all night and then be alert and vigorous the next day. (This is still expected of doctors in training.) After several months of these awful schedules, we felt only half alive, but we were able to function fairly well. New mothers go through this type of initiation too. It's not fun, but it can be done.

Stay away from substances that artificially alter your sleep cycle and cause the time you do sleep to be less restorative. Alcohol is the chief culprit here. Even a glass of wine before bed can disturb your sleep. However, sleeping pills, especially if used chronically, can be hurtful. (Also, caffeine before bedtime bothers some people.)

Exercise daily. The half hour you spend in vigorous aerobics or jogging or speed walking while pushing the two-year-old in the stroller with the baby in a backpack will pay off by allowing you to sleep less at night but making the sleep more efficient.

Take catnaps. Close your eyes for five minutes during your coffee break. Sit in the car, relaxed, for ten minutes after work, before you pick up the kids. These little naps can have tremendous restorative value.

And, of course, sleep in on weekends . . . if you can!

How Your Children Feel About Your Work

Babies and small children want to be with their parents. Children in their middle years want to check in with their parents from time to time, especially when things aren't going so well. Teenagers need more freedom and, coupled with this, the knowledge that their parents still care more than anything for them. In other words, children want to feel they are a top priority in their parents' lives. How closely the bond between parent and child is expressed depends not only on the age and developmental stage of the child but also on the child's own personality.

When there are several children in a family, these children learn how to make room for one another's needs although this may not come easily to all siblings. With a little reinforcement from Mom and Dad, they also learn how to parent each other. That is why children in the large family often have an easier time of it when both parents work outside the home. They are bonded to one another and don't feel completely abandoned when the parents are gone.

In an ideal world, a parent (usually the mother, for biologic reasons) would be at home with each child until that child reached school age, and then that parent would work part-time until the child was a teenager. The other parent, although working full-time, would have weekends and evenings for the family. Maybe the parents would switch off.

Most large families are far from this ideal situation, however. (Financial considerations and the parents' own goals are important factors.) How then can employed couples help their children grow up feeling as secure as possible?

First of all, parents must keep telling and showing their children how much they love and miss them. Rather than go off in a corner when you return from work, take five minutes for hugs and to hear about how the day went for your children. Use your coffee break to call and just say hello to each one. Plan something special every day, such as ten minutes of reading or singing before bedtime. If you notice that one child seems more glum than the others, take her aside, touch her hair or hug her, and ask her why. (The hug is because body language tells you so much. If she won't hug, she's probably feeling really sad.)

If your children are preschool or younger, choose a sitter who is warm and motherly above all else, even if she doesn't speak their language too well or won't teach them to read by the time they are three. The children should feel that the sitter thinks they are terrific and loves being with them. A day-care center whose teachers stress feelings and learning how to relate to other people satisfactorily, one where self-esteem is a top priority, is far better than one with rigid academic expectations, especially for the children of dual-career parents.

Explain to the children why you have to work. Children are very egocentric and may feel your working is somehow their fault or that they're bad, so you go to work to get away. Or they cost a lot, so you have to work. They need to be told that, yes, having a large family is expensive, but each one of them is so valuable to you that you are happy to do whatever it takes to provide for them. If you enjoy your work, they need to know that too. It helps them to see that work can be a pleasurable and interesting part of life. After all, they will be working one day too.

Instill a sense of unity and pride in your children. When they are together, even if you are not thère, they are a family. They are never alone when they have each other.

Try not to let work commitments interfere too much with your family. Draw lines at work as to how much extra you are willing to do. This makes good sense even for people who don't have a large family. For those who do, learning how to say "no" firmly and politely is a necessary skill. (You don't have to explain to your boss why you can't stay until nine o'clock tonight either.) Do your job well and help out at work as much as you can, but stick up for your personal needs too.

Work for the day when on-site quality child care is offered by every enlightened company, flexible-time jobs will be available to all employees who desire them, and job reentry will be a realistic option for the parent who chooses to spend some years at home with the children.

A Sick Child

Precisely because so many children are shedding viruses and bacteria even before they show signs of illness and because little children drool on toys picked up by other little children (and for several other reasons too), day-care centers are good places for exchanging germs. The first year in day care, children can expect to have at least one or two more infections than children kept at home.

Before you start to feel guilty about these facts, it's important to realize that there are actually some benefits. Some diseases cause much less trouble when children get them early in life. After a child has had such an infection, he builds up immunity and usually will not get the same infection when he is older, when it would hit him harder.

Be that as it may, you still have to deal with what to do

with a sick child who cannot go to day care. Because of situations like this, some parents prefer home day care. Day-care mothers who have only a few children under their care may have facilities that allow them to isolate a mildly ill child, so the working mother needn't miss a day's work.

Sometimes a mildly ill older child can even be brought to work. A seven-year-old with a strep throat, for example, could safely be kept in the back room of a small business where Mom works. Mom could check in on the child periodically and be there to give the antibiotics as prescribed. Some parents with large families will occasionally ask a teenager to stay home from school with a sick younger child if it will not hurt the older child academically.

When a child is really sick, of course, just about any mother would want to stay home.

It is important to think about what you will do when your children become ill. You need to consider the nature of your work. Do you have sick days you can save up? Will you be docked a day's pay? Are you a critical part of the work operation, or will they get along just fine without you? What is the attitude of your co-workers? Will they cover for you if you reciprocate? Can your husband get off easier than you? Can you take off half a day and your husband the other half? Can you take work home when your children are ill? Can you do the necessary parts of your job by phone? Can you make up your work on the weekend? Will you be fired?

Once you have looked at your work to see how easily you can take off if your children become ill, you need to come up with alternatives. Here are some suggestions:

1. If your younger children are in a day-care center or home day care, find out in advance what the rules are regarding illnesses. (This may be a factor in choosing child care in the first place.)

2. Let your child's doctor know you are employed. He/she can give preventive immunizations, advise you about the special health needs of day-care children, if applicable, and tell you whether or not a particular illness is one you should stay home for. He/she will be happy to write a note to your employer too, if requested.

3. Line up backup babysitters. You may have a relative or neighbor who can look after your children when they are mildly ill. There are even drop-in day-care centers for sick children only. If you or your company use these, take your children to visit *before* they get ill. There's nothing scarier for an ill child than being forced to stay in totally unfamiliar surroundings without a parent present. (It helps if siblings are there too.)

4. Find out your company's written and unwritten (that is, attitudinal) policies regarding parental sick leave.

5. Discuss with your husband how the two of you can best handle sick children. You may wish to alternate staying home or devise some other strategy that best meets the needs of your family.

6. Recognize your responsibility to your children. If you feel they are really sick, you are entirely justified in being with them. Some of us feel just a little guilty when we stay home from work with an ill child, but we should not, providing we do not abuse the privilege. Instead, we should use the time to give special attention to the ill child. After all, it's rare that the working mother of a large family gets time alone with just one child. Make the most of it.

7. If you leave a mildly ill older child (say a teenager) at home alone, check up often by phone and give him/her your work phone number.

Temporary Leave of Absence

Another issue concerns what to do when a family emergency arises. Many women save their sick time and some vacation time for these unpredictable events. A husband and wife may each be able to take a little time off consecutively, but sometimes it is necessary to request a temporary leave of absence—for a child who needs surgery, an aged parent, or even a special family trip. This is easier to do in some situations than in others. Find out the policy of your company before making any requests. Will your job be in jeopardy? Will the lost wages be a problem? Can sick leave be used? Who will do your work in your absence? Maybe you can do some work while you are at home.

Only when you have worked out the details and considered the consequences should you present your request to your supervisor. That way you will know how far you can negotiate and what the bottom line is for each of you. You will also be far more likely to be perceived as a responsible employee.

When Quitting Is Best

The entire family is involved in Mom's career. Some families cope well, even thrive. Some families wouldn't survive without two incomes, while other families pay an enormous emotional price for Mom's job. How do you know if your family is in the latter category? Here are some of the symptoms of family distress.

Degenerating marital relationship: Many wives who start back to work after being at home for several years will notice a bumpy period as their husbands get used to new roles (however supportive the husband may be). This is very different from a husband's progressively severe resentment because he feels his wife's job is taking her away from him. Positions that require a lot of travel or threaten a man's perceived status as primary provider tend to cause more friction in some homes. Maybe the wife is too tired for sex or requires her husband to share in the housework in a way that the husband perceives as being unmasculine.

While it is true that some men are not bothered at all by having a wife who outearns them or by being the one to prepare dinner, others are. In assessing the stress your job places on the family, you have to know how your husband feels. Often these feelings arise out of childhood experiences, so they can be quite resistant to logical discussion and compromise.

Depression, change in behavior, or failure of normal development in the children: Some children need little parenting while others need a good deal. Some children, at certain periods of their lives, need their mothers more than usual. A pervasive sense of loss and sadness in a child or acting-out behavior that is getting him into trouble could be signs of depression. The child with a learning disorder or a chronic illness or a restrictive day-care situation may need his mother to devote more time to him, at least temporarily. Sometimes a mother will notice that all her children seem to be having a hard time coping in her absence because her job has taken her away from them emotionally as well as physically. All of these situations may demand that you reevaluate whether you need to work now.

Mom is depressed: If you don't feel good about your job, if you feel exhausted all the time or guilty or resentful at missing all of the things that are happening each day to your children and spouse, your feelings will definitely affect the family. That's a strong reason to consider being a stay-at-home mom, at least for a while.

Marisa had four children, and the oldest two were in grade school. Her one-year-old had started group day care at the age of eight weeks. Marisa had been working eight hours a day, five days a week for as long as she could remember. It was hard having to spend the whole weekend cleaning and shopping instead of having time with the children.

Often she worried about her relationship with her husband. Since she was so tired most of the time, she wondered if someday he would decide to go elsewhere for companionship. But it was the look on her little baby's face each day that finally tipped the scales for Marisa. He was the last baby they would have, and Marisa was missing him even more than he was missing her.

Marisa decided that life was too short to miss the really good parts, and so she resigned from her job. When the kids are older, she will be back.

The job has changed: You and your family may have done just fine before your promotion. Now you must travel at least once a month, and it takes you and the family a week to recover from each of your trips. Or your new boss habitually asks you to stay late, and the children are very hungry and cranky when you arrive home. Whatever the reason, a once satisfactory job may turn sour. This may be the time to be a career homemaker pro tem.

If you notice any or all of the above signs in yourself or in your family and can possibly survive a hiatus in your career, you may wish to give notice or, failing that, look for a step-down job. You will need a lot of self-confidence, especially if part of your identity has been built around your work, but if quitting is right for your family, you will experience an enormous sense of relief at the correctness of your decision. And you can find support from the many mothers in your community who will not permit society to take their mothering years away from them.

CHAPTER
12

"Going Crazy"

"GOING crazy" is sort of the parental equivalent of the terrible twos. The parent experiences a mixture of anger, poor judgment, self-pity, battle fatigue, and frustration. Consequently, little things get blown out of proportion. (At times a parent may even lash out physically, feeling great remorse later.)

Sunday evenings were always the worst for Jo Anne. The house was invariably a wreck, and Jo Anne knew she had to pull things together before Monday, when she had to be at work. Even though the six children helped a bit, it was an awesome task, and Jo Anne knew that every Sunday evening at five o'clock she would "go crazy." She would get this awful, out-of-control feeling brought on by too much to do and not enough time to do it in. And she would start yelling. The kids would scatter. Even her husband, who did his best to help out, was affected by Jo Anne's Sunday night frustrations.

For Sally, it was bedtime that made her "go crazy." Tired from a long day at home with a baby and toddler and having to get through dinner while helping the three oldest with their homework, she just wanted to crawl into bed. But Jeff, her husband, didn't get home until eight, long after the children had eaten, so she had to prepare another dinner for him in addition to bathing the children, supervising homework, doing a load of wash and the dishes, and trying to get the little ones settled for sleep.

When mothers of large families were asked the question "Are there times when you 'go crazy' dealing with all your kids' needs and wants?" 98 percent said yes. It goes without saying that it is frightening to children when a parent "goes crazy" because they expect their parents to be always clear-thinking and fair.

Older children realize that sometimes a parent will be tired or stressed, responding in a way that he/she wouldn't normally. If "going crazy" is just an occasional thing, accompanied by shouting and growling (but never by physical violence), it's probably not too harmful. Children need to understand that Mom and Dad are human and can have bad days just as they do.

If a parent is out of control a good deal of the time, however, children will definitely suffer. A parent may realize that a significant life stress, such as being laid off from work or losing a grandparent, has made him/her vulnerable. If this is the case, the parent needs to find someone to confide in as he works through his loss. The parent should also share the reason for his behavior with the children so they will not feel guilty for having somehow caused the problem. (As we have said, children, especially young ones, have an egocentric view of the world; if something goes wrong, they tend to think they are to blame.)

Sometimes a serious family problem, such as alcoholism, is at the root of the stress. There may be problems at work for the parents, and they are bringing the tension home. A parent may be overwhelmed with the responsibility of dealing with several children at various stages of development, or there may be some anxiety about finances. If you suspect that a fairly serious problem is making you (or your spouse) chronically snappy and irritable, it is very important to get help because the problem will pass on to your children if you do not.

Fortunately, most of us have a much milder form of "the crazies." For example, some days you just aren't functioning as efficiently as usual, but you don't know quite why. When you get behind, the chores you still have to do loom larger than ever. Little things you would ordinarily take in stride upset you more than you like to admit. Maybe you have the feeling that no matter how hard you work, you'll never catch up with all you have to do today, or you rebel at the frustration of having to clean up the same mess over and over. An unexpected complication such as a flat tire may ruin a carefully planned day. Sometimes you even get angry at yourself for not being able to do the impossible *each and every day.*

And then there are the little, predictable annoyances that just get to you because no matter how easily preventable they seem to be, they *keep on happening.* For example, the mother of eight who gets angry at herself when she over-commits to volunteer activities and becomes exhausted. Or the mother of four whose kids always seem to remember they need something from the store "for tomorrow" when she has just finished her shopping. Or the mother who "goes crazy" when her four children's needs and wants keep piling up until they suddenly seem overwhelming.

Let's assume that you have the garden-variety of parental "crazies." Many parents can pinpoint times when an attack is more likely to occur. Not getting enough sleep may do it. So will attempting a diet and feeling hungry all the time. Outside stresses such as problems at work or an ill grandparent create home pressure. Some women experience premenstrual tension, which can make them feel irritable, fatigued, and bloated for days or even weeks before their periods.

Solutions

If you were to ask Rosemary what was the most awful day in her life, she would tell you about what happened one day last July. She was at work when she received a call midmorning from one of her four children that went like this: "Mom, the ambulance just came for Jason, and the paramedics think he broke his leg. They're taking him to the wrong hospital—the one where you don't have insurance."

The last time Rosemary had seen eleven-year-old Jason was when she had dropped him off at summer school on her way to work that morning, and he had seemed fine.

As the story unfolded, it appeared that Jason and a large ball had had an inopportune meeting while Jason was working out on the trampoline. He was thrown off balance and fell, breaking one of the bones in his lower leg. Rather than disturb her at work, someone had called her eighteen-year-old son.

Rosemary tore out of work, drove frantically, and was able to intercept the ambulance and convince the driver to take Jason to the hospital where she had insurance coverage. After receiving a temporary cast, Jason went home. At dinner that night he began to complain of stomach pains. Rosemary thought the pains were related to his leg, but they weren't. And they got worse and worse. So Jason went back to the hospital, where a surgeon examined him and admitted him for observation, suspecting appendicitis.

Rosemary spent all night in Jason's hospital room, along with the worried surgeon. The good news was that Jason got better the next morning and didn't need surgery. His mother also recovered. Today she is able to laugh about that awful day.

Actually, humor and an attitude of "this too shall pass" are the best ways to survive one of those dreadful, miserable, awful, terrible days that most parents of large families experience with some regularity. Children also benefit when their parents devise mature ways of dealing with especially stressful events. The children learn techniques that they can apply in their own lives and will probably use when they become adults.

How to Defuse "the Crazies"

If you find yourself "going crazy," there are some steps you can take to feel better yourself and to prevent your children from being victims of your stress.

Analyze the situation. Think about what you can do to resolve things temporarily. That's what Marty did when she had to pick up her two older children from school late because of a crisis at work. Arriving home she was greeted by an impatient babysitter who had evening plans of her own. The baby was screaming to be nursed, and the toddler quickly got into a fight with her older brother. Marty, still smarting from the rough time she had had at work, knew there was no way she could get through dinner preparations and retain her sanity. So she took the baby into the bedroom, locked the door, and nursed her for ten peaceful minutes, then piled everyone into the car and took them to a fast-food restaurant for dinner. Once the kids were fed, they were a lot easier to deal with. And Marty could prepare a small dinner for her husband at her own pace.

Don't get angry at yourself. Everyone has bad days, and children need to know that parents are human too. (One teen thought that her mother never made a mistake and felt she could never live up to such a role model. This adolescent was very relieved when Mom completely lost her cool one day and used a string of words her daughter didn't know were in her vocabulary!) Sometimes getting angry at yourself makes the situation even worse. As your own self-esteem plummets, you yell still more at the children.

Baby yourself. Before you lose control, tell yourself it's time for some self-indulgence. Then fill the tub with warm water and soak or read a book or go window shopping.

Let the children know you're having a bad day. In this way the children will know your anger isn't directed at them personally. They'll also probably be more careful of their behavior.

Eliminate situations that trigger "the crazies." One mother of four just hated having to return to a store she had just been to because a child forgot to mention he needed school supplies. She finally refused to do it. Her children received a few poor grades on projects, but they soon learned a valuable lesson about planning ahead.

Exercise daily. Exercise is a great stress and anxiety reducer. You say you don't have time? Be creative. One working mother of seven, with a baby who nursed every two hours through the night, went jogging every day after the baby's 5:00 A.M. feeding. A second mother, who also had seven children, went walking with a friend at 6:00 A.M. each day. Both women experienced an increase in their energy levels.

Keep up your own interests and friends. There's nothing

self-indulgent about this. When you are happy and involved, you'll be a much better parent.

Recognize biologic stress. Children might get into fights
when they are hungry, tired, or slightly ill. Their snarling
and teasing may trigger an attack of "the crazies" in you.
This happened to Elaine, who would delay the family's
dinner on those occasions when her husband worked late.
If the children had to wait, they got very hungry. They
started fighting. Elaine, hungry herself, would start screaming at them. By the time her poor husband got home, the
whole place was in an uproar. Elaine stepped back, took
a look at the situation, and decided to feed the children
earlier. When her husband didn't have to come home to a
difficult household, his late times began to get earlier.

Stephanie, like most mothers, thought she was never
supposed to get sick. She would struggle through bouts of
flu, cystitis, and even migraines, snarling at everyone and
getting no sympathy. Then one day she developed hepatitis
and had to take to her bed. The family rose to the occasion,
and the house didn't fall apart. Stephanie, although feeling
nauseous and with a bad stomachache, really enjoyed her
illness. She read, watched TV, and slept. She's a little disappointed that you can get hepatitis A only once, she jokes,
but now she's much easier on herself when she doesn't feel
well.

Support your mate when you notice he/she is stressed.
Beverly's husband is a salesman with his own business. He
works over seventy hours a week to support his family of
six. When he gets home from work, he really needs peace
and quiet . . . at least for a little while. Beverly recognizes
this need and accommodates it. So do the children, at her
insistence.

Carol, who has thirteen children, feels the stress periodically. Her husband, a pediatrician, is tuned in to her
needs, and just before she completely "goes crazy," he will
suggest they go on a "micro-mini" vacation alone.

Most people can recognize stress in their spouses. It may be brought on by business pressures, hunger, noise, or something that has caused a loss of self-esteem (the promotion of a rival at work, for example, or a cluster of new wrinkles).

Whatever the stress to which your mate is vulnerable, you can be a good listener, relieve whatever stress you have any control over, and reassure your spouse of his/her value to you.

If you are a person with religious beliefs, pray. Many parents do this in anticipation of problems or when they're in the midst of difficulties. They say it helps them greatly.

You may be relieved to know that "going crazy" is a perfectly normal phenomenon. It's brought on by being a hardworking, caring parent who is doing an important time- and energy-consuming job with precious few fringe benefits. (In fact, the only mother among my study families who denied ever having an attack of "the crazies" was blessed with a houseful of servants.)

So take it easy, breathe deeply, give each kid a cavity-promoting candy bar, and retreat to the privacy of your bathroom with a frivolous novel or Erma Bombeck's latest book. (Take a candy bar for yourself too.) The remedy for a routine attack of "the crazies" is discreet, well-timed self-indulgence. If you have the time, that is.

CHAPTER
13

Fathers

UP until now most of what we've talked about has related to mothering. What about fathers? Aren't they important? Are they just out there to make a living for the family? Actually, if there is one factor you can use to predict how well a family will weather the teenage years and how successful the children will be in choosing life goals, that factor is probably Dad.

Most fathers in strong families take great pleasure in their offspring. Doug, father of four, tells us:

> I had always intended to have a large family because I felt that we would have a better community and more fun, and

would feel like a real family, not an isolated, introverted mini-unit.

The children all bring me joy, pride, and love, but at times they try my patience.

I think that personal growth comes only as we stretch our inner resources, and having four mouths to feed and to be responsible for does just that for me.

We go camping as a family, and these trips are our best fun times. The kids often fight, and that makes life challenging.

I would hate to grow old and have no children or grandchildren to share Christmas with.

Children are great self-fulfillment because fulfillment comes from giving; and to have four kids you have to give a lot, but it's worth it. I wouldn't swap my role as a father of four for all the money/careers/life-styles in the world.

Other fathers find that having many children actually adds new dimensions to their lives. A self-employed father of seven comments: "I tend to be a loner, but my children's activities have drawn me into interaction with people and groups that I never would have had otherwise, and for the most part, it is informative, positive, and enjoyable."

An investment firm executive with ten children is quite frank: "The initial shock gives way to appreciation of the benefits children can derive from a large family . . . the interactions, mutual support, learning to share, teamwork, and respect for one another."

Career and Financial Obligations

A husband and wife can be rather liberated about who helps with household chores and the kids, and about the wife's work outside the home. Nonetheless, most couples still feel, when push comes to shove, that the husband has the greater obligation to provide most of the financial support for the family. A man's sense of himself can be tied up in his work, whereas many women, even career women, see themselves as making their most important contributions through childbearing and rearing.

Young fathers do worry about making it financially. They know that in order to succeed at work they sometimes need to put in extra effort. If they don't, they may not get the promotions that mean a higher salary. When they are in a profession or building a business, they have even more demanding pressures. If they don't put in the time and effort, everything may collapse.

Career obligations can and often do come into direct conflict with family needs during the early years, and it doesn't matter what kind of work you do. There will be times when Dad can't make the parent-teacher meeting because he's out of town on a business trip or has to have plans drawn up for a presentation tomorrow or is still seeing patients. Maybe he hasn't been home before eight or nine for the last several weeks because it's hard to work at home with all the noise and confusion there.

It can be hard for wives, especially nonemployed ones, to understand the pressures of a competitive job. They miss their husbands and resent being responsible for all the dinner preparation and cleanup, as well as for getting the kids to bed, and maybe even making another whole dinner when their husband does get home later on. They begin to see themselves as losing some kind of ill-defined competition with their husband's job. (One woman thought that everyone at her children's schools must think she was a single mother because her husband had to work evenings as well as days and didn't make a parent activity for several years.) So when Dad finally does get home, he's hardly greeted as a warrior returning from doing daily battle for the family.

This is an area where many spouses find it difficult to find a solution. Dad is working long hours for the family

(Why would he be killing himself with a twelve-hour day if it weren't for the family?), and Mom feels abandoned (Doesn't he care enough about us to even eat dinner with the family?). It may help to realize that many families are going through the same difficulties. Possibly the majority of husbands miss family dinner at least once a week. Many come home late a lot more often than that. These dads love and miss their families, but they want to be able to put all three children through college or buy a house big enough so that four children don't have to share one bedroom.

Husbands and wives *must* talk about their work obligations and discuss the politics of career advancement. When each understands the other's pressures (and these pressures cannot be intuited, they must be expressed), it's much easier for husband and wife to figure out how they can help each other. It doesn't hurt to share job stresses; for example, if a wife knows that inventories must be done in January or that an important case is coming to trial next month, she'll be much less upset when her husband is late for dinner several weeks in a row. After all, the whole family depends on this kind of cooperation.

When their husbands are under work stress, wives can help in the following ways:

1. Don't take it personally.
2. Give some extra TLC, even when you think it's you who should be on the receiving end.
3. Try to get some rest during the day so you will be less droopy when your spouse does get home.
4. Come up with easy-to-reheat meals for Dad. (This is where a microwave really comes in handy.)
5. See if you can eke out some special time for Dad and the kids to share, even if it's only fifteen minutes.

6. Allow Dad to unwind when he does get home. Don't immediately present all the household problems to him.

When they must work late, on weekends, and so forth, husbands can do the following:

1. Let your spouse know when special projects or obligations are coming up at work.
2. Call each day you will be late and give an estimated time of arrival so she will know what to do about dinner and evening obligations.
3. Tell your wife often how much you appreciate her and the way she handles things when you have to be at work.
4. Make special time on weekends for the kids and for your spouse.
5. If you have worries about work politics or ethical issues or your competition, it can help to discuss these issues in confidence with your wife. She needs to know you're human and that you have worries and fears too.

Does your wife work outside the home? If she does, you're probably happy about the extra income and pleased that she's doing something she likes, but you may feel that you and the children don't get all the attention you would if she were at home full-time. You may also feel a little insecure about her "other life" at work, and you may resent having more family obligations than your co-worker whose wife stays home with the kids.

Does your wife stay at home with the children? If she does, you are justifiably proud of your ability as a bread-winner and glad you can give your children a full-time mother, but you may be resentful that she does not contribute financially to the family and worried about what would happen to the family if you were incapacitated or lost your job. Maybe you feel that wives who work outside the home are more understanding of their husband's work obligations than are stay-at-home wives. (You may even feel they are more interesting as people.)

Whatever your family situation, there are downsides as well as upsides to dual-career families. Each family has to decide what's right for it, without worrying about what others are doing. Each family must also be flexible enough to make changes as the situation warrants.

Maintaining a Satisfactory Love Life

One Saturday afternoon Pete and Mary put their four little ones in their fenced backyard, with the six-year-old in charge, and retreated to the bedroom of their one-story house for some private time. They had just gotten into bed when Pete happened to glance at the bedroom window. There, noses pressed to the window, were their four children, the baby having been lifted up so that she could also see what her parents were up to. Everybody was waving to Mom and Dad. That was the end of afternoon soirees for these parents.

It's a wonder that any family has more than two children since it is so difficult for parents to find time and energy to be together. This is especially true when both parents work. But spousal time must become a priority in the large family. You and your spouse are what is going to make this family work, and your needs are very important to the whole family. So take the time to laugh, joke, flirt, and have an active love life, and don't feel bad about the time you may take away from your duties. If need be, take a nap in the afternoon so you will be rested at night, or consider taking a few moments first thing each morning for each other.

Lovemaking isn't the only cement that binds spouses, however. Mutual support and concern are every bit as important. And it really can last a lifetime.

Spouses grow to know what each other's needs are over the years. They develop the capacity to put their own worries aside momentarily when the other's seem more pressing. They learn to look at things from their spouse's perspective. They even evolve their own key words and forms of communication. Of course, these things don't happen overnight.

Take Ann, for instance. Her babies came quickly after her marriage, and as a stay-at-home mother she was often starved for adult talk. When her husband arrived home after a day at work, all he wanted to do was spend a few quiet minutes reading the paper with no interruptions. Ann sulked, pouted, but then started to see things from his perspective. Her husband, who had been coming home later and later, responded by appreciating how lonely Ann's day had been. When they both realized how the other was feeling, they were able to help each other out. Ann's husband now has "reentry time" at night, and Ann gets his uninterrupted attention after that. The kids are much happier, and not only that, Ann and her husband have a prototype for handling future problems.

Carol remarks how her husband always seems to sense when the stress of her thirteen-child family is getting to her. Helen's husband is "quiet, loving, the calming influence in the family." In each of these families, wives and husbands communicate their needs with the expectation that these needs will be of concern to their spouses. And they are seldom disappointed. Each spouse is also mature enough to know when he needs to forget his own problems momentarily to focus on those of his/her mate.

How to Talk to Each Other

When one couple got home from work, the toddlers were hungry, dinner had to be cooked, the wash had to be done, and office material had to be prepared for the next day. Conversation was limited to what was necessary for daily survival. Several times, information about out-of-town business trips was not discussed until the day before the trip. After a few of these flubs, the couple arranged for their secretaries to call each other and pass on information about their respective business schedules.

If you don't want this to happen to you, you'll need to devise ways to communicate with your spouse (whether or not you work outside the home). Here are some methods:

1. Find the best time to transmit practical information and the best time to discuss things with more emotional content. For example, breakfast may be a good time to review the day's events, but Saturday afternoon is a better time to talk about how to handle your teenagers' taste for loud, disagreeable music.
2. Use a bulletin board or log to prevent scheduling two things at once. Important events must be written down.
3. Devise telephone rules so that someone will not take a message and forget to deliver it for several days or months, or not at all.
4. If you have really important issues to discuss, such as returning to work or having another child, take a weekend away from the children to devote to that particular issue without interruption.
5. Recognize that some topics are difficult for men to discuss or to bring up. You may have to be patient when you and your spouse work out how

to communicate on these important issues where compromise is essential.

6. If you feel that your communication skills are in urgent need of improvement, consider something like Marriage Encounter, sponsored by many religious denominations to make a good marriage better. Or get a recommendation from your doctor for a marriage counselor.

Involvement When the Children Are Small

As mentioned before, lots of fathers are busy building careers when the children are small and don't have time to get deeply involved in child care. Some fathers have trouble relating to a child when it has not yet evolved into a little person. It's not unheard of for a father of six or eight children to be unfamiliar with how to change a diaper, but it should be considered a crime!

On the other hand, many fathers are very involved with their young children, sharing bathing, feeding, and bedtime rituals as well as playtime.

A third group of fathers seems to grow into child care. These are dads who wouldn't have dared to put a new diaper on their first baby even if the poor child hadn't been changed for a week. They're a little better with the second. By the time the third or fourth arrives, they're right in there—changing diapers, walking the floors at night, even volunteering at the preschool carnival booth.

Men, it has been shown, handle babies in a slightly different manner from their wives. They're often a little more active and vigorous with them. Babies come to enjoy these times with their fathers and almost certainly gain a lot developmentally by playing with them. Mothers who intuitively recognize this will go to considerable lengths to give the children some time with Dad at the end of the day.

Interacting with Teenagers

There is no time when good fathering is more important for children than during the teenage years. There are several reasons for this. Sons need to separate from their mothers if they are to become autonomous men. That makes it very hard for them to accept advice or discipline from their moms. Dad must become the major counselor and disciplinarian during these "separation" years of adolescence. One wise mother of thirteen expected her adolescent boys to go through a period where they viewed her as a real handicap. She said that as soon as the boys reached eighteen or nineteen and were on their own, their whole attitude toward her improved remarkably. They no longer needed to struggle against their attachment to her because they had achieved independence. But before that maturity occurred, she made sure that the boys had lots of contact with their father, and she tried to step out of the picture temporarily.

Adolescent boys seek a role model in their dads. This means that Dad must be available on-site for talking, maybe shooting a few baskets now and then, and discussing from time to time his philosophy of life.

Adolescent girls have their femininity reinforced by their dads. They also need a chance to talk about things and to learn about what their father's expectations are for them. The masculine perspective they gain from their fathers during adolescence will help them with future relationships.

And, finally, mothers aren't the greatest of disciplinarians for teenagers. This doesn't mean that the majority of teenagers aren't respectful and obedient toward their mother. Most teens in large families are, in fact, quite cooperative. Dads are just usually more effective when heavy-duty discipline is needed. They're bigger, have deeper voices, and when Dad is mad, brother, you'd better watch out! If Dad gets involved, it has to be important.

The Influences of Fathering

You can pick up just about any urban newspaper and see the effect that a lack of good fathering has on adolescents and the community. Teen crime, pregnancy, noncompletion of high school, even accidents are all much more prevalent in dysfunctional households, and dysfunctional households are often those with no father or where the father has a problem, such as alcoholism, that renders him a less effective parent.

Fathers aren't important only in large families. The one- or two-child family also benefits from good fathering, but in large families the father's involvement becomes even more crucial. Many mothers have said they didn't know how they could have survived the teen years without the help of their husbands.

Effective fathers are the spiritual leaders in their families. The moral codes that they espouse and practice become very important to their children. Sometimes an adult child will remember, years later, how Dad always went to church or synagogue with the family every Sunday or Sabbath, or how Dad helped the teenager down the road get a summer job. The adult child may not have had religious connections for years, but the memory of his dad's beliefs or ethics or kindness to others will return to motivate him.

Competent fathers generally have a pretty direct way of handling adolescent problems. They're accessible enough to their kids to sense changes in behavior, and they act on these changes, perhaps by taking a walk with a child to talk things over or even confronting him or her if the problem is serious. They know that while adolescents shouldn't be repressed, they do need fairly strict guidance at times.

Sometimes children don't have the talents or interests that their father wishes they had. He may have been the captain of the football team in high school, but has sons who like art or music. The wise father wants his children to develop those talents they were born with, even if they're not the same talents he has. In the small family there's sometimes much more pressure on the child to conform to Dad's expectations. (I recall a soccer coach who yelled at his only son when that child failed to give a stellar performance on the soccer field.)

In the large family the father knows that if one child does not share his interests, another probably will. He can sit back and relax, encouraging the activities of each of his children even if they're different from his own. Of course, if he happens to have five children who love basketball . . . voilà!

Fathering the large family is a lifelong avocation. It takes a true investment of quality time. If the father is really sensitive to the needs of his children, he'll try to find a special area where he can relate to each child. One might like to play baseball with him, another to go for hikes, a third to have him admire her prowess at gymnastics. Dad values each of his children as unique human beings, and his style is to try to bring out the best in each. This kind of parenting doesn't stop when the children leave the nest. It can extend for a lifetime, changing with the evolving maturity of each child.

Learning How to Father

Certainly, being available for three, four, or nine children isn't easy, especially when you probably have to work longer hours and earn more money than the father with

one or two children. Some children are going to need more
of your time and attention than others; some children will
make you prouder than others; and you still have to treat
them in such a way that they're not jealous of one another.
You may feel that one of your sons is just like you were,
a champion baseball player or great at math. You and he
can joke around, and you're on the same wavelength all
the time. But you know that you have to give some attention to the little guy whose main interest seems to be art
and reading. And you may have no idea what eight-year-
old girls like to do, but you learn to talk and relate to them
on their level anyway.

It isn't easy learning how to father a variety of children.
If you were lucky enough to have a great father yourself,
you may just be able to follow his pattern, but if he was
aloof or away often, or you were an only child, you may
have very few memories to guide you.

Parenting a large family requires the same attention to
the children's needs that parenting one or two does, but
your time is more limited and you have many more needs
to consider. There may be times when you long for a moment's peace, a little less noise and confusion. Sometimes
you might even want to spend some time with your wife
but find you are competing with a hungry baby and raucous
toddlers for the attention of a very tired spouse. If you and
she actually get some time alone, she'll probably fall asleep.
Where are the instructions on how to do it all?

You are a critical influence in the lives of each of your
children. Even when each is a baby, he or she will enjoy
playtime with you because you probably make everything,
even a toss in the air, exciting. Since mothers and fathers
handle babies differently, your young children learn a lot
from your different styles, so take the time to cuddle and
bounce your toddlers, perhaps change and bathe them, and
be a presence in their lives from infancy onward.

Notice how each of your children acts in your presence.

Is one of them particularly interested when you are repairing something around the house? Does another enjoy talking about sports with you? Your acceptance and encouragement of each child's interests is a strong stimulus to his future performance.

Be accessible for serious discussions. Children and teens, even if they seem rebellious at times, look upon you as the one individual who can best explain to them how they should relate to the wider world. (This may be why success has been shown to be tied to the involvement a person's father has had in one's life.)

Let your kids know you are proud of their accomplishments. You probably remember how much it meant to you when your dad praised something you had worked hard on. Moms didn't seem to count quite as much; they always thought that whatever you did was wonderful. But dads, they were harder to please, so their comments carried much more weight!

All in all, good fathering involves providing security, motivation, and direction to all your children, enjoying each one for his own special accomplishments and letting each one know you will always love him and be there for him.

Profiles

Here's what three fathers have to say about having large families.

Tom is the father of eight children ranging from a kindergartner to young adults. He is self-employed in a small business he started many years ago. If he had one piece of advice to give young fathers starting out, he would tell them, "Don't be afraid of the future. Things usually take care of themselves."

Tom's family was not exactly planned, but he and his

wife were "not unhappy when they came." Now that he has a large family, however, "I don't go out of my way to tell people I have eight kids and have to defend it." He feels that most people's attitudes about large families "lean toward negativism; they can't understand it and don't know why anyone would do that, too darn much trouble. People like to joke and make snide remarks."

Founding and running his own business suits Tom's personality and the needs of his family. He thrives on the autonomy and finds he can schedule things so he is with the kids when they need him. You can't be afraid of responsibility when you have your own business and when you have eight children.

With his children he says he's "sensitive to the needs of each child" and doesn't "favor one over the other." The kids respect their father and do what the parents want. "We never had a major problem." The children all acquired jobs once they turned sixteen and helped pay for their own cars and education. "We don't have an excess of money," Tom says, "but we've always made it." The older children have all attended or are attending local colleges, commuting from home.

Tom gives his adult children practical advice about their future. He strongly believes in productivity. "Lots of people with Ph.D.s couldn't produce anything," he tells them. "You have to use education as a tool to further yourself and increase your productivity. Work hard to do the job right. Don't let education be the end-all." Needless to say, all Tom's children are hard workers.

Tom and his wife intuitively support each other. She works part-time, and he tries to be with the kids those after-school times when she is busy at work. If the children have a disciplinary problem, the parents "don't really sit down and have a family conference. If there are problems, one or the other of us will make a decision and the other goes along."

This couple also tries to get away together, if only overnight, every few months.

Tom's family is the most important thing in his life. You can tell how much he enjoys them just by talking to him. He has faith in the future and confidence in his own and the family's ability to make it, but he still hasn't figured out after decades as a father how to keep the kids from fighting.

Brad's five children are all under nine. He and his wife both came from large families, and he knew he "wanted a large family but wanted to be able to afford them. I made some decisions early on that involved some sacrifices with the family." In those early years Brad worked very hard to establish his career as an investment counselor, and had to be away from the children more than he would have liked. He still worries if this might have had a negative effect on the little ones.

In the last three or four years, however, he has become well enough established that he can let his partners carry some of the load. Weekdays he still leaves for work very early, and he doesn't get home until eight, but weekends are for his wife and children.

Brad is also very sensitive to the needs of each child. In fact, during his long commute each day he even thinks about the children and what he can do to help them. Brad says, "Some of the children are more readily there for you. One child is always the first one to greet me. He's the one who runs up to grab my hand. I have to make a conscious effort to think about the different kids and who needs what. One child is quieter, never gives hugs. Last night we went camping, so he was the one who slept in the tent with me."

Brad's kids fight too. "The natural jealousy among kids can get pretty bad. I figure I'll be deaf by the time I'm forty, and that's that," he jokes.

Brad and his wife are both strong, intelligent personalities who like to take charge and control the situation. They've learned to compromise.

> I've had to work to tone down my desire to take charge and just to steamroll things through. I've had to learn that there's a lot of ways to do things, and as long as the end result's the same, it doesn't matter. I have to watch how gruff I am. I've found that it's best for my wife and me if we can emotionally distance ourselves from the situation —we're both strong and "take charge" people—so we work at sitting back and discussing things. If one person steps up to discipline the children, we pretty much let it go at that.

When one of them is having a bad day, the other will step in to give the spouse some space and will take over caring for the children.

Even though Brad is often tired after his long day and just wants to stay home for dinner, he realizes his wife has had an equally long day cooped up with the children. Once a week they both make the effort to get out, and even though "you have to force yourself to do it, I'm always glad afterward," Brad says.

To sum up: "You have to be ready to give of yourself. It all boils down to love. You have to love those kids. You have to enjoy seeing others have a good time."

Now that the oldest of his five children has become a teenager, Dave is finding that his day doesn't contain enough hours to do all he would like. "The things that happen in one day," Dave says, "are unbelievable." Saturday morning might involve a Brownie "Daddy and Me" hike followed by chores in a co-op nursery school cleanup day, then home to do household maintenance and watch the children while Mom goes to her part-time job.

"Be sure you have sufficient time to do all of this," Dave

would caution other fathers. "You can't do this and take a job that requires frequent travel. If you don't want to put the time into it, don't have a large family." Dave is a salesman, and he has little doubt that his career would have moved along more swiftly if he were willing to be away from his kids.

> The choices I made hurt my career. The boss wanted me to entertain clients every weekend. If I do that four times this year, it will be a lot. It would enhance my financial gain. My house is falling apart, I drive an old car, but that's the choice I've made [to spend more time with the children]. It seems we're always in the red. At times you aim a little higher at work, take a few more chances to gain a little more financially than you would [without the financial pressures of a large family].

Being with his children has given Dave the opportunity to know their talents and interests. "I see special talents and try not to let that influence how they should go. I might be steering that child away from what he or she would be happiest doing. Career choice starts early. I try to instill in my children that at any given time they can be anything they want to be."

Dave also came from a family of five. He feels that parenting is "basically intuitive. Some things my father did I said I would never do. He was not active with his children, but I have taken a very active role in my children's lives. My dad had a lot of integrity—honesty was a big issue— and he had a good Irish work ethic. I try to emulate that. I want to do a good job of parenting, and the rest kind of falls into place."

Dave says that he is

> disappointed if the children don't do as they're told, and it happens frequently. At any given time one child is doing

something that disappoints me and another is doing something that makes me proud.

There's a constant challenge because they're all different. What works for one does not work for another; you are constantly challenged on how to communicate with each one. For instance, we had a track meet at the city park last week. Sean [one of the eleven-year-old twins] really wanted to win. He did his best but came in eighth in the softball throw, fifth in shotput, and last in track. His twin sister went out and without trying got two gold medals. How do you make that up to him? But then this week he finished first in his whole school in a math contest, and his twin sister was not even listed [as finishing with honors].

Since the oldest girl has turned thirteen, he's learning about how to deal with adolescents. His first clue about what lies ahead came when he arrived home from work one day and found her sunbathing in a two-piece bathing suit in the yard in chilly weather.

But he enjoys this child. "She's older, and we can talk," he says, but "she knows how to push my buttons too!" His philosophy about teenagers is that "no parent ever won an argument with a thirteen-year-old. So don't argue," he tells his wife when she and their daughter get into the inevitable hassles that almost all teen girls and their mothers have.

Dave feels that the pressures his family faces really cut into his personal time with his wife. "I believe there truly is less time now than there was when the children were younger. I've given up on [having much time alone with his wife]. That's the way life is right now. Don't let it chew you up."

In spite of all the pressures and stresses, Dave still says that the family is the most important thing in the world to him. "They're my favorite subject. I could talk about them twenty-four hours nonstop."

* * *

It's pretty obvious that fathers of large families nowadays are just as involved as mothers, albeit in a different way. Almost all feel real pressure to be good providers, and they recognize that they are tugged in opposite directions by their desire to earn more money for their families through career advancement and their need to spend time with their children.

As more women work outside the home and as we grow to recognize the vital needs fathers meet in the creation of responsible, happy adults, the role of fatherhood will continue to evolve. This change is happening in both large and small families, but the greater number of individuals in the large family makes the change more challenging and more essential.

CHAPTER
14

The Gradually
Empty Nest

DO you ever wonder, as you go through your busy day, what it's going to be like after all your children have grown up? What will you do for excitement? Who will give you your hugs? Will you remember how to act in a fancy restaurant or how to carry on a conversation that doesn't involve kids?

Most of us who have several children do so because we really enjoy them. As the years go by, they play a bigger and bigger part in our lives. Soon we forget how we managed to exist and filled our time before they came. And then one day they start leaving. At first it's a gradual attrition. One child goes off to college or joins the service, but he comes back for holidays and gives the home address as his official place of residence. Then another child leaves, and the same thing happens. Eventually one child brings somebody home for you to meet, and you realize that a new family is about to be created.

You're probably not anywhere near that stage yet. You may, in fact, be just planning your third pregnancy. You may be chasing toddlers around or driving grade schoolers all over the place. Some days you probably say to yourself that you can hardly wait until they're all grown up so you can take a bath in peace or read a book at one sitting. Or your children may all be teenagers, and when you look at them, you realize they will not be around too much longer.

Wherever you are in terms of your family's development, it's not too early to think about the future. When your family is young, you invest very heavily in it. Your time is consumed by the needs of these children, and all your dreams and plans are tied up in them.

Yet your goal as a parent is to make yourself obsolete. You are constantly teaching the skills they need to survive on their own. You pat yourself on the back when your children are able to do things earlier or better than other people's children. You may get angry at yourself as a parent when one of your children doesn't seem to be able to fend for himself.

So you find yourself dealing with two contradictory issues: your mission to make your children autonomous and your desire, at least at times, to have them be small, cuddly, and dependent.

But they do grow; it's inevitable, and you really wouldn't have it any other way. Knowing this, you have to grow too. Granted, there's not much time when the children are small to develop your own skills and interests, but it is something you need to think about. If you have held on to your own interests and have planned for the future, you will be able to give your children their independence in a gracious manner when the time comes. You won't feel that you cease to be important as a person after your parenting role is over.

Mothers have in the past had more problems with the empty nest than have fathers. A generation ago fathers had their jobs as well as their families to back them up. For women, the family was the job.

The current generation of parents may prove quite different. Most of us, mothers and fathers alike, are used to working. Mothers may put their careers on hold when the children are small, but the idea of going back to work when the children get to be teenagers or college age is pretty much accepted and expected.

One mother of five laughed when she was asked about the "empty nest." "There's never an empty nest in the large family," she said. "The older children keep coming back, and even if they didn't, I could always find something to keep me busy because that's the kind of person I am."

The "empty nest" is supposed to be that time in parents' lives when all the children have left home and the mother, who is probably going through the "change of life" around this time, becomes sad and depressed. Some people assume that mothers who have chosen to have several children have a bigger part of themselves tied up in these children and are hit harder when the little ones are grown and gone. Does this "empty nest" thing really happen in the large family?

Sometimes, yes. Some women feel sad when they don't have little babies and cub scouts around anymore, when they know that a hectic and productive stage of their lives is gone forever. Fathers miss their children, too, especially if they feel a little guilty for not having been around enough when the children were young. Some mothers and fathers express remorse for "not having been a good enough parent." Of course, just about everybody feels a twinge of sadness at the thought of the kids growing up and leaving, but the parents who are most likely to have serious problems are those who have not planned ahead for this transitional stage, who have not held on to a sense of themselves as individuals.

Contrary to popular opinion, parents of large families may be less likely, on the whole, to suffer "empty nest" syndrome than parents of small families, probably because the nest never actually empties if you have a big enough family.

Late one evening when I was working in the emergency room, things quieted down for a time. The staff on duty all had teenage children, and one physician got on the subject of his oldest son going away to college. It seems that this man had two sons, a year apart in age. His wife had been home with the children and had few other interests. When the first son went away, she became quite dejected. She couldn't even walk past his empty bedroom without almost crying. She knew that the second son would soon be going away, too, and then there would be nobody except herself and her husband left in their big, beautiful house made for children.

This woman was probably just a little older than I was because my first child would be going to college the same year as her younger son, but my son's leaving would in no way empty the nest. I was still in the process of weaning the baby. In fact, when my son did leave the next year, there wasn't even an empty bed. One of the other children laid claim to it before it was even cold.

In the small family mothers and fathers make major investments in just one or two children. When these children leave, the parents' lives can be profoundly changed. In the large family the child-rearing period is longer just because there are more to raise. If you have your last baby in your early forties, and many people do, you'll still be going to grade school plays and Little League games when you are eligible to join the American Association of Retired

Persons. Sound depressing? Many parents of large families find the idea exhilarating!

By the time parents are putting their youngest child through college, many have a grandchild or two. They can enjoy little ones all over again but without the responsibilities. Some grandparents even care for their grandchildren during the day when their own children are at work (a great solution to the child-care problem if everybody involved can work together). One mother who is doing this says she goes to great pains to let her children do their own parenting. Her tongue is black and blue from all the biting she's had to do, she quips.

One of my patients, I'll call her Lupe, had thirteen children of her own. She was now a widow in her seventies and living with one of her daughters. One day she came in for her appointment accompanied by this daughter and the daughter's two babies. I had known Lupe only as a little old lady who had several chronic medical problems, but as she cuddled and soothed a crying three-month-old, I saw her very briefly as a beautiful teenage mother on a remote rancho in Mexico holding her firstborn son. Lupe was a mother and would be to her dying day.

The Family Compound

Several very large families have come up with a living style I call the "family compound." These families live in the same neighborhood, the same block, and sometimes even in the same house with married children and grandchildren. The parents often employ some of their children in the family business.

The family compound can come into being when young marrieds cannot afford housing. The parents allot their children and spouses space until they have a down payment on a house. Other times teenagers will marry, have a baby, and need some help to hold the whole thing together as they mature a little more. Then there are the families where Mom, now Grandmom, helps raise her grandchildren while their mother goes to work, and it's just more convenient if everybody lives close by. One family of sixteen had such a huge house that three married children moved into apartments within the house and are raising their children there.

When Your Youngsters Won't Leave

Large families can provide a lot of social support to their members. Grown children may have less incentive to go out and look for their own group of friends. Why should they go elsewhere when it's so much fun at home? So some parents experience the problem of pushing their children out of the nest. Much as they love their children, it gets pretty tiresome cooking twenty or thirty meals a day for forty years. These parents find themselves saying "enough already" while at the same time feeling guilty about it. One mother of six says she finally offered the family heirlooms to the child who went out, got married, and produced a grandchild first. (It worked; her grandchild is now three years old.)

Preparing for the Future Now

What do you, a young parent in the throes of childbearing and child-rearing, do now to prepare for a time when the children are older? Your investments in your family (and here we are speaking of both physical and psychological investments) are enormous. You realize, of course, that your job is to get these kids to a point where they're able to take care of themselves. But that's in the dim, remote future, isn't it? Besides, you don't have any time or energy to imagine life A.K. (after kids).

Hold on! There are things you can do so that you won't go into a tailspin when the last child packs her clothes for college (don't laugh!). More important, these things will allow you to give your children the freedom they need to grow and separate when the time comes.

Make your marriage a top priority. Play with your spouse from time to time. Let the kids see you playing. If your husband has had a bad day, let your children skip an evening event so you can spend time with him. Take your wife on a twenty-four-hour getaway even if the kids wail that the babysitter is too mean and strict. Kids feel much more secure when they see strong bonds between the parents. And you and your spouse will, it is hoped, have each other long after the kids are gone.

If you have a career or a hobby and are at home with the children, try to keep your skills or interests current. That way you can reenter the working world when you want to or become a volunteer and use your talents to help others. Believe it or not, your kids will benefit too. When they see that their parents really get pleasure out of an interest or job, they'll expect to do the same eventually.

View your life in stages. The Bible says, "To every thing there is a season, and a time to every purpose under heaven." Your childbearing season will eventually pass. What will the next "season" bring? It could be tremendously rewarding if you let it!

Get all the joy you can out of every moment with your family. Relish the time spent nursing your babies, reading to your toddlers, and having your first graders, in succession, read to you. But don't forget that listening to a teenager as she grapples with ethical concepts or discussing career plans with a young adult is just as important. Most of us have "favorite ages." We like our kids when they're babies and helpless, or when they're third graders and make cute little Christmas gifts for us. We need to learn to enjoy every stage our children go through and be there for them as much as, but no more than, they need us.

Don't worry about how you parented in the past. Just do the best you can now. My kids get awfully sick of my saying, "All you can do is the best you can do." Was I ever surprised to find that several other parents of large families said very similar things to their children!

None of us is perfect. We do our best. (If we were too good, our kids would be intimidated, and we wouldn't want to do that to them, would we?)

Keep a sense of yourself as a person. You are not an extension of your children, and they are not extensions of you.

Don't plan on depending on your grown children to meet all of your needs in the future. One woman I knew figured that because she had "sacrificed her youth" to raise four children, they owed her a guarantee of happiness. She badgered the poor kids all the time about how sick she was, how she needed to be driven here and there, how her house needed repairs. Some of the kids just tuned her out, leaving one or two to dance attendance on her. They didn't have much time left over for their own families. She and they would have been a lot happier if she had taken responsibility for her own life.

Reminiscences

Sometimes the best way to find out what it will be like for you when your children grow up is to talk to mothers who are going through that very experience right now. Here are the thoughts and reminiscences of two mothers:

Anne: She is in her late forties and had three children, two girls and a boy, within thirty-one months. They are now in their late teens and early twenties. A fourth child was born seven years later. "They are so close and such good friends," she says.

> I didn't have to work, and so I could be with them all the time. Now I volunteer so that I can actually be with my twelve-year-old in school. It was a hassle sometimes, but I thoroughly enjoyed having them all around. I think we had no problems because they are very sensitive and loving children. I was more directive with the older ones, but I backed off with the little one because it's a different world we're living in. The older ones got hurt by being too nice.
>
> I was always very open with them.
>
> I think the best thing that ever happened to the three older ones was the little one. I used to do everything for the older ones, but when the baby came, they had to become more independent.
>
> We are very family oriented. There are five children in both my husband's and my family. When we have holiday celebrations—and we do this for all major holidays—there are twenty or thirty people from each family.
>
> Our marriage has gone through some difficult times in the past six years due to family stresses. My husband's dad had Alzheimer's disease, and his mother had tumors on the brain. He was the oldest son and had to do everything for his parents, but the last year of his father's Alzheimer's disease actually brought my husband and me closer. We're

at a time now where we enjoy doing everything together and enjoy the kids' being gone. The youngest would rather be doing something with her sisters and brother anyway. We use the time to play golf together, something I've liked to do for many years. We bicycle together too. Every year we go to Hawaii and stay with friends. We hope to travel more in the future.

I went back to school this year and took a computer programming class at the local junior college. I might take a part-time job as long as I can be home when the little one gets home from school. I think if you have to work to put bread and butter on the table or to give the children a better education, fine. But if you're working just for luxuries, it's not worth it. It's too important to be there when your daughter's coming home from school if someone has been mean to her. She needs you then and there. You have no energy left to be sympathetic if you've been working all day. I just think that if mothers don't have to, they shouldn't work when the children are small.

I always wanted to get married and raise a family. We want our girls to be prepared because the divorce rate is so high that they have to be able to take care of themselves. It's a different world they're growing up in, and they must be able to make a living if they have to. It's just as important for a daughter to graduate from college as it is for a son. Our girls are very bright too. Maybe they would be bored if they had to stay home, and it's so expensive to raise kids nowadays that you need two incomes.

Helen: She has six children, three of each sex. Her youngest, now in high school, was born when Helen was nearly forty-seven years old. Helen remembers:

We sort of expected we'd have a family that was larger than usual. I listened to the children and enjoyed them; it was just a big adventure. It was exciting and really a wonderful time. I came from a family of three girls. Having boys was something new. It was more fun than I thought it would be.

I'm not a person who's wild about caring for tiny infants. I really enjoyed them more as they became older and had something to say.

We had all of our children involved in a swim team program. They learned to compete only against themselves. We really enjoyed their parochial school. It was a loving umbrella.

They all had hobbies. They still have things around the house that I'm trying to get rid of. They all had piano lessons and then went into other stuff—guitars and drums. We went to museums and national parks. The children were the ones who were leading us. There was an electricity that we took from them, I think, rather than the other way around.

We're three thousand miles from our relatives. It was up to us to do everything. We were a unit that had to be self-propelled, and the children did their share.

I guess I differ from other people. All of our kids have come back home. We would not support them in another house or apartment. If you're not earning enough to support yourself, we told them, you'll have to come back home. Our oldest daughter finished college and then returned and began teaching school—not a well-paying job. Later she married. Our second daughter is still at home. She's a musician and teaches senior citizens and handicapped children, among other things. She doesn't drive, due to a birth injury, but she's handling it well. Her room is a nightmare because she collects junk.

Our first son is a lawyer and the second son is a dentist. Both used our house as home base when they attended graduate school. We're a family that's used to accommodating one another.

We have eight grandchildren and relate very easily. We're

all heading to a local mountain resort this summer to rent places close together. Our children don't ask us to babysit too often. They know we're so busy. The job has fallen to the other sets of grandparents to do heavy-duty babysitting. Besides, our teenager has friends over all the time. The older children complain that we had never let them do what she does!

We really haven't been able to take off and do things, just the two of us together, as much as we see our contemporaries doing. We kept thinking it would change, but it hasn't. My husband said at one time he was supporting three generations: his parents, ourselves, and the children. There should have been some way for us to have a special time together but there wasn't. Will we have enough strength to do the things we want to when we finish the job of raising children?

I feel so sorry for young mothers today who have to spend so much time at work. They miss the fun. But it costs ten times as much now to put a child through private school as it did when ours were little. It's much more expensive to raise children nowadays, and I feel young parents are trying to look at this much more realistically than we did.

About our marriage: We just enjoy each other's company and always have. We're not alike in just about every respect, so we always have a lot to talk about. We try to understand the other person's point of view. We still love each other, and we never expect the other to be the same as ourselves.

*E*PILOGUE

FIRST of all, a big thank-you to the parents who made it possible for me to write this book.

We as a culture often choose movie stars, politicians, and sports figures as the people we admire most. Allow me to suggest that the MVPs in our society are not these individuals at all but, rather, the parents who are out there making daily sacrifices to have and raise good children. I have had the chance to become acquainted with some of these fine parents in the course of my research on successful large families. The parents who were the most generous with their time and suggestions were usually those with the most children or the busiest schedules. Why did they participate in the research? Almost invariably, they wanted to help others who were thinking about having more than two children.

And they were all terrific people. They shared their pains and struggles as well as their triumphs. I saw a community come together to support a mother and father as they dealt with a serious illness that had overcome their sixth child. I met a mother of thirteen who went back to work to support her family after three decades as a homemaker. I saw parents overcoming alcoholic problems, educational handicaps, even the death of a child. Through it all, I saw the courage of people who believed in the importance of the family, of working hard for others, and of values that could not be measured in material terms.

The United States and most other industrialized countries already have birth rates below what is needed for population replacement in the next century. This being the case, parents who make a conscious choice to have more children are actually helping to preserve the generational balance. Why is generational balance so important? Because each generation has obligations to those who come before and after, to nourish the young and care for the aged and infirm.

Every couple should make a responsible choice about the number of children they wish to conceive and bring into the world. They need to consider their own resources consciously, to be sure that they are capable of parenting a large family responsibly, if this is what they have chosen to do. Both large and small families have their own unique advantages, and the existence of both kinds gives us strength. Healthy, intact families, whatever their size, will always remain the basic building block of society.

$\mathcal{I}$NDEX